Benton County Tennessee

Administration, Guardian, Clerk, Trustees, Probate of Deeds, Records of Wills, Scholastic Population

1836–1855

WPA RECORDS

Heritage Books
2024

HERITAGE BOOKS

AN IMPRINT OF HERITAGE BOOKS, INC.

Books, CDs, and more—Worldwide

For our listing of thousands of titles see our website
at
www.HeritageBooks.com

A Facsimile Reprint
Published 2024 by
HERITAGE BOOKS, INC.
Publishing Division
5810 Ruatan Street
Berwyn Heights, MD 20740

Originally published 1937

International Standard Book Number
Paperbound: 978-0-7884-9051-4

ADMINISTRATION - GUARDIAN CLERKS -TRUSTEES
PROBATE OF DEEDS-RECORD OF WILLS- SCHOLASTIC
POPULATION- 1836-----1855- BENTON COUNTY

INDEX....COUNTY COURT CLERKS OFFICE.

P 1.   C.

INDEX

INDEX COUNTY COURT CLERKS OFFICE.

(F)

INDEX

MINUTE BOOK
BENTON COUNTY
1836----1855

P 1.   An Inventory of amount of sales of Estate of James Holland
Deceased, on May 18th 1836.

Willie Norman	To bed and furniture	$ 13.62
Josiah Puckett	1 Bed stead and cord	.75
John Hall	1 Bed and furniture	10.00
Wyly Holland	1 Bed stead and cord	1.12½
" "	1 Bed furniture & cord	13.75
" "	1 Large Spinning Wheel	4.00
John Brown	1 Blowing horse	.75
John Holland	1 Chest	2.00
John Milton	1 pr sheep shears	.75
Josiah Puckett	1 pr. candle sticks and snuffers	.50
John Holland	1 slate	.31¼
" "	1 Biber sacred will	.89½
John Hawley	2 Books	.50
William W. Wheatly	1 Box	.87½
John Mattn	1 Lot of tools	.50
John Askew	1 Bay Bill tooth palicans	.25
John Hall	1 Shovel and sticks	2.00
John Brown	1 Hone	1.37½
William Bakin	1 Razon & Case & strop	1.12½
Pong Milton	1 Razon glass & Brush	1.00
Kenist Reddick	1 pr horse fleam	.50
William Baker	1 Box & articles	.26½
John Hall	1 Grid iron	.12½
John Holland	1 pr fire irons	1.50
Wyly Holland	1 skillitt	.56½
" "	1 pot hooks	.81½
" "	1 Over	.37½
John Holland	1 Churn	.89½
Sion Nelson	1 Frying Pan	.62½

P 2.

Wyly Holland	1 Coffee Mill	.26½
John W. Hill	1 Coffee Mill	1.50
James Rutherford	1 Lamp	.25
James Reavs	1 Skillett & lid	1.12
Wyly Holland	1 trunk	.25
Willy Holland	1 trunk	1.06½
" "	1 candles tallow	.75
" "	1 Trunk	.06¼
" "	1 Lap robe	1.31
James Cooly	1 Box	.63¾
William Holland	1 Butter dish and plates	3.12½
Willy Holland	1 Pot hanger	.37½
John Holland	1 dish & 3 plates	1.75
John Milton	1 Bason	.50
" "	1 "	.08¾
" "	1 "	1.06½
John Pafford	1 dish	.87½
John Hall	1 pitcher & bowl	1.50
Nutle Perkins	1 set plates	.43¾

P 3 Continued.

William Wheatly	6 bowls	$ .88
Robert Cherry	6 bowls	.31¾
Wm. H. Holland	Teaspoons	1.85
Nathiel R. Parker	Cup & Saucers	.43¾
Samuel Benton	Cup saucers & bowls	.25
William Baker	Vines	.31½
Samuel Benton	1 Pitcher	.25
Wm. W. Holland	Bowls and vines	.12½
Henry Milton	3 bottles	.25
James M. Ridus	2 bottles	.38
John Milton	1 set spoons	.42½
Kenneth Reddrick	3 Tumblers	.37½
Robert Cherry	Knives & forks	.50

Inventory & amount continued

Richard Holland	1 Bottle Ink	.25
Lynday Cateman	1 Coffee Pot	.31½
Wm. W. Wheatky	1 gourd & salt	.13
Henry Milton	1 dresser	3.75
Robert Cherry	1 Flat Iron	.50
Nelly Shares	2 slugs	1.00
John Holland	1 Flax Hackle	2.31½
Wm Holland	1 Harness & slay	1.00
Willie Holland	1 Umbrella	.25
Wm. W. Holland	2 Coffee pots & 2 pr shears	.37
Richard Holland	3 Gallon Jugs	1.12½
Syndid Latmore	1 small Jug	.12½
Milton	1 Jug	.75
Willy Holland	1 Chest	1.00
Bruton George	2 Reap Hooks	1.00
John E. Williams	1 Rifle gun & pauch	5.12½
Willy Holland	1 Pigeon	.27½
John Holland	1 Water Pail	.08½
Willie Holland I	1 Piggon	.50
Lyndy Latamore	1 Tar Bucket	.62½
Richard Holland	1 Kittle	.87½
John Melton	1 Pot	.37½
Berry W. Wheatly	Overset of hooks	1.00
James Rutherford	1 Shaving Skillett	.37½
Berry W. Eheatly	1 Large Pot & Hooks	2.00
Berry W. Wheatly	1 Washing Tub	.50
Rush Reddick	1 Weeding Hoe	.87½
John W. Hill	1 Club Axe	1.62½
Charles I. Wheatly	1 Bucket	.13
Charles I. Wheatly	1 cat	.25
John Milton	2 pitchforks	1.00
Willie Holland	1 tub	1.62½

Inventory Continued
Page 3

Berry W. Wheatly	1 reel	2.00
Willie Holland	1 reel	2.00

P 3-Continued

Wood J. Cooly	1 churn	$ .50
Berry Vester	1 stand racks	.56¼
Berry W. Wheatly	1 keg vinegar	.75
Neely Shove	1 Slay & harness	.50
Samuel Benton	1 Bee Gum	.50
Willie Holland	1 Empty Barrell	.43½
William W. Holland	1 deer skin	.26
Willie Holland	1 sifter	.50
Willie Holland	1 bead tray	.50
Willie Holland	1 harness	.68½
John Melton	2 bowls	.12½
Samuel Benton	2 boxes	1.00
Willie Holland	1 table	.25
Willie Holland	2 chairs	.62½
Berry Vester	2 pr cards	.50
Richard Holland	1 bee gum	.12½
Nicholas Brown	1 pail	.06½
David Benton	1 plow stock	.43½
Seion Melton	1 lot chairs	1.12½
John Melton	3 chairs	1.25
Rebecca England	1 dining table	2.56½

Page 4 - -----

John Hall	1 ink stand	.12½
James M. Cooly	1 Man saddle	8.00
John Pipin	1 curry comb	.25
John Melton	1 pr gloves	2.75
William W. Holland	1 trot line	1.00
Adye Hall	1 Bee gum	2.52
James Rutherford	1 cow & calf	14.00
Scion Melton	1 calf	3.00
Elizabeth Parker	1 cow	1.00
James M. Reeves	1 heifer	7.00
" " "	1 heifer	6.37½
John P. Benton	1 heifer	3.06½
Samuel Benton	7 heads of hay 1 chair	20.00
John King	16 heads of hay 22 chairs	18.00
Berry Wheatly	1 lot pigs	1.00
John W. Hall	1 pr truck wheels	3.00
James B. Hill	1 horse	32.50
Scarabon J. Cooly	1 Filly colt	20.75
" " "	1 " "	21.75
Parker, Nathan	1 bee stand	1.75
Berry Wheatly	1 side sole leather	2.06½
Perry Melton	1 side sole leather	3.37½
John Hall	1 cross cut saw	6.00
John Pipin	1 plan mole	.75
John Hill	1 hand saw	1.62½
Wm. W. Wheatly	1 hand saw	1.87¼
Wm. W. Holland	1 tennon saw	1.00

Page 4 continued.

John Howard	1 Whip Saw	$ 5.00
William W. Holland	1 square	.40
Willie Norman	1 small saw	.38
John Pippin	1 box tools	3.50
William W. Holland	1 drawing knife	.25
William W. Wheatly	1 drawing knife	.31½
William Holland	1 Axe	1.25
John Holland	1 Axe	1.00
John Milton	1 carving knife	.37½
William Holland	1 Box tools	2.31¼
Willie Norman	1 lot tools	.50
John Milton	1 lot irons	.25
Adge Hall	1 iron wedge putter	.75

Inventory & amounts continued

Page 6.

William Pafford	1 cotton plow	.25
Berry Vester	1 steel guard	1.50
Joseph M. Benton	1 well bucket and irons	2.43½
John Pippin	1 set flumes	3.50
William W. Holland	1 barnard axe	.50
S. Milton	1 lot shut iron	1.25
David Benton	1 lot iron	1.68½
John Milton	1 axe	.50
David Benton	steel	.50
John Hall	1 grind stone	3.50
S. Milton	1 set blacksmith tools	50.00
G. Sealman	1 set timbers	9.64
Bonny Vester	1 bill	1.06¼
Nathaniel B. Parkin	1 sack	.25
K. Reddick	----	8.00
Susan Holland	1 tub and soap	2.12½
John Milton	1 Gunn salt	.12½
Willy Holland	1 stand	.25
William W. Wheatly	1 stand & soap	1.18¾
William W. Holland	1 rope leather & tools	.75
One note James C. Guttry due the 15th day of March 1832 --		11.50
Cash Found		1.30
One note on John Askew May 1st 1836		9.00
One on Martie & B. Castin-Due Jan.1st 1837 for		30.00

ACCOUNTS

Janus Gavin Acct	3.60
John G. Savage Acct.	1.00
Thomas Wheatly Acct.	2.00
David F. England Acct	2.62½
David Farmer Acct	1.00

ACCOUNTS

William W. Holland Acct.	1.12
John Hall acct	1.75
James Jonus Acct.	.25
John Mays Acct.	.12
John Pafford Acct.	5.00

MINUTE BOOK
BENTON COUNTY
1836----1855

Page 8 Continued.

James Holland Acct.	3.74
John Askew Acct.	.25
Samuel Benton Acct.	.62½
David D. Thomas Acct.	.25
George W. Farmer Acct.	.87½
John P. Benton Acct.	.25
Charlie J. Wheatly Acct.	.37½
Berry W. Wheatly Acct	1.12½
Thos. Sanders Acct	.25
Kinnith Reddick	.50
Nathaniel B. Parker Acct	.75
William B. Wheatlu Acct	.12½
Saley Pulley Acct	.25
Assessment by Robert Cherry Acct	2.00
John Melton Acct	3.12½
William Carvill Acct	1.62½
John W. Melton Acct.	.75
TOTAL AMOUNT--	$482.42¾

Page 7 Continued.
State of Tennessee, I william H. Holland do hereby certify that the foregoing is an inventory & amount of sale of the estate of James Holland
deceased So far as yet come to my hands   ' William H. Holland,Adm.
Sworn to in Open Court, June Term 1836-   TEST.

                                        Thos. H. Burden, Clk.

State of Tennessee, Benton County---We the Committee's appointed by the
County Court of said County on the 18th of May 1836, and as agreed to
lay off and set aside for the widow of James Holland, deceased two barrels
of corn, 100 wght four, 150 wght four, 150 wght bacon, 20 lbs of lard, one
buchel of salt, $5.00 worth of sugar & Coffee, one pound of pepper and one
lb of spices.   Samuel Benton
                                     David Benton
                                     Martin Carton

Page-8.
A true list of property of Cyrus Council deceased on this 9th day of
November 1839. On a credit of six months. This a residue of the for sale-
First lot of hogs, Evans Jordin------------- $13.25
2nd lot of hogs, Jessie Hammonds   5.95
3rd lot of Hogs, Jackson A. Jordin.   5.12½
                        Total $24.12½

                 Jessie Hammonds, ADM.

May 17th-1836
Amount of sale of James Cottons Estate

1-Log chain	$ 2.25
1 Cow and calf	7.12½
1 Yoke steers	29.00
1 Cow and calf	11.00
1 Cross cut saw-$3.95-1 lot timbers $2.16-total	5.85

MINUTE BOOK
BENTON COUNTY
1836----1855

Page 8 continued.

1 Heifer-$3.75- 1 horse $65.00	$ 69.25
Page -----9	
1 Bridle .18¢----1 saddle and blanket $4.25	4.43½
1 Auger 25¢. 1 axe 25¢, 1 shot gun 7.12½	7.62½
1 Slate-25¢, 1 plow 2.12½, 1 auger 75¢	3.12½
1 Hose & axe 75¢, 2 chairs 62½¢ 1 pr gurs 75¢	2.87½
1 chire 25¢, 1 pr steel carts 62½, 1 axe 1.50	2.37½
1 chevis and stoop 37½, 2 wheat stones 37½¢	.75
1 axe 50¢, lot iron 1.00 1 single tree 25¢	1.75
1 iron wedge 25¢- 1 geography slate 75¢	1.00
Life Doctor Franklin 50¢, Lewis & Clark 25¢	.75
1 lot salt 1.50 1 goard cords 75	1.31½
1 gourd cord 25¢, 1 bucket cord 37½¢	.87½
1 skillett & lid 87½¢ 1 rope 3.00	3.87½
3 chairs 87½, 1 grindstone 2.00 1 piggon 12½¢	3.00
1 book 50¢, 2 books 2½¢, books 50¢	1.12½
1 lot books 50¢, 1 lot do 25¢, 1 do 6¼	.81¼
2 books 25¢, books 12½, 1 pr saddle boys 4.37½	4.75
1 umbrella 25¢, 1 clock 10.25 L inst 56½	11.06½
1 pitcher 2½, 1 shot & cord 12½, 2 hides 1.25	1.50
1 hoe 25¢, 1 cart 2.95, 1 sheep 87½	3.89½

Page 9

James Daniel	3.12¼
John Weir	.50
George McDaniel	1.75
Jessie Jones	.50
John W. Weir	.25
Amount brought up	182.35
William Lindsy	.25
Lewis Blankhorn	1.18¾
James Stagnr	1.87½
John Lindsey	.75
Jacob Shilling	1.37½
James McDaniel	.62½
One note on B.R.Grissom due Dec.25th 1836	11.50
William Ebear Accountress	.37½
Abonor Johnson Account,	.50
Page 10	
Gabriel Holmes Acct	.25
John Barnes Acct.	.62½
John Anderson, acct.	.37½
William McAuley acct.	.50
	$ 202.53¾

This amount of property and claims filed in my hands, sworn to in open
court, July 4th 1836. Richard Crosswell, Adm.

Page 12. Continued on   page 7-

An amount of sales of the estate of Merritt Holland, Deceased.

John Johnson	Dr. to	One Hoe Weeding $	.37½
Britton George	" "	" Grubbing Hoe	.65
James Holland	" "	" Hand Axe	1.50
" "	" "	" Hand axe	1.95
John Pafford	" "	" Jack Plane	1.93¾
David Benton	" "	" Smoothing Plane (Paid)	.75
Samuel Benton	" "	" Drawing Knife	.51
William Wheatly	" "	" Scythe & Cradle	4.06½
John W. Hall	" "	" Club axe	2.76
John Hall	" "	" Farming Tools	1.06¼
John Pafford	" "	" Farming Tools	2.13¼
Nicholas Brwen	" "	" Log cabin	2.00
William W. Wheatly	" "	" Set traces	1.62½
John Milton	" "	" Rifle, Pouch & Note	14.00
Britton George	" "	" Grind stone	1.76
Richard Holland	" "	" Cotton Plow	1.06½
Adyr Hall	" "	" Shear plow	2.25
" "	" "	" Single Tree	.13
Charlie T. Wheatly	" "	" Saddle & Blanket	11.00
James Holland	" "	" 2 Deer Skins	.31¼
Mathir Holland	" "	" One pr Saddle Boys	4.50
Charlie T. Wheatly	" "	" Hand Axe	2.18¾
Randinck McClowd	" ".	" Iron Wedge	.50
Bowy Visitor	" "	" Pr Montinfels (PAID)	.31½
Robert Cherry	" "	" Razon Box	2.25
Adye Hall	" "	" One DNK	.43¼
John Milton	" "	2 cakes soap	.12½
Richard Holland	" "	One Box	.63
Susannah Holland	" "	" Four sitting chairs	1.00
" "	" "	" Bed & Furniton	8.50
" "	" "	" " "	5.57
John Hall	" "	" Loom	5.50
Susannah Holland	" "	" Spinning Wheel	.50
" "	" "	" Clock Reel	2.00
" "	" "	" Trunk	.75
" "	" "	Two Pots & 2 skilletts	2.00
" "	" "	One Pr day irons	1.50
" "	" "	" Iron & Griddle	.87½
" "	" "	" Shelf Wain	1.50
" "	" "	" Pair & Pigon	.50
" "	" "	" Piece leather	.50
Adge Hall	" "	" Lot boxes	.64½
Susannah Holland	" "	" Cow & Calf	12.00
" "	" "	" " "	11.00
Matthew Wilson	" "	" Bay Horse	40.00
Andrew Benton	" "	" Horse Colt	32.62½
James Holland	" "	" Black Mane colt	17.35
Susannah Holland	" "	" Blade Stack	1.50
" "	" "	" Lot corn	15.00

MINUTE BOOK
BENTON COUNTY
1836----1855

Page 12 continued.

Robert Cherry	Dr.	To	One Lot 6 barrels	$ 10.56¼
Nathaniel B. Park	"	"	" " " "	10.25
Susanah Holland	"	"	8 Head Sheep	12.56
" "	"	"	4 " Hays 1st choice	4.01
Richard Holland	"	"	6 " " 2nd "	6.10
James Holland	"	"	50 Doz Oats	5.00
Ayed Hall	"	"	2 Hays	4.25
Susannah Holland	"	"	2 "	4.00
John Askew	"	"	9 "	10.75
Joanas Holland	"	"	1 calf	2.00
Adye Hall	"	"	1 Fiddle	.87½
John Askew	"	"	9 Head hogs	8.00
Susanah Holland	"	"	One Pr sheep shears	1.00
" "	"	"	" Claw hammer	.25
" "	"	"	" Churn	.50
" "	"	"	" Tub	.50
" "	"	"	" Table	.25

Page 13

N. B. Parks paid to Susanah Holland	5.00
James Holland to Money	17.50
James Garener paid Susanah Holland	1.00
Berry Vester Acct	.25

I Susanah Holland do certify this to be a true inventory
of Merritt Holland Estate, sworn to and subscribed to in open
court this 6th day of September 1836.

                              Her
                    Susanah X Holland
                         Mark.

Page -13

Inventory and account of the sale of the Estate of Abel Rushing
Deceased.November 4th 1836.

Property Sale	To Whom Sold.	
Bed stead and furniture-	Nancy Rushing	$18.00
Saddle & Bridle	" "	19.00
Bed and furniture	Sarah Rushing	15.00
" " "	William G. Rushing	15.00
One bureau	Sarah Rushing	12.00
One sugar chest	Nancy Rushing	9.00
One clock & case	John B. Carson	5.62½
One cupboard & Furniture-	Sarah Rushing	1.50
Ten chairs	Sarah Rushing	3.00
One rifle gun	Wm. G. Rushing	13.50
Two tables	Sarah Rushing	2.00
One Bed & Furniture	Jack Rushing	15.00
" " " "	Robert Rushing	15.00
One hand saw	William W. Holmes	1.50

Page 13-Continued

Property Sale	To Whom Sold	
One hand saw	William W. Holland	$ .31½
One axe	Berry Vester	1.12½

Page 14....

One auger	William Baker	.25
One axe	Jack Taylor	.03½
One auger	Joce Taylor	.12½
One iron wedge	Jonas Watkins	.75
" " "	Sarah Rushing	.62
" axe	" "	1.50
" claw hammer	Berry Vester	.12
" drawing knife & hoe	Abner Smalley	.25
" spinning wheel	Lewis Brewer	.31¼
" " "	Sarah Rushing	2.50
" flax wheel	" "	5.00
" pr steel cards	Elbert Wiggle	1.81
Three gallons Timothy seed	V. W. Burton	.81¼
One side saddle	Sarah Rushing	5.00
One man saddle	Elbert Wiggle	2.06¼
" " "	Ephriam Perkins	5.50
" " "	Sarah Rushing	3.00
One Loom Bar	" "	6.00
One chisel	T.W.Burton	.18¾
One lot Leather	Aborin Smalley	.52
Three plows, 3 pr guns 3 hoes	Sarah Rushing	13.00
One ox plow	Bonney Howin	4.00
One caulder	William Pearce	.75
One cutting knife & box	Alfred Ballard	3.13½
One Krune plow	William Pearce	2.17
One mattress	W. R. Vester	2.56½
One cavy plow & churn	W. R. Vester	1.27½
One spade	W. R. Perkins	.25
One hand axe	Abner Smalley	.43½
One horse harness	J.L.McCracken	3.75
One side sole leather	James Ballard	3.75
One side sole leather	John Presson	1.56¼
One side sole leather	James Alexander	4.00

Page 15 ------

One side sole leather	Sarah Rushing	2.31½
Three deer skins	Elijah Alsup	1.25
One lot barrels	Sarah Rushing	1.00
One lot cuslings & coopers	" "	7.00
One bay mare & colt	W. G. Rushing	75.00
One sorrell mare	Sarah Rushing	40.00
One sorrell one year colt	James McGill	46.25
One bay colt	Sarah Rushing	50.00
One sorrell horse	Thomas McGill	51.00

MINUTE BOOK
BENTON COUNTY.
1836----1855

Page 15 continued.

Property Sale	To whom sold	
One Bull	Abner Smalley	$ 8.00
One white & Black cow and yearling	Benjamin Bradly	10.00
One cow and calf	John McGill	11.31
One bull	Isaac Ballard	5.75
One lot cattle-5 head	Sarah Rushing	38.00
One red heifer	Nancy Rushing	11.25
One black heifer	Isaac Ballard	5.00
Five 1st choice sheep	Sarah Rushing	7.50
Four 2nd choice sheep	Lewis Holland	6.37
Three sheep	Thos Ward	4.00
On account claim, Robert Rushing		37.00
One large chair,	Isaac Ballard	4.00

Property sale on December 30th 1836

One book of Lafayette	J.H.Burton	.62
One lot of books	Thos. Wharton	.31
" " " "	" "	.50
One geography	Robert Rushing	.20
One Life Marion	Thos. Wharton	.12
One arithmetic	Jos Greer	.20
One dictionary	Stephen Rushing	.75
One Life of Washington	Thomas Wharton	.31
One pr harness	L.D.Pierce	.18¾
One pr guns	W. R. Hudsons	.75

Page -----16

One cheese	Elijah Alsp	.12½
One auger	Joel Taylor	.31¼
Four bee stands	Sarah Rushing	2.00
1/3 of a wheat fan	Sarah Rushing	3.00
Three heard of geese	" "	4.00
One stack of fodder	S.W.Barton	2.37
" " " "	" " "	1.68¼
" " " "	Sarah Rushing	5.00
One lot of oats	" "	1.00
" " " hay	A smaley	.75
One ox cart	Sarah Rushing	10.00
One yoke oxen	John Faulkner	65.00
One pr steel cards	Sarah Rushing	.50
One lot of corn	A. Smalley	7.50
One lot 5 barrel corn	A. Smalley	7.50
" " " " "	Jno. Pierce	7.48¾
" " " " "	R. C. Petty	9.18¾
" " " " "	J. J. Rushing	7.18¾
" " " " "	R. C. Petty	7.50
" " " " "	Stephen Rushing	7.18¾
" " " " "	Nancy Rushing	6.87½
" " " " "	John Wood	7.30

MINUTE BOOK
BENTON COUNTY
1836-----1855

Page 16- Continued.

Property Sale--	To Whom sold	
One lot of 5 barrel corn	John Wood	$ 7.25
" " " " " "	Robert Rushing	7.18¾
" " " " " "	Stephen Rushing	7.18¾
" " " " " "	S. H. Burton	7.18¾
" " " " " "	R. C. Petty	7.18¾
" " " " " "	John Wood	7.90
" " " " " "	S. H. Burton	7.00
" " " " " "	Joshua Ove	7.20
" " " " " "	Joshua Ove	7.20
" " " " " "	Thos Beavens	7.18¾
" " " " " "	John Jackson	7.20
" " " " " "	S. H. Burton	7.50
" " " " " "	John Jackson	7.20
" " " " " "	L. D. Pierce	5.25
First " " " "	Joel Taylor	19.37½
Second " " " "	Burrell Rushing	15.25

Page 17 -----

Property Sale	To Whom sold	
Three lot 10 head hays	John Warren	$13.12
Four " 16 " "	Wm. G. Rushing	16.00
Five " 6 " "	John Warren	15.51
Six " 10 " "	John H. Warren	9.50
Seven " 1 " "	Cash	5.00
Eight " 6 " "	Jack Edward	24.50
Nine " 2 " "	John Havaman	3.23
Ten " 3 " "	John Bill	14.25
Eleven " 4 " "	L. D. Pierce	7.00
Twelve " 14 " "	Sarah Rushing	14.00
Thirteen 3 " "	James Hancel	6.00
One occupant claims	Joel Rushing	20.00
One negro woman & 12 children		
hired 12 months	Sarah Rushing	200.00
One Negro man (Ben)	Joel Rushing	79.00

A list of notes and accounts and cash found in the possession of Abel
Rushing, December, at the time of his death, follows, to wit:
One note on James C, Brown due March 1st 1839 for $125.00 this note is
very doubtful.
One note on James Melton for eight barrels of corn, Doubtful.
One note on J. L. Lashalason for $4.00 due May-doubtful.
One note on D. Rushing for $13.33 due Sept. 3rd 1836.
One account on W. R. Vester for $5.00.
    "   "   "   Benton Rushing   2.00
    "   "   "   Elizabeth Thornton 9.46
Cash on hand   100.00
Page 18.
We the undersigned administrators of the estate of Abel Rushing do

Page 18 Continued.
hereby certify that the foregoing contains a true inventory and accounts
of sale with the notes accounts and cash of said estate which has come into
our hands or knowledge of to the present time.
January 2nd 1837.

HER
Sarah Rushing-Admr.
MARK

Joel Rushing Administrator .....A supplementary Inventory of Jonas
Holland deed the rent of the land for the year 1836. Amounts to the
sum of Forty Dollars $40.00.
Wm. W. Holland.

Page 19.

An inventory and amount of sale of the Estate of William Combs, Deceased.

Articles sold	To Whom Sold	Amount
3 bedsteads & furniture	Mary Combs	$ 20.00
1 Lot kitchen ware	Mary Combs	5.10
28 head hogs	Mary Combs,	25.00
1 saddle mare	Mary Combs	30.00
2 cows	Mary Combs	15.00
6 sheep	Mary Combs	5.00
1 set plows and gurs	Mary Combs	2.00
2 Bee Gums	Mary Combs	2.00
1 Lot of Tobacco	Mary Combs	.50
1 hand saw	Mary Combs	.25
12. Head gear	Mary Combs	1.00
1 Padlock	Mary Combs	.25
1 Yoke Oxen	Marvin Sayles	14.00
1 Gray Mare	Charlie Sarratt	51.25
1 Sorrell colt	William Swindle	20.25
1 Sorrell colt	James Cooper	16.12
1 Crosscut saw	Matthew Williams	7.12
1 saddle	William Northington	18.00
1 Rawhide	James Shirley	1.37½
3 Plain Pots	James Cooper	1.03½
1 steel trap	Jonathan Smith	1.50
1 spread	William Matin	.37½
1 lot iron	James Shirley	1.43½
1 Wagon	S. H? Davidson	27.00
1 Gun	Thos Hubbs	9.62½
1 plow	James Willey	1.00
1 Set B.S.Tools	William Camp	37.25
1 Square	James S. Sayles	.62½
1 lot iron	James Cooper	.25
1 lot bricks	James Sayles	6.25

MINUTE BOOK
BENTON COUNTY
1836----1855

Page 20

The whole amount of sale of William Combs. Died 24th day of October
1836. --------- ------- $333.09½
October 1836. Received of James Wyly...... 2.51
Cash .75
Cash 5.00
Cash 1.75
Amount of Shop accounts 71.91
We Mary Combs administrator and James S. Sayles administrator of
Estate of William Combs, do hereby certify that the foregoing is a
true inventory.of the amounts of sales of the Estate of William
Combs, Deceased. Also notes accounts and cash. That has come to our hands
as yet.January 20th 1839.
Mary Combs
James S. Sayles.

State of Tennessee.Benton County. We the committee appointed
by the Honorable Court. At the October Term of 1836. to set apart
a sufficient quantity of provisions to save the widow and family
of William Combs, Deceased.
We do find, fix, set apart the following provisions-
Twelve Hundred weight of pork. Or Sixty Dollars. Twenty Five Barrels of
corn or $36.00. Sixteen dollars for sugar & coffee, four bushels of salt or
three dollars. Two sides of leather or six dollars and fifty cents.
Fifty lbs of picked cotton or eight dollars. One hundred pounds of soap
or six dollars. Three bushels of oats or $1.21½. $2.50 for potatoes
150 lbs of flour. or $4.50, $3.50 for whisky, spice, pepper, ginger, the
milk of the two cows or $5.00. Nothing on hand but 12 barrels of corn
October 24th 1836.
James Wyly
William Thompson
Healloway Key.

Page 21........

State of Tennessee, Benton County. We the undersigned committeemen met
on the 1st day of December according to an order of court
authorizing with said committeemenx to lay off and set apart to
Sarah Griffin her dower of land in the county aforesaid. Beginning
820 Poles, south 96 poles, H. Wades south east corner. Surety.
640 acres, beginning at a stake 3 white oak and 3 sweet gum and
a chestnut pointers, running 33½ poles to a black gum thence north 33½
poles to a dogwood. Thence east 48 poles to the beginning.Corner it
being 10 acres.
Range 6 section 4. and also five acre tract lying--Range 6 section 4 beginning a dogwood 56 poles, south of the southwest corner of entry.
No 1662 for 10 acres, running thence south 4 poles to a stake. Black
oak dogwood and gum pointers. Thence west 20 poles to a dia oak Hickory
White Oak & Gum Pointers, thence north 4 poles 40 poles to a stake maple gum
White oak pointers thence south 20 poles to the beginning.Corner
and also one track of fine acorns,beginning one pole south of south

Page 21 Continued.

East corner of entry No.11662 on a stake poplar dogwood, and black
gum, with two sweet gum pointers thence west 40 poles to a poplar
black gum and black pointers. Thence north 20 poles to a stake 4
poplar pointers thru east to the beginning corner which we the
commissioners hereunto set our hands and seals this 1st day of Dec.1836.

                         Levin Cottonhame
                         John F. Johnston
                         John Elmore
                         E. W. Lynch

Page 22

A list of doubtful notes and accounts of the Estate of Aswill Matlock,
Deceased.
One note on Robert Brady made payable to Z. Thompson for $73.00
due October 1824.
One receipt J. P. Wall as Constable Regnoble.
One note to William Henderson for Eighty Dollars made payable to
Benj Atkins.
On the 25th day of December 1834, assigned over by Anderson Carson
on 23rd of October 1835.
One note on Mandy Armour six dollars made payable to squire Evans
on 20th December 1836.
One note on squire Evans from Neal Dalton made payable to John L.
McCracken, due Sept.23rd 1836.
One note on Jon McDaniel for $10.00 note made payable to squire Evans
Due Dec 25th 1835.
Page 23.
One Account on Jesse Newman for Nine Dollars. Dated February 1835 with
a credit of two dollars on account.
One on Wallis Beard for nine dollars and 25 cents dated January 1835.
One note on John Sayle for six dollars,made payable to John McCracken.
Due February 26 1836.
One account on George A. Kornegay & Irvin B. Carnes for ninety nine
dollars and fifth cents. Dated January 1st 1836.
One account on Anderson Bivens for seventy seven dollars & fifty cents.
One account on Squire Evans due 1836. for $3.43. One account on John
Sayles. $10.43 due 1835. One account on William Conrad for $1.00.

Page 24.

One account on James Martin .12½. One account on James Walker 25¢.
A list of notes & accounts that Caswell Matlock deeds possession of.
One note Rob Carson Forty Dollars. Due Jan 1st 1836. One receipt on
James Holmes. Claiming for one note of Fifty Dollars & fifty cents on
Irvin B. Carnes. Due January 1st 1836. One on H. Z. Minor Steel for
Forty Dollars. Due February 1836. One note on John Griffin Twenty
Five dollars. Due January 1st 1836. One account on Elizabeth Wood for
ten dollars August 1835. Account on John Johnston for $2.46. One account

Page 24 continued.
on James Massey for 25¢ due 1835.
Account on Mansfield Barnett-due 1835 for .06¼¢
Account on Michie Fry due 1835 for   1.06¼¢
Cash on hand Twenty Dollars ...

State of Tennessee, Benton County,-An inquisition, Kirkman Ferry
said county on the 20th of January 1837.Before George Camp Coroner
for and of said county aforesaid, upon the virs of the body of an
infant.Alone and thin lying deceased upon their oats who hung
sworn and cranged to inquest on the the point of the State aforesaid,
when how and in what manner the said infant was murdered upon the oats
present and say that they believe that the infant was murdered
in witness whereof as will of the aforesaid have to this inquest put
the seal on this August and year aforesaid.

George Camp   William Thompson-Foreman
Coroinn   James Arnold
                      Wm. Morrison
                     Jonus M. Camp
                     Joel Camp
                     William Northington
                     Thomas Wiseman
                     Absalom Smith
                     T.A.Noel
                     Henry C. Camp
                     William Brush

State of Tenn, Benton County, With commissioners appointed by the court
to set apart an addition to what has hereto aforebear, set apart, serve
the widow and family of James Holland, Deceased, met and say she be allowed
Twenty Five dollars cash. February 6th 1837.

                              John Jackson
                              Lewis Brewer
                              William Rushing

Page 26.
An inventory amount of sale of the estate of Burrell Alsop December
23rd 1836 and February 1837.

Purchasers name	Items	Price
Nicholson Brown	1 Flask	$ .43¾
Eligah Alsup	1 Flask	.06¼
Eligah Alsup	1 Shoe Brush	.18¼
Isham Jones (Note)	1 Hone	.75
Elisha M. Hewer (Paid)	1 Set shoe tools	.81¼
Hugh Alsup	1 Razor	.25
Samuel Alsup (Note)	1 Box & Brush	.75
William Johnson	1 Brush	.50
Susan Alsup	1 Butcher Knife	.25
Jesse Roseberg	1 Pocket book	.31½
Susanah Alsup	1 Butcher Knife	.25

Page 26 continued..

Purchasers name	Items	Price
Hugh Alsup	1 Bottle caster oil.	$ .25
Mary Alsup	1 Umbrella	1.00
Samuel Alsup	1 Trunk	1.50
Jefferson Murray (NOTE)	1 Pr saddle bags	.38¼
Hugh Alsup	1 Mans saddle	9.50
Asa Price (NOTE)	1 Blanket	2.00
L. W. Brewer	1 Bridle	.56¼
Wm. H. Johnson	1 spelling book	.06¼
John W. Tilley (PAID)	1 Ink Stand	.18¾
David Brown (Note)	1 pr gun	2.93¾
Hugh Alsup	1 Hay	3.18¾
Jesse Roseberg	1 plow	3.00
Eligah Alsup	1 single tree	1.00
Samuel Alsup	5 barrels corn $1.50 per B	8.00
William Carmack (Note)	5 " " " " "	7.81¼
Laughlin Branton "	5 " " " " "	7.81
Daniel Buchanan	1.56 per barrel more or less	2.29½
Robert Jones (Note)	1 Clevis	.37½
Thos. L.Floyd	1 Truck cutter	.25
Daniel Buchanan	1 Lot corn 81¼ per barrel	1.54½
James Alsup	1 Occupant	5.00
Jacob Edward	1 Sorrell Horse	85.06½
George Cathey (PAID)	1 Curry Comb	.12½
Delton Shellberg	261 Bundles of Fodder	1.81¼
Cash		.49
		$205.33¾

I, Eligah Alsup do certify that the within is a just and true inventory of and amount of sale of the Estate of Burwell Alsup, Deceased. So far as yet come to hand, given under my hand this 3rd of April 1837.

Eligah Alsup

Sworn to in open court, April 3rd 1837. Tho.H. Burton, Clerk.

Page 27.

State of Tennessee, Benton County, A list of notes and accounts due the Estate of Harvey Hatley, Deceased. Also the ready cash belonging to the aforesaid estate, both solvent and insolvent. In June 1837. And notes and accounts not yet due belonging to the sole Estate aforesaid with their sworn dates and one judgement on Heasley Holloway for Twenty One Dollars with interest from the 26th of December 1836... $21.40
Also judgement Absalom Swift for with interest from the 1st day of April 1837 20.00
One note Redding Hallowell for nine dollars-Apr 7th 1837 9.00

MINUTE BOOK
BENTON COUNTY
1836-----1855

Page 27 continued.

Elisha Tedders note for Fifty Five due the first day of January
1839... $55.00
Also the same for $27.50 due the 1st Jan 1837.   27.50
One note Garrett Swindle and Jones Marchbank due Sept 1st
1837 ....   7.50
One note William Pull due December 29th 1836 for Two
Dollars.   2.00

Page 28----
One note Pleasant Mullinks due Dec 25th 1837   39.00

One note Richard Hicks for fifty cents.Due July 15th-36   .50

One account Elisha Tedder for Seven Dollars   7.00

One account on Hyram Curfew for one dollar eighty seven cents   1.87

One account Allen Mulinkis   1.75

One account Garrett Swindle   2.50

One account on Joel Tedder for Twelve Dollars   12.00

One account on Daniel Waggoner   2.50

List of property such live stock household furniture
farming articles, belonging to the Estate of Hardy Hatley
Deceased, on the 30th day of June 1837.

The widow- 1 bull, cow yearling		8.00
" " 1 Cow and calf		7.00
James Cooper one cow		12.12½
Dewey Reeves, 1 black calf		10.50
The widow 1 black heifer		5.31¼
Alfred Lewis-1 red heifer		7.12½
The widow	1 black heifer	5.00
" "	1 dove "	1.50
Henry Camp	1 black steer	3.37½
Edward Simmons	1-Black bull	6.87½
Henry Camp	1-Black heifer	3.87½
The widow	1-Yoke steers	40.00
Luke Hatley	1-Lot hogs	9.00
Hyman Swift	2 sows and ten pigs	8.31½
The widow	34-Head hogs	10.00
Page 29		
The widow	Plows and grass hoe	1.50
" "	1-Lot	.25
" "	1-Lot kitchen furniture	3.00
" "	1-Rifle gun	8.00
" "	4-Bedstead & furniture	25.00
" "	1-Side saddle	5.00

Page 29 Continued

Eli Halley	1 man saddle	$ 5.00
The widow	1 mans saddle	.12½
" "	25. Head gus	1.25
" "	11 head sheep	7.00
" "	1.Lot plank	.25
" "	1.Scythe and cradle	.50
William C. Coward	1 Sorrell horse	62.00
The Widow	1.Sorrell mare	30.00
Eli Harley	1.Sorrell Colt	15.00

Page 30----

Luke Hatley	1 Sorrell horse and saddle	50.00
The widow	1 Lot tools	1.00
" "	2 Sides leather	1.00
Joel Tedder	1 Spotted sow and 4 pigs	4.12½
William Morrison	1 Sow & pigs	4.00
Eli Hatly	1 sow & 9 pigs	11.50
Wm. Hatly	1 Sow and 7 pigs	5.12½

The foregoing is a true account of notes and accounts with the sale
of the property together with the cash on hand belonging to the estate
of Hardy Hatly Deceased so far as has come to my hand. Sworn to and
subscribed in open court this 3rd day of July 1837.

                                              Edward Hatly.

State of Tennessee, Benton County. Agreeable to an order of the
honorable court of said county, we have this date met at the late
residence of Hardy Hatly, Deceased to lay of years provisions
for the widow and family which we have done and beg leave to report
as follows.

Twenty five barrels of corn, fifteen pounds on the place, also forty
dollars to buy pork, 12 bushels of wheat, 180 lbs of bacon found on
place, 4 bushels of salt, $1.50

40 lbs of coffee	$ 8.00
50 lbs sugar	5.00
2 lbs pepper	.75
1 lb spice	.37½

Sixty one dollars. Sixty two to come out of proceeds of sale.
This 29th of June 1837.

                                 Committeemen
                                 Pleasant Mullinks
                                 Amos Bruce
                                 George Camp

MINUTE BOOK
BENTON COUNTY
1836-----1855

Page 30 Continued ...

A supplementary inventory of the Estate of James Holland, deceased,
for tents in the year 1837 to amount of $29.50 of returned
May term 1838 on oats---open court---

W.W.M.Holland.

Test. THOS. H. BURTON-CLERK

Page 31..

State of Tennessee, Benton County, a list of property belonging to the
Estate of Sherod Hatly, late of North Carolina, and commissioned in
papepeon of the subscribe and Guardian, of the for said Sherod Hatly.
The year of our Lord 1838. and first Monday of AugustBeg)

1. Negro man (named Albros) about 37 yrs
1. Negro woman (named Nancy) about 30 yrs.
3 small children making five in all.
1. Bed and furniture.
2. notes on Monk Hatly amounting to twenty four dollars and seventy
seven & ½ cents. One said note for 12.50 comes due Nov.25th 1839
the other due first day of January 1838.-Edward Hatly, Guardian,
Sherrod Hatly.

An account of the Esate of Rebecca England, Deceased, Sold 17th February
1838.

Property Sold	To whom sold	Price
1.Oven and lid	Alfred Brown	$ 1.25
1.Pot and hooks	Sterling Brown	1.43¼
1.Washing tub	Calvin Reddick	1.65

Page 32.

1.Kittle	Jonas Gorman	2.00
1.Axe and piece of metal	John Miller	.25
1. Lot tools	George Cather	1.06¼
1.Bell	John Phifer	.18¾
1.Skillitt	Jonas Gorman	.40
1.Tin bucket	James T. Farmer	.43¼
1 Water Pail	John Noble	.50
1.Piggin	W.W.Wheatly	.31¼
1.Table	Sterling Brown	2.62½
1.Mashur ½ bushel	W. W. Wheatly	.32½
1. Clevis & single tree	Peter Hubbard	.75
1.Hoe	John Milton	.12½
1.Spinning wheel	John Nobles	1.81¼
1. Plow	Jonue Benton	4.00
1. Loom	Calvin Reddick	1.25
1 Pr gun	Peter Hubbard	2.25

Page 32 Continued.

Property Sold	To Whom	Price
1. Churn	James Garner	$----
1.Slay	" "	.75
1. "	S. Miller	.75
12.Slay & hames	John Melton	1.00
1.Bag Cotton	James Alsup	1.81¼
2.Sitting chairs	A.J.Benton	.73
2 " "	Rob Jonus	.56½
2.Barrels	Benjamin Brewer	.12½
1.Sife	John Milton	.30
1.Barrell	James Garner	.25
1. Chest	William Falkner	2.50
1.pr cards	John Lehapher	.69¾
1 Basket & lid	John Melton	32½¢
1.Box	S. Milton	.50
" "	" "	.50
2.Books	Robert Jones	.37½

Forward amount brought over

Page 33.

2.Books	Dan C. Brewer	.43¾
2.Books Hugh Alsup	Hugh Alsup	.12½
1.Bottle & crock	Robert Jones	.25
1.Looking Glass	John Phiphin	.30
1.Bottle	Peter Hubbard	.20
1.Coffee Pot	James Garner	.12½
1.Coffee Pot	John Melton	.12¼
1.Tugg	George Bell	.32¼
1.Chest	John Melton	3.62½
1.Lot Cotton	James Garner	.25
1.Crock	Andrew Benton	.12½
1.Lot wares	William Wheatly	.37½
5.Plates	Jessy Rasberry	1.00
2.Plates	James Garner	.12½
1.Dish	John Phifer	.50
1.Table	John Melton	2.37½
Knives & Forks	Edward L. Hattamon	2.06½
1.Bed & furniture	James Garner	17.00
1.Stead	John Nobles	1.80
1.Bed & furniture	James Garner	19.50
1.Stead	John Nobles	.30
1.Pot rack	Thos.Wheatly	2.12½
1.Bed & furniture	David Brewer	20.00
1.Stead	Wm.W.Wheatly	1.00
1.Flat Iron	Chas. B. Reddick	.75
2.Bowls	James Garner	.25
1 Cow & calf	Hugh Alsup	16.50

Page 33

Property Sold	To Whom	Price.
1.Cow & Calf	John Bell	$16.81½
1.Heifer	John Askew	4.31½
1.Steer	John Askew	4.25
9.Head of Hogs	John Askew	18.37½

Page 34.

1.Sow & Pigs	Robert Cheney	4.00
1.Black Sow	George Castra	3.94
3.Head of Hogs	John Askew	9.00
1.Small Mare	Daniel Brewer	67.50
1.Colt	Joseph Askew	23.12½
1.Mare & Colt	William Carmack	28.12½
1.Lot of Meat	William Wheatly	4.25
1.Bee Gum	John Askew	1.00
1.Bee Gum	John Noble	.25
3.Geese	S.Wheatly	.87½
1.Club Axe	John Phifer	1.00
1.Bell	George Bell	---
1.Axe	John Phifer	1.82
160.Bundles of Fodder.	James Garner	1.62½
1.Occupants Clam	John Nobles	11.60
1.Occupants Judgement	James Garner	50.00
	Total Amount	$ 388 .14

State of Tennesse, Benton County,This day James Garner Administrator
of the Estate of Rebecca England,Deceased.Came before me Geo W.Farmer
one of the Justices of in said County.After being duly sworn, according
to law.Says the above within is an inventory and accounts of sale of the
personal Estate of Rebecca Englad so far as yet come into my hands.An
knowledge of the Administrator sworn to and subscribed before me this
11th day of June 1838.

Test...George W.Farmer::: James Garner.

Page 35.

Name	Property Sold	Price.
E.Leais	1.pr cat cards	$ .50¢
Isaac Lynch	3.Coffe Mills	.62½
John B.Presson	3.pr cotton cards	.50¢
Hardy Rushing	4.Curry Combs	.10
Ephriam Perkins	1.Pr Cast Butts	.50
" "	5.Pr blk hoes	.41
" "	3.Pr Lastig Shoes.	.76
H.S.Daniel	3 " " "	.89½
J.W.Utley	3." " "	.93¾
Joy Presson	30.¾ Domestic.	.10

MINUTE BOOK
BENTON COUNTY
1836----1855

Page-35-Continued.

Name	Property sold	Price
William Sykes	31¼.Calico @	$ .27¢
Edward Lucas	28. Calico @	.27
Ephriam Perkins	14. Calico @	.21
" "	14½. Calico @	.28
" "	9½ Calico @	.38
John H. Williams	27½.Calico @	.17
G. W. Beard	1. Not ridden	6.50
T. James	6. pr hoes	.33
Tomas Hicks	4. Tuck Combs	.31¼
John Haywood	8 " "	.13
" "	5.Shaving Box	.64¢
Isaac Lynch	10½ Doz.Buttons	.12½
John Bayc	I. Lot Gun Flints	.50
E. Smith	6 razor Strops	.28
Ephriam Perkins	7½ Yds of Calico	.17
" "	30½ " " "	.30
" "	5¼ " " "	.18
" "	10¼ " " "	.41
Isaac Lynch	32 " " "	.31¼
James Hicks	13¼ " " "	.23
Isaac Lynch	4¼ " " "	.10
R. H. Burton	2¾ " " "	.16
H. W. Barker	19¾ " " "	.26
T. H. Burton	28 " " "	.32
Jas McCard	4¼ " " "	.12½
Robt Homes	8¼ " " "	.16
John Williams	10½ " " "	.19
Page 36		
H. M. Brown	21¾ " " "	.16
John R. Lewis	28 " " "	.34
H. W. Barker	28 " " "	.22
Truon B. Carns	31¼ " " "	.25
James Hicks	7½ " " "	.31
James W. Utley	31 " " "	.19
John Haywood	13 " " "	.26
" "	20 " " "	.27
H. S. Daniel	10 yds blk cambric	.14
James Hicks	15½.Calico	.20
S. H. Burton	10 "	.30
Irving B. Carns	15¾ "	.13
H. W. Barker	17 "	.13
A. G. Hunt	19¾ "	.27
G. A. Noles	41/ A.Checks	.17
H. W. Barker	12½ Calico	.32
Jon Haywood	21¼ "	.12½
John Ballard	26¼ "	.28
J. W. Utley	15¾ "	.23
Edward Louis	17½ "	.43¾
John Davis	7. "	.31
G. W. Beard	¾. Blue Cloth	5.25

Page -36- Continued.

Name	Property Sold	Price
J?W.Utley	17½. Calico	$ .22
" " "	6¼. "	.30
" " "	24½. "	.15
S.Tass	32½. "	.38
T.M.McCord	4¼. "	.18
John Jackson	22½. "	.20
H.Short	9½/ "	.40
E.Lewis	3 .Flannels	.37½
Irvin B.Carns	34¼. "	.32½
John Jackson	11 .Calico	.42
John Flowers	3½.Blue Cloth	8.00

Page -#- 36

Wyatt Arnold	5¾..Blk Cloth	5.50
S.H.Burton	3½/Calico.	.16
C.C.Roe	22½.Calico	.20
J.W.Utley	7 .Pr Suspenders	.80
Hardy Rushing	21¾.Domestic.	.31
A.Ballard	28¼. "	.26
S.Ross	33. "	.30
Harvey Rushing	21¼ "	.34
J.Jackson	26 . Yds Calico	.39
J.W.Utley	10. " "	.28
A.G.Hurt	1./Bed & Furniture	18.00
Isaac Lynch	1.Meat	3.00
H.Short	1.Meat	3.00
John McAuley	1. "	4.76
J.W.Utley	1. "	3.37¼
S.Ross	1.CarryYou & Harness	51.24
Thos McGill	1.Saddle & C.	17.50
John Haywood	1. Mare	72.50
John Jackson	20¾.Calico.	.22

Page 37-

J.W.Utley	28 .Calico/	.17
Wm Sykes	18¾. "	.32
John McAuley	6 . "	.34
John Haywood	32 "	.15½
John Utley	.Tobacco.	.18
John Boyd	1 .White Hats	3.00
James McCord	13¼/Cosinet	1.32
J.W.Utley	24 .Lb Spot Morino.	.43
W.McAuley	2½.Block Clothe	4.17
" "	11¼.Cosinet	1.13
Joh Haywood	5 .Cork Ink Stands	.30
J.H.Burton	½.Doz Snuff Boxes	.25
John Jackson	3 .Ink Stands	.73
E.Jordon	5 .Snuff Boxes	.13

Page 37-Continued.

Name	Property Sold	Price
James McCord	25½. Domestic.	$ .14¢

Page 38..

John Haywood	1. Japan Chest	.31¢
Jonus Alexander	1. Doz C. Buttons	.69
J.Haywood	1 S Brush	.09
J.Alexander	3. Doz C Buttons	.30
T.Jonus	1.Pr Teaspoons	.12½
S.Rogers	7. Boxes Wafers	.07
N.Hampton	1½ Teaspoons	.16
Hume Darby	4.Razors	.61
Cash	1.Doz B.Teaspoons	.62½
John Haywood	3.Snuff Boxes	.03
" "	7.Tuck Combs	.09
" "	4. " "	.87
W.Stuart	4. " "	.30
John Haywood	5.Pr S.Combs	.06
J.S.Sayles	4.Pr S.Combs	.06
John Boyd	5.Pr S Combs	.08
H.Darby	12.Wood Combs	.23
John Haywood	1.Doz C Butts	.41
G.Jonus	5. Box L.Caps	.16
T.Alexander	2. Pr Brass Knucks	.82
E.Perkins	1. Pr Brass Knucks	.87
Hume Darby	4.Pocket Knifes	.32
Cash	4.Table spoons	.50
G.Jones	4. " "	.50
T.Alexander	3.Doz Bolts	.21
Y.Jones	4.Ink Stands	.16
J.W.Utley	5. Pkg Staves.	.12
E.Punknis.	1.Doz C. Butts.	.52
E.Lewis	5.Paper Tocks	.09
T.Boyd	9. " "	.12½
J.Utley	1.Doz Pocket Knives	.36
T.Jonus	2.Sets B.Teaspoons	.21
J.W.Utley	8.Chest locks	.11
" " "	10.Pad Locks	.20
" " "	4.Stock Locks	.65
Irvin B.Carns	1.Doz C.Butts	1.25
S.S.Madden	9.Gun Locks	1.00

Page 39----

J.W.Utley	5.Ban H.Pins	.11
Cash	5 " " "	.12½
G.Flowers	7 " " "	.16
Cash	2.Paper Tocks	.12½
J.W.Utley	2.Sets Knives & Forks	.81
" " "	4. " " " "	.88

Page 39-Continued.

Name	Property Sold.	Price.
J.W.Utley	6.Sets Knives & Forks	$ 1.00
" " "	7.Pr Scissors	.38
J.McAuley	3½.Doz Gin Buttons	.84
E.Perkis	2. Papers urrd scruado	.38
J.Haywood	3 " " "	1.00
J.W.Utley	1. " " "	.25
" " "	1.Lot needles	3.13
" " "	9.Papers of fish hooks	.18¢½
S.Rogers	4.Insect Powders	.11
J.W.Utley	5½.Doz Lasling Buttons	.38
" " "	3 .Pr Wood Combs	.03
" " "	3 Pcket Knives	.20
" " "	3 Pocket knives	.39
" " "	3 Pr side combs	.11
N.Short	11 Fine comb	.08
J.Haywash	1 Pr shoe brushes	.18¾
J.W.Utley	4 " " "	.16
H.Roberts	1 Brass C.Slick	.58
J.W.Utley	6 Shaving Brushes	.09
" " "	2½ Teaspoons	.13
J.S.Sayles	2 Curry combs	.14
J.W.Utley	1 Lot sundries	1.18
Cash	1 Corn T Stand.	.11
A.Lashlee	6 Iron squares	.44
J.W.Utley	1 Black Hat	3.87
" " "	1 " "	2.12
J.Alexander	1 " "	2.82
J.W.Utley	1 " "	3.12½
" " "	1 " "	2.25
S.Rogers	1 " "	3.00
N.Strickland	12.Yds calico	.37½
J.Alexander	2 Pr Fancy Hoes	.67
J.W.Utley	5 Yds Gingham	.67

Page 40..

Name	Property Sold.	Price.
J.W.Utley	8 Pr White hoes	.39
J.W.Utley	10. " " "	.62½
" " "	18½ Yds of Gingham	.38
" " "	21 " " muslin	.40
" " "	5 " " gingham	.35
H.S.David	15½ " " padding	.29
J.W.Ulley	2½ " " vesting	.56
" " "	2½ " " "	.53
" " "	18½ " " pink cambric	.22
" " "	15 " " tuck combers	.67
J.Ballard	1 ###### shawl.	1.11
J.Burton	1.Shawl	1.07
T.Viach	2.Shawls	.89

Page-40-Continued.

Name	Property Sold	Price.
H.Roberts	5. Cas Handles	$ $.33¢
H.Wtley	1½.Yds of Bobinet	.58
E.Jordon	7/8.Yds" "	.50
C.M.Sarratt	1.Stock	.93
J.Haywood	1.Stock	1.00
J.W.Utly	1.S.I.Friels	1.01
" " "	1.Seamies silk	.09
H.S.Daniel	4.Pr Scissors	.20
J.W.Utly	9. Combs	.25
" " "	.Thimbles	.77
Cash	1.Set thread	.90
J.Brown	2½.Yds cambric	.43
H.Roberts	12. Combs	.67

Page-41-

J.W.Utly	30.Gee Corntis	.11
" " "	5-3/8 -Yds Vesting	.63
" " "	1-3/8- " "	.88
" " "	2. S Duck	.31½
" " "	10.Yds muslin	.48
" " "	7½ Yds B. Muslin	.52
J.H.Burton	9½ " " "	.45
" " "	2½ " Domestic	.35
T.Veatch	2 " "	.13
E.Lewis	8. Bro "	.19
J.W.Utly	1½ Flax Linen	.12½
Y.Jonus	17½ Bucksana	.12½
J.W.Utly	8 Yds gingham	.31½
W.H.Hampton	2.Blk Cloth	5.50
J.W.Utly	10. Cat Handkss	.16
" " "	6. Silk "	.18
" " "	2 " "	.87½
" " "	10 Cat "	.14
Cash	1 Cat shawl	1.45
H.Derby	5/8-Vesting	.63
J.McAuley	26 yds lace	.13
J.Y.Presson	3½ " home spun	.26½
J.W.Utly	6. Cat handkss	.14
G.W.Beard	9. Razor strops	.23
J.H.BURTON	5½ Wall paper	.15
J.W.Utly	2½ Packs of pins	1.01
J.W.Utly	1. Lot tape	1.18
W.H.Barte	3.Pr hoes	.18
J.W.Utly	8.yds pink gingham	.27
" " "	9 " " "	.26
G.W.Beard	1¾ P.Muslin	.62½
J.W.Utly	23. Muslin	.25
T.Ballard	4.Checks	.24
Cash	.Cat velvet	.12½

Page 41-continued.

Name	Property Sold.	Price.
J.T.Presson	1.Pr socks	$ .37½

Page-42-

H.M.Brown	1.Blue silk	.29
H.M.Butler	36.Footing	.13
S.H.Burton	1 .Lot of lace	1.50
T.Browning	81.Footing	.12½
D.Butler	13½-lace	.13
J.W.Utly	27-Lace	.11
" " "	4½.Pr gloves	.18¾
" " "	4½.Trest linneon	1.00
T.Veach	1 . Lot combs	.19½
J.W.Utly	1.Lot tape	1.00
Cash	.Combs	.06½
A.Lashlee	1.Lock	2.00
T.A.Nall	.Pepper	.21
J.Hicks	.Spice	.26
G.Flowers	1.Star & Stock.	.52
T.McCann	1.Razor	1.00
J.W.Utly	1.Sanddras	1.06¼
Y.Jones	3.Seives	.50
J.Ballard	3.Hammers	.41
W.H.Burton	1.Brush	----
S.H.Burton	1.doz tumblers	1.00
Cash	11.Glass Tumblers	.90
G.Beard	1 .½ doz mugs	.66
Cash	1. Bowl	.12½
Cash	1.doz glass plates	.50
John Haywood	1. " " "	.50
J.Alexander	1. " _ " "	.50
H.M.Brown	11. Plates	.58
J.W.Utly	½ .doz salt sellers	.15½
" " "	7. Salt sellers	.15
" " "	4. " "	..19
" " "	5. Pepers.	.25
S.H.Burton	3. Creamers	.24
S.Razons	1. Hammer	.43¼
S.H.Burton	10½.Doz Cat Woods	.50
J.W.Utly	.Spice	.15
T.McCord	1 .Table	1.12¼
S.H.Burton	1. Bed stead	1.77
J.W.Utly	1.Bonnett	1.06¼
" " "	1.Scales and weight	3.25
Irvin Lewis	2. Chairs	.80
Isaac Ballard	24 yds-domestic	.30
J.W.Utly	.Store License	4.25
" " "	2 . Barrels of sugar	46.00

TOTAL.......... .. $966.08½

Page 42-Continued.

I certify the within is a true return of the sale of the property of Edward Haywood,Deceased

S.D.Strayhorn

Sworn to in open court---January Term-1838.

Page--43---

An account of the Estate of Bartin Coats ,Deceased--Sold 1838.

Property	To whom sold.	Price.
1.Horse	Elijah Rogers	$31.00
1.Saddle	E.L.Mattock	12.00
1.Pr chain & cleaves	Elijah Tedder	2.00
I.Axe	John Runneon,Jr.	1.75
2.Hoe & Axe	" " "	.75
1.Plow & Share	" " "	1.75
1.Cow & Calf	Anna Coats	15.50
8.Sheep	" "	12.12½
2.Saws,9 ,head of pigs	" "	13.00
4.Spotted Hogs	" "	16.50
4.Hogs	Lewis Runneon	16.23¾
1.Bunch Oats	John Davidson	2.12½
1.Wagon Tongue	John Runneon	2.41
1.Watch	" "	3.75
1.Pr Boots	Lewis Runneon	2.56¼
1.Pr Saddle Bags	W.M.Morrison	3.62½
1.Side saddle	John Runneon	4.31¼
1.Auger	Anna Coats	.50
1.Rule	John Runneon	.37½
1.Churn	Anna Coats	1.00
1.Pr hens	Elga Tedder	.18¾
1.Side Blade	Hencher Nunney	3.00
1.Spinning wheel	Anna Coats	2.18¾
1.Cowhorn Oven	John Runneon	.43½
1.Lot kitchen implements	Anna Coats	3.50
1.Loom	" "	2.62½
1.Lot gunns	John Runneon	1.68¾

Page 44--

1.Looking glass	Lewis Runneon,Jr	1.62½
1.Table	Anna Coats	1.31½
1.Lot shelf ware	" "	3.12½
1.Lot shaving tools	John Runneon	1.87½
1.Bureau	" "	13.62½
1.Overcoat	Lewis Runneon	1.31½
1.Bed & Furniture	Anna Coats	13.50
1." " "	George Flanagan	14.12½
1.Hat	John Runneon	.12¼
1.Pr shoes	" "	.18¼

Page 44-Continued.

Property	To whom sold.	Price.
1.Trunk	Sim Rodgers	$ 2.41
4.Chairs	Anna Coats	1.25
1.Flat Iron	" "	.75
1.Pr shears	James Garrison	.12½
1.Lot quills	Anna Coats	3.75
	TOTAL............ ....$12.78½	
	Cash on hand	330.00
		542.85

State of Tennessee,Benton County,Personally appeared in open court Anna
Coats,Administrator of the Estate of aforesaid,whom being duly sworn
according to law doth dispose and say,the foregoing is a true statement
of the sale of the personal property of the Estate of the Estate of
Barton Coats,Deceased,late of said county of Benton.

Her

Anna X Coats --Adm Estate of B. Coats.

Mark.

Sworn to and subsribed in open court this October A.D.1838.G.R.Kelsey
Clerk--#######

A true inventory of the personal Estate of Joel Taylor,Deceased--
2.Bed steads..2. Boxes..Shelf and furniture..1.Table.4 chairs..3 water
vessels..1 .churn..1.wheel..1 pr cards..1.Check reel..2 pots.. 1 skillett
1.kittle..1 oven.. 1 griddle..1 flat iron..1 candle mates..6 head of sheep
7. Head of cattle..1 horse .. 1 lot of books..1 pr guns..1 old hand saw
1 hand axe..1 patent clock..1 slate... 4 head of geese..1 looking glass
1 bread tray.. 1 salt barrel..1 weeding hoe..1 coffee pot..1 case of
knives and forks..

This is amount of notes due the above estate   -------   ------

1.Note on Young Adonis & Enous Jordon-Due Dec 25th Next...	$ 31.60	Page 45
1.Note on Henry Adams & Jessie Hammonds(credit $40.00) due December , Next......	55.00	
1. Note on Elisha Petty-### with credit for $5.87½...	12.50	
Due bad debts on Young Adams-Due Dec 25th 1839...	8.50	
1.Note on Stephen Taylor-Due Dec 25th Next.	20.00	
1.Note on Jonathan Fuller-To be paid in trade-Due March 1st Next--	35.00	
1.Note on Gillian Adams-Due Dec 25th next.	11.00	
1.Note on Pleasant Pritchard-Dec 25th 1839..	100.00	
1.Note on S.Rodgers-Due October 1st 1838.Bad debt	12.00	
1.Note on William Hallowell-Due Jan 1st. last.	3.00	

Taken in by Jonathan Fuller, administrator,on account of said, made of
the personal property of Joel Taylor,Deceased at his late residence,
in Benton County,after having administered accordingly. to law.

Page 46

1.Lot of boxes & contents	-Widow Taylor	$ 5.00
1.Bead	Elizabeth Taylor	10.25
.Shiff & Furniture	Widow Taylor	2.00
4.Chairs	Widow Taylor	.50
4.Water Vessels	" "	.50
3.Head of cattle	" "	23.25
1.Cow	Elizabeth Taylor	10.62½
1.Yearling	Charlie Taylor	4.75
1.Cow	Charlie Taylor	12.00
2.Candles	Widow Taylor	.50
3.Sheep	Jessie Hall	6.00
1.Ram	Jessie Hall	1.50
1.Saddle	Widow Taylor	.50
1.Clock	Widow Taylor	3.37½
3.Books	Edward Jordon	.75
.Books	" "	1.12½
"	" "	.37½
"	" "	.25
"	" "	.43¾
1. "	" "	.75
1.Sorrell Horse	Widow Taylor	5.00
	TOTAL....................	.$88.67¼

The foregoing is a full and perfect account of the sale of all the
property on the Esate of Joel Taylor,Deceased.Directed by law to be sold
notes with good securities due twelve months after date were taken   the
purchaser,this 27th of October 1839.

                    Johnath Fuller- Adm.

Returned November term 1838 on Oath in open court.

                    Test--G.R.Kelsey- Clerk.

Page-47--

We the commissioners appointed by the county court of Benton County
at September Term1838.To examine the accounts of Susannah Holland
Administrator.Of Merril Hollan ,Deceased.and to make settlement with heirs
her administration of the said estate how performed that duty and return
following settlement.We find the said Suseanah Holland,charged with the
following items(viz)first amount of sale and inventory $320.65

We find the said Susanah Holland had maid the following disbursement which
entitled to credit.(viz)

Thence No 13,Paid Nicholas Brown,proceeding short.	$30.00
No 2. Paid Dr Brown	2.00
No 3, Paid services to clerk	2.35
Paid services to clerk recording settlement	.50
Paid committee's to make settlement	1.50
Total............	46.25

Page 47-Continued.

The committee thinks proper to allow the administrator for services
collecting and paying out the amount of $30.00

Leaving a balance in the hands of the administrator,belonging to the
Estate Mirret Holland,Deceased to the amount of Two Hundred and Eighty
Five dollars and ten cents

$283.10

Page 48.

In the name of God,Amen.

I Peozy Ferrell of the County of Henry and State of Tennessee being weak
of body but sound of mind, and memeory and calling to mind the uncertainty
of this transitory life and proving that it is appointed for all men once
to die. to publish this my last will and testament.Manner and form as
follows to wit......
I give and bequeath unto my beloved wife,Susanah two hundred and fifty
acres of land on Tennessee River.Wherein I now live.Two hundred Head of
Horses.All my stock Cattle and Hogs.All my household and kitchen furniture
in during her natural life after my last debts are paid.After the death of my
wifethe land where I know to belong to Thomas R.Cheatham and his heirs forever
I turn after death of my wife.the horses cattle and hay.Household and kitchrn
furniture are to be equally divided between Patsy Grason and Thomas R.
Cheatham.I also nominate constitute and appoint,James Watkins and Henry
H.Winns Executors of my last will and testament.In testimony when of I have
unto set my hand and seal 6th October 1832-Swpt 18th-

Pazey Ferrell
His mark.

Witness
David A.Askew
Drewery A.Askew.

Page 49-
State of Tennessee, Benton County..This day being the 23rd of October 1838
Sarah Rushing Administrator of the Esate of Able Rushing ,Deceased,by her
Agent Joel Rushing.Made application to make a settlement with Mr George R.Kelsey
clerk of the County Court of Said County.and administrator of said Estate
which I beg leave to make report as follows to wit.First I find the
administrator charged with the sum of Twelve Hundred and five dollars
fifty seven and three fourths cents,on accounts of sale of said Estate
$1205.57¾.Ssecond I find her charged with the sum of One Hundfed and forty
three dollars and twenty cents on account of notes and cash-$143.20
I also find in the of Joel Rushing one of the legatees of said deed which
he has administered and submits to go in this settlement the sum of Five
Hundred and Twenty Five Dollars.$525.00. Also in the Robert Y.Rushing
in like manner the sum of Two Hundred and Eighty Seven Dollars.
And in like manner the hand of Jackson Rushing the sum of One Hundfed and
six dollars

Page 49-continued.

Also for rent for the year 1837, th e sum of $62.50.--2.5

Making in all the sum of Twenty Three Hundred,Twenty Nine Dollars
and twenty seven and three fourths cents.$2329.27¾

I also find the administrator should have the following credits to wit
Thirteen dollars and twenty five cents $13.25
Abner Smalley proven account for the sum of Seven dollars
and twenty one cents.   Marked No 1.   7.21
Thomas L.Floyd ,receipt for crying property for the sum of
three dollars marked No 2.   3.00
Thos H.Burton clerk for the sum of One dollar sixty two and
one half cents. Marked No 3.   1.62½
John Cheatham from Account for seventy five cents marked No 4   .75
Thirty Three dollars administrator furnished   33.00
Shiff received for Tores 1836.Five dollars thirty four three
quarter cents.   5.34¾
Same for 1837.Five dollars seventy two & one half cents. No 7 5.72½

Clerk received one dollar ,marked No 8   1.00
Clerk for settlement   2.00
Marked in all the sum seventy two ninety and ninety and one
half cents.   72.90½

Page 50.

I also allow the administrator for trouble and expenditures of
management of sale of estate   50.00
                                                                122.90½

Which will leave in the hands of administrator the sum of
Twenty One Hundred & Ninety Six Dollars thirty seven & one half
cents,which is respectfully submitted.
                                                                2196.37½

Page##### 51

December 26th 1836.
John F.Johnson ,Guardian of the minor heirs of William B.Griffin
Deceased,appointed this day for settlement with Mr George R.Kelsey
clerk of the county court of Benton County, and I find in his hands
seventy three dollars eighty five and three fourths cents $73.85¾
Interest for the same for twenty months   4.43¼
                                                          $78.29¼

1st I find him charged by J.F.Johnson as follows for services
rendered into year 1838
2nd To attending court at Camden and giving bond to run thier
business $q2.00
3rd to drawing copy of bond & order.   1.00
4th to taking entering and delivering same at Waverly   2.50
5th.To paying taxes for land   .43¾

Page 51-Continued.

6th.Clerks fees for settlement	$ 1.00
7th.For entering some on record	.50
Amount in hand of Guardian,Seventy Eight Dollars,Twenty Nine and one fourth cents.	78.29¼
Charged by Guardian,Seven Dollars,forty three and three fourth cents.	7.43¾
The Guardian the same.	70.85⅝
All of which respectfully sunmitted....	70.85⅝

1.Man saddle	$10.00
1.Pr Marlingales.	.75
1.Saddle Blanket	.37½
1.Lot Books	.65
1.Pr studyards	.75
1.Oil stand.	.45
1.Umbrella	.43½
1.Pr saddle boys	1.68¾
8.Lbs tobacco.	2.00

Page 52--

1.Gun & Pouch	8.50
1.Gun	.12½
2.Gugs	.87½
1.Hat	.23¾
1.Looking	1.37½
4.Chairs	.75
1.Iron Wedge	.75
1.Axe	1.25
1.Set Shoe Tools	3.00
1.Lot Tools	5.06½
1.Bead	10.75
1.Fraw	.66¼
3.Bee Gum	3.00
1.Mullock	1.93½
2.Hoes	1.00
1.Plow	2.25
1.Plow Mold.	2.00
1.Plow	2.00
1.Hackle	.25
1.Grind Stone	1.87½
2.Plains	2.25
1.Lot hogs	36.00
1.Lot hogs	6.12½
1.Harness	30.00

Page 52..

1.Bell	1.25

Page-52-Continued.

1.Set gurs	$5.25
.Due the Esate of Vezy Ferrell by Thomas Weiners	9.50
	$155.00

I Thomas R.Cheatham do hereby certify that the above is a true account
of the property sold at the sale of the Estate of Vezy Ferrell,Deceased
given under my hand this 22nd day of December 1838.

T.R.Cheatham.Executor.

Page 53.

An account of the sale of the property of the Estate of William Lee,
Deceased.Made at the house,Samuel B.Pierce in Benton County.After having
advertised as directed by law,this January 29th 1839.

1.Lot copper ware.	Hugh Darby.	$ .37½
Pots and hooks	Sam Little	1.25
1.Skillett & Lid	" "	.87½
1.Weeding Hoe	Sam Ross	.50
1.Saddle	Hugh Darby	1.50
1.Axe	Reuben Mitchell	2.50
1.Lot plain gear.	Sam Tottle	3.06½
1.Chest	Robert G.Lee	4.00
1.Bottle	Hugh Darby	.50
1.Set cups and saucers.	Sam Ross	.75
1.Set plates	Nancy Hicks	.37½
1.Pistol	William Robertson	1.00
1.Rifle shot bag and moles.	Sam Ross	9.12½
1.Pr suspenders	Hugh Darby	.26
1.Ink stand	Nelson Pearce	.31¼
1.Pocket Book	Hugh Darby	.25
1.Shaving glass	Rubin Mitchell	.56½
1.Razor case	Sam B.Pearce	.50
1.Set knives & forks	Needham Short.	1.56½
1.Bell	Ben Mitchell	.50
1.Curry Comb	Tom Sevendell.Pd	.37½
1.Claw Hammer	J.F.Johnson	.25
1.Ladle & Lead.	Hugh Darby	.25
3.Spoons	A.Teller .Pd.	1.24
1.Lot shoe tools	R.Michie	.25
Powder,copper and whess-	John Anderson	.25
1.Set shoe brushes	Sam Ross	.18¾
1.Shoe Brushes and strops.	Sam Tottle,	.12¾
1.Pocket Book & Knife	Darling Pearce	.18¾
1.Handerkerchief &Cravat	B.Michie	.71¼
1.Mans cloak	Hugh Darling	5500

Page 53-Continued.

1.Hat	B.Michie	$ .37½
1.Mans dress coat	Hugh Darby	6.12½
1.Vest	A.G.Holt	3.00

Page 54.

1.Coat & Pantaloons	Sam Tottle.	.06½
1.Plow	Willy Gilcloth	.50
1.Blanket	Hugh Darby	.12½
1.Bed tick	" "	2.00
1.Meal Bag	J.F.Johnson	.50
2.Chickens	Jacob Hicks	.12½
1.Hog	Sand Tellett	2.00
1.Lot shucks	N.R.Williams.	.93½
1.Lot pork	Halloway Ree-Pd-	.12½
5.Barrels corn	Green Adams	12.50
5.Barrels corn	Hugh Darby	15.00
The residue of corn @ $3.00 per barrel		4.31¼
1.Fodder stack	E.W.Lynch	2.89½
1.Fodder stack	Hugh Darby	----
1/2-Stack fooder		1.62½
1.Bay mare.	A.G.Holt	50.00
1.Bay horse.	Ansal Peorse	36.75
1.Bridle	A.G.Holt.	.25
1/2 stack fodder	Green Adams	3.31½
1.Pr Trucks	N.R.Williams	7.37½
The residue corn, 6 barrels 1½ bushels shelled.		18.90
1.Note on hand,on N.Peons		11.20

AMT BILL.... $222.58¾

Claim against Loyd Cole(doubtful)   6.50
William Lee, witness, attendance care of V.Armonia
vs L.Cats 3 days.... $ 2.25
$231.25 -1/3

Page 55--

State of Tennessee, Benton County,This day being the 11th day of March
1839.Sarah Rushing ,Administrator of the Estate of Able Rushing,Deceased,
by his agent ,Joe Rushing,made application to make settlement.,that could
not be made--The last of the date October 2nd 1838 by the paper not being
properly arranged.stated for rents and heirs of negros--1838---
Said Rushing now make settlement with me George R.Kelsey,Clerk of the
county board of said county.As the administrator Estate which I beg
leave to report as follows....

1 St stan for rent of land in year 1838...	$54.00
2nd, for heirs of negroes	191.00
I also allow the administratrix for trouble & expense	5.00
Clerks fee for settlement	2.00
Clerks fee for two entrances of settlement	1.50

Page 55-Continued/

A list of the amount of sale of the property of George W.Barnett,Deceased
Acpts,&cash ,notes on hand.This January 28th 1839.

Jeremiah Odle.	1.Mare & Saddle.	$56.50
John Johnson	1.Yearling Colt	16.50
John Walker	1.Saddle	18.00
David Barnett	1.Saddle	5.00
Eligh Wood	1.Martingals & Whip	.37½
William Hubb	1.Briar Hook	.31½
Eligh Wood	1.Saw	.12½
William Crabb	1.Steel trap.	.25
John Johnson	1.Pr hames & chains	1.25
Alfred Wesson	1.Shot Gun	1.25
Henry Camp	1.Silver watch	7.31½
C.L.Matlock	1.Knife.	8.00
S.Utley	1.Silver pencil	.75
Jas Grayon	1.Razor strop	37½
William Johnson	1.Barrell Gun	1.50
Henry Walker	2.Pistol Barrell	3.50
M.C.Barnett	1.Bedstead	4.00
" " "	1.Press	3.62½
S.Utly	2.Bors head & shot.	.31½
John Johnson	1.Box tools	.56¼
E.L.Mallory	2.Lasts.	.12½
Lucy Fry	1.Profile	.25
Henry Walker	1. " "	.12½

Page 56.

Henry Walker	1.Profile	.18¾
Michie Fry	1. "	.25
" "	1. "	.31¼
Wm Johnson	1.Shot pouch	.65¾
James Evans	9. Barrels Corn	29.00
M.C.Barnett	1.Chicken	.25
C.L.Matlock	1.Gun Lock	1.50
		$176.68¼

One receipt on Michael Fry for Four Hundred Twelve Dollars & Twenty
five cents.With a credit of Forty Dollars,which Mr Fry is to have equal
half of said amount which leaves the sum of coming to Mr Barnett $186.12½
One note on D.T.Sayles & P.R.Lewis   24.24
One note on Edward and Wilson   40.00
One note on A.B.Wilson & Others   8.00
One judgement on David Henry   48.00
                                                              $306.36
                                                               177.18
                                                              $483.54

Which private Estate sworn to in open court,April 1st,1839. J.Walker-Adm.

Page 56-Continued.

An Inventory and accounts of sales of Thomas McGill,Deceased,Sold on
the 31st of March 1838.

Thomas Ward,Jr.	1.Single Tree & Chains	$ .87½
John McGill	1.Iron Wedge	.87½
Andy Rushing,Jr.	1.Set plow gears	2.25
S.H.Burton	1.Polo Axe	1.00
John W.Chandler	1.Shear plow	.89½
Mary Mc Gill	1.Polo Axe	1.00
" " "	1.Lot pot ware.	1.00
William Presson,Jr.	1.Shovel Plow	2.89½
L.Cottingham	1.Corig Plow	5.06
Mary McGill	2.Bed stead & furniture.	15.00
" "	1.Lot cupboard ware.	1.00
" "	1.Water pail	.25
" "	1.Coffee Mill	.18
James Mc Gill	1.Man saddle	19.00

Page 57.

Mary McGill	1.table & lot ware.	1.00
" "	1.Big wheel	1.00
" "	2.Salt barrels	.06
" "	1.Cow calf & bull.	5.00
William Rushing	1.Cow	19.00
John Thornton	1.Small yoke of steers	18.00
T.Presson	1.Lot hay & wheat.	22.00

Page 58

S.Presson.	1.Lot hay & 7 heads	6.12½
" "	1.Lot hay & 12 head	8.12½
John Mc Gill ,Jr	1.Black mare	5.00
Thomas Ward	1.Young horse	47.00
Mary McGill	1.Lot hay & 7 head	3.00
" "	5.Head sheep	5.00
John McGill	1.case of razors & strops	2.87½
Mary McGill	5.Chairs.	1.00
A.Harris	1.Lot fodder	1.25

Debts doubtful Estate.

Jonus McGill	29.17
Thomas Jones	1.00
A.C.Presson	1.50
	228,37¾

Page 58 Continued.

I certify that the foregoing contents is a true inventory with the amount
of sales of the property,belonging to the Estate of Thomas McGill,Deceased
so far as has come to my hands or knowledge.Also the accounts due the said
Estate.Given under my hand this 4th day of June 1838.
                                        John D.Rushing-Adm.
Sworn to and subsribed in open court, this 4th day of June 1838.
                                        John Runneon.D.C.

An inventory of an accounts committee.My home.Since the sale of the
property of Thomas McGill,Deceased of which I wish to render an account of
tp this court.Of which I am administrator.of said Thos McGill,Deceased
One account of Seventeen dollars & fifty cents and one half.   ..$17.58 ½

                                        John D.Rushing-Administrator.

Page 59-

In the name of God, I Nathaniel Townsend of the State of Tennessee,Benton
County.Being of weak body but sound mind and memory,considering the un-
-certainty of this mortal life.Blessed be the Almighty God for the same.
To make and publish this my last will and testament,in the manner and
form following.That is to say after my debts are all settled,I give and
bequeath unto my beloved wife..Mary Townson,all of my Estate,horses,cattle
hay,household and kitchen furniture,all of my claims to occupants land to
raise my small children up on.And at my wifes death Mary Townson,I will
the remainder of the property if any, be divided equally among my child-
-ren.I will and hereby appoint my beloved wife Mary Townson,Executrix of
this my last will and testamwnt.And hereby revoking all former wills by me
made.Witness whereof I have hereunto set my hand and seal in the year
of our Lord One Thousand Thity Eight Hundred and Thirty Nine and the 7th
day of March.
                                His
                          Nathaniel Townson
                              Mark.
Signed sealed and subscribed by the above named Nathaniel Townson to be
his last will and testament in the presence of those of us who have hereunto subscribed our names as witness in the presence of the Testator.
                          Attest...Nathan Williams
                                William Gilbreast.

Page 60--

State of Tennesse,Benton County-Court May Term,1839/Then was the within
Last Will and Testament of Nathaniel Townson,Deceased produced in open
court.And the due execution thereof proven by the Oath of Nathaniel
Williams and William Gilbreast,subscribed witness there to and ordered
to be recorded.   Test-G.R.Kelsey-Clerk.

Page-61.

State of Tennessee,Benton County,Agreeable to a Joint Resolution
of Both Branches of General Assembly of Said State.We the undersigned
Ephram Perkins,Nicholas Brewer,George W.L.Hudson , and Amos Bruce
proceeded to lay off said County of Benton In Districts convenient size
for the purpose of election justice constabulary to the provisions of
said act of assembly, and make report as follows(To Wit)

District No 1.Beginning at the Tennessee River on the Southeast Corner
of the County running west to range line dividing seven and eight thence
N rth with said line,Birdsong Creek which is at the mouth of Ammons Creek
thence down said Birdsongs Creek to the mouth.Thence up Tennessee River
to the beginning and say the uction.Said district be held at the hose of
John Runneon.

District Number 2 commences at the southwest corner of No 1 runs north
with said Range Line to Birdsongs Creek at the mouth of Ammons Creek
thence up Ammons creek,Garlands old place,on the Natchez Trace.To the
County Line thence south with the County line to the corner thence east
to the beginning.And say the election in said district be held at the
house of C.

Page 62

District No 3 begins at the mouth of Birdsongs Creek runs up Creek to the
mouth of Ammons Creek ,thence up Ammons Creek to Garlands old place
on the Natchez Trace.Thence northward running with the ridge,round the
head of little Birdsong to Lewis Barkers on Cypress Creek.Thence northward
private way leading by Berry Williams to Thomas Jones.Huntingdon road
thence east with said road to Cane Creek thence down said creek to the
mouth, and down Cypress Creek to Ammons.Bridge across said Creek thence wi
-th road to Kirkmans Ferry thence up Tennessee River to the beginning and
say the election in said District be held at Chalk Level.

District No 4-Beginning at Garlands old place on the Natchez Road runs
northward with the ridge round the head of little Birdsong to Lewis
Barkers.Continuing Northward by a private way from said Barkers leading by
Berry Williams to Thomas Jones on the Huntingdon Road.to the county line t
thence south with the county line to the Natchez Road.Thencewith the
Ntachez Road to the beginning.And say the election ij said district shall
be held at Berry Pearses.

District No 5.Beginning at Kirkmans Ferry on the Tennessee River on the
lower corner of No 3.Runs west with Kirkmans Ferry Road to Ammons Bridge
a Creek Cypress.Thence up said creek to the Mouth of Cane Creek. and up
that creek to the Huntingdon Road. and with said road to Thomas Jones the
-nce northward with ridge round head of cane creek To the ridge dividing
Tennessee River and Sandy Watsons.Thence with said ridge to the point Mason
round and with said road.To where it began to leave the ridge to the Paris
Road.Including Wallace Rushings.Eastward with the Paris Road to the Thompson Ferry Road. and with that road to the top of the ridge dividing

Tennessee River and Sandy Watsons.

Page 62-Continued.

Tennessee River and Sandy Waters.Thence round with said ridge between
Harmons Creek and Beaverdam including John Milton & William Pafford
to strike Tennessee River at the Mouth at the mouth of Cypress Creek
thence up the River to the beginning.And say the election for said
district shall be held at the house of Wyatt Arnold.

Page 63-

District No 6.Begins at Thomas Jones on the Huntingdon Road,runs northward with the ridge round the head of Cane Creek to the ridge of
Dividing Waters of Tennessee and Sandy.And with said ridge to the point
Mason Raod and which said road to where it begins.,to where it begins to
leave the ridge and with said that ridge to the Paris road thence westward with said road to the county line thence south ard with said line
to the Huntingdon Road,thence with said road to the beginning.And say the
election for said district shall be held at the house of Thomas McGill.

District No 7.Begins on Tennessee River on mouth of Cypress Creek.The
lower corner of No 5 runs westward the ridge dividing the Waters Beaverdam and Hammons Creek thence round with said ridge,excluding John Melton
and William Pafford. to the ridge dividing Tennessee & Sandy Waters.
And with said ridge northward with the county line thence east with said
line to the Tennessee River.And up River to the beginning.And say the
election shall be h eld at the house of David Benton.
Page 64
District No 8.Begins on the County Line on the northwest corner of No 7
runs west and south with the county line thence eastward with the said
road to the Thompson Ferry then with that road to the top of the ridge
dividing the waters of Tennessee & Sandy.Thence northward with said Ridge
to the beginning.And sy the election for said district shall be held at the
house of Nicholas Brewer.

District No 9.Begins at the Bank of the Tennessee River on the lower
corner of No 8. Runs down the river to the lower bank of Lick Creek.There
come between Benton & Henry County.Tence est up Sandy River thence up
Sandy Road,leading from Paris to Point Mason, and with that road to the
old county line. and thence with same to the beginning.And say the election
in said district shall be held at the house of Stogals

Given under our hands this 6th day of January 1836.
                         G.W.Hudson
                         E.Perkins
                         Nicholas Brown.

State of Tennessee, Benton County,Clerks office.June 6th 1836.There was a
deed of bargain and sold from Levy Braly to Sam Braly,Alfred Braly,John
Braly,James E.Glenn and Sally Glenn to James Arnold for 125 acres of
land in this county.Produced in myn office an authenticated from the clerk
from the county of Warren and state aforesaid and the state tax tereon
being paid.So let it be registered.

Page 65.

Sate of Tennessee,Benton County,Clerks Office,Jan 6th 1836.There was a
deed of bargain & sold from Mark M.Combs to G.W.L.Hudson   for 150 acres
of land,this county,duly autenticated in Humphrey County and the sate
tax thereon so let it be paid.So let it be registered.

State of Tennessee,Benton County,Clerks Office ,Jan 6th 1836.There was a
deed of bargain & sold from John Wiggle & Ruth Wiggle for 150 acres of
land in this county was produced in my office and duly proven.John Barn-
hart and W.E.Hudson and the state tax thereon.Being paid so let it be
registered.

State of Tennessee,Benton County,Clerks office,June 6th 1836.There was a
deed of bargain and sale from Anderson Lashlee "and John Call for 50
acres for 50 acres of land in this county, was produced in myn office.
and said Anderson Lashlee acknowledged before me Thos H.Benton,clerk of
the County aforesaid and acknowledged the execution thereof,and the State
Tax being paid the reon ,so let it be registered.

Page 66.

State of Tennessee,Benton County,Clerks Office June 21st 1836,There was a
deed of bargain & sale from William Wood to R.N.Wood 55 1/6 acres of
land,in my office, produced in my office.duly autenticated from the clerk
of Humphrey county. and the state tax being paid so let it be registered.

State of Tennessee,Benton County,Clerks Office July 4th 1836.There was
the within deed of bargain & sale of 40..120/oo.acres of land in the
County produced in my office and proven by the oaths of James Malin &
William M.M alin to be the act and deed of the within bargain for the
purpose thefein contained that day it reports to have been done and the
state tax being paid. so let it be registered.

State of Tennessee,Benton County,Clerks Office July 4th 1836.There was the
within deed of bargain and sale of---- acres --- of land this county
produced in mmy office,produced in my office and proven by the oaths of
James Mail & William Malin. to be the act and deed of the within bargain
for the purpose to have been done.And the State Tax having been paid.So
let it be registered.

State of Tennessee,Benton County,Personaly appeared before me Thos H.Burton
Clerk of the County Court,Able Rushing with whom I am well acquainted
and who acknowledged he executed the within deed to 10 acres of land in
this county. for the purpose therein contained,and the State being paid so
let it be registered.Witness my hand at office,August 1st 1836.
                                        Thos H.Burton, Clerk.

State of Tennessee, Benton County,This day was a bill of sale from
George B.Kornegay to Line Smith twenty acres therein contained and
produced in my office duly certified from under the hand of the Clerk
of this County. of the County Court of Carrol County and by me certified
for registration August 9th 1836.

Page 66-Continued.

State of Tennessee, Benton County,this day was bill of sale from Crom
Earps--- and Cullen Novel to Zachariah Baker for a negro girl slave and
proven to be the act and deed of said bargain for the purpose therein
contained.By the oaths of Simon Pope a subsribing witness this August
9th 1836. Test,Thos H.Burton..Clerk.

Page 67.

State of Tennessee,this day was bill of sale from Benton County.----
From Solomon Copland to Zachariah Baker for a negro girl slave named
Vina, and proven to be the act and deed of the said bargain or for the
purpose there contained by the oath of Mary K.Hubbs,a subscribing
witness,This August 1st 1836.Thos H.Burton, Clerk.

State of Tennessee,Benton County,Clerks Office September 5th 1836,There
was a bill of sale from Elizabteh Phillips to James Hansel for a negro
man slave"Ephriam".Produced in my office and duly proven by the oath of
Ephriam Perkins and Nicholas Brown.Subsribing witness thereto to her act
and deed for the purpose therein contained.Therefore let it be registered.

State of Tennessee, Benton County, This day Anderson Lashlee,personally
appeared before me Thos H.Burton ,Clerk of County Court of said County
who having prayed and obtained a license to retail spirits at his
establishment in said county and make oath in due formation of law.That
he will not sell any spirits to any negro slave or Agent during his
license.

Page 68

with then present without a written permit from his or her master or
overseer and in all things comply with the law in that made and proved
sworn to and subsribed to this 14th day of September 1836.
Anderson Lashlee.
I do further swear that I will not knowingly permit or allow any gaming
or betting for whisky wine or money or other things or other valuable
things in the house which I may retail spirits or on my premises,but that
if anyone should game or bet to my knowledge I will give in for matter
thereof to the grand jury at next term of circuit court for my county.
Sworn to and subscribed to before me this 14th day of September 1836.
Thos H.Barton-Clerk.....Anderson Lashlee.

State of Tennessee, Benton County,Personally appeared before me Thos
H.Burton,clerk of the county court of said county-Dowley P.Hudson
and" Anderson J.B.Hudson subscribed witness to the within deed from
Edward H.Hudson for 650 acres,when after being duly sworn say they are
acquainted with the above named bargainor and that he acknowledged
the foregoing to be his act.Dedd for the purposes therein contained
on the day it purports to be dated,given under my hand,at office this
7th day of November 1836. Thos H.Burton- Clerk.

Page 69.

State of Tennessee,Benton County,This day Elijah Lowery personally
appeared before me,Thos Burton,Clerk of The County Court, of said
County.Who having prayed and obtained license to retail spirits
at his establishment,in said county and makes oath in due form of law
that he will not sell any spirits to any negro slave by himself
during his license which begins dated equal with the presents without
a written permit. from his or her master or overseer, and with all
things comply with law.That case made provided sworn to and subscribed
to this 10th day of November 1836.   E.M.Lowry.

Page 70.

I do further swear that I will not knowingly permit or allow any gaming
or betting for whisky,wine or money,or other things to drink or eat.Or
other valuable things in the house which I may retail spirits on my
premises.Or but if anyone should game,or bet, to my knowledge with,
I will give information thereof to the grand jury,at the next term of
the circuit coutt.For any county sworn to and subscribed to before me
this 10th day of November 1836,.....Elijah M.Lowry.

State of Tennesse, Benton County, S.S.The the undersigned committeemen
appointed by the county court of said county. to lay off and set apart
a suffidy of provisions to save the widow and family of Able Rushing
Deceased,One year met this 4th day of November 1836,on the premises of
said ,deceased, and have laid off and set apart the following provisions-
(Viz)...One hundred barrels of corn, about 15 bushels of wheat,what
potatoes are on hand,one beef, one milk cow,and twenty four hundred
pounds of pork,which we find on hand.Also that administrator and
administratrix also furnish said family with twenty five dollars worth
of sugar and coffee.five dollars worth of salt,beside what is on hand.
Two dollars worth of pepper,and one dollars worth of spice,All of which
is respectfully submitted.
                        D.P.Hudson.
                        'Ephriam Perkins   ---Committemen--
                        J.B.Carson.

State of Tennessee, Benton County,This day was a deed of gift from James
Presson whom I am personally acquainted,produced in my office,and who
acknowledged the execution thereof for the purposees therein contained,
to wit-- the gift of a certain colt to Daniel C.Benton,Minor son of
Providence Benton,of the County aforessaid .Witness my hand and seal
this 29th of November 1836.
                        Thos H.Burton Clerk.

Page 71.

State of Tennessee, Benton County, Clerks Office,December 12th 1836.
There was a deed of bargain for fifty acres of land from Mitchell
Childress,Sheriff of Humphrey County, to John Cathingham in this County.
Same being acknowledged and certified by the clerk of the county of
Humphrey.County and state tax being paid.So let it be registered.

Page 71- Continued.

Sate of Tennessee, Benton County,This day Britton Barker,personally
appearded before Thos H.Burton,clerk of the County court of said county
who having prayed abtaineth license to retail spirits, at his establish-
-ment in said county, and makes oath in due form of law that he will not
sell any spirits to any negro slave by himself or agent,during his
license.Which bears   date equal with this without a written order from
his or her master or mistress or overseer, and in all things comply with
the law.In that case made and proved sworn to this 16th day of January
1839.Britton Barker.

I further swear that I will not knowingly permit or allow any gaming or
betting for whisky,wine money or other things to drink,or eat or other
valuable things,in the house which I may retail spirits,or on my
premises,but that if any should game or bet to my knowledge, I will give
information thereof to the grand jury,at the next term of the circuit
court,for my county,Sworn to and subsribed before me this 16th day of
January 1837,.Britton Barker.

Page 72,

State of Tennessee,Benton County, This day Richard Rushing,personally
appearded before me Thos H.Burton,Clerk of the County Court of Said County
who having prayed and obrained a license to retail spirits at his
establishment in said county.And makesoath in due form of law,that he
will not sell any spirits to any negro slave,by himslef or agent during
his license which was the same date,equal with these presents,without
written orders from his or her mistress or overseer,or master.And in all
things witch the law in that case made and provided,sworn to this 4th of
February 1837,.....Richard P.Rushing.

Page 73.

I do further swear that I will not knowingly permit or allow any gaming #
or betting for whisky wine or money,or other things to drink or eat or
other valuable things in the house,which I may retail spirits or on my
premises,But that if anyone should game or bet to my knowledge I will
give information thereof to the Grand Jury at the next term of the circuit
court,for my county.Sworn to and subsribed before me this 4th day of
February 1837,

Sate of Tennesse, Benton County,This day William Baker personally appeared
before me Thos H.Baker,Clerk of the County Court of said County.Who having
prayed and obtained a license to retail spirits at his establishment in
said County,, and makesoath in due form of law that he will not sell any
spirits to any negro slave by himself or agent during his license which
bears date equal with these presents,without a written order from his or h
her master or mistress or overseer,in all they comply with the law in
that case.Made and provided sworn to this--- day of February 1837.
                          William Baker,

Page-74-

I do further swear that I will not knowingly by permit or allow any
gaming or betting for whisky wine or money.Or otherthings to drink or
eat,or other valuable things in the house which I may retail spirits
or on my premises.But that if anyone should game or bet to my
knowledge I will give information thereof to the grand jury at the
next term of court for my county.Sworn to and subscribed before me
this 2nd day of February 1837.

State of Tennessee, Benton County,This day John H.Williams personally
appeared before me Thos H.Burton .Clerk of said county.court of said
county.Who having prayed and obtained a license to retail spirits at his
establishment in said county. And makes oath in due form of law that he
will not sell any spirits to any negro slave,by himself or agent during
his license,which bears date equal with these presents,without a written
permit from his or her master or mistress or overseer.And in all things
comply with the law.That case made and provided sworn to and subscribed
before me the 14th day of February 1837...John H.Williams.

I do further swear that I will not knowingly permit or alow any gaming
or betting for whisky wine or money or other things to drink or eat,or
other valuable things,in the house which I retail spifits or on my
premises.But that if anyone should game or bet to my knowledge I will
give information to the Grand Jury at the next term of circuit court.
for my county.Sworn to and subscribed to before me this 2nd day of
February 1837.

State of Tennessee,Benton County,This day John H.Williams personally appear
ed before me Thomas H.Burton,Clerk of said County Court of said county
who having prayed and obtained a license to retail spirits at his
establishment in said county.And makes oath in due form of law.That he
will not sell any spirits to any negro slave by himself or agent during
his lecense which bears date equel with these presents,without a written
permit from his or her Master, mistress or overseer and with all things
comply with the law.In that case made and provided sworn to before me
this 14th day of February 1837....John H.Williams.

I do further swear that I will not knowingly permit or allow any gaming or
betting for whisky wine or money or other things to drink or eat,or other
valuable things in the house which I am retailing spirits,or on my
premises.But that if any one should game or bet to my knowledge I will
give information thereof to the Grand Jury at the next term of the Circuit
Court,for my county.Sworn to and subsribed to before me, this 14th day
of February 1837.... John H.Williams.

State of Tennessee,Benton County, Personally appeared before me Thos H.
Barton,Clerk of the County Court,of said Benton County.William Sykes,ith
whom I am personally acquainted. and acknowledge that he signed the
within bill of sale for the purpose herein contained.This given under my
office February 6th 1839.Thomas H.Burton. Clerk.

Page 75

State of Tennessee, Benton County,Clerks Office--This was the within
deed produced before me in open court duly on then------from clerk
of the County.Court of Stuart County.So let it be registered.

State of Tennessee,Benton County,Personally appearded before me Thos H.
Burton.Clerk of County Court of said County John McIllwain with whom
I am personally acquainted and who acknowledged that he executed the
within deed for the purpose therein contained.Witness my hand of office
this 3rd day of October 1836...Thos H.Burton-Clerk.

Page 76.

Abbegal McIllwain ,female,Court also personally appearded before me
privately and apart from her husband,John McIllwain and acknowledged
that she executred the within deed voluntarily and understandingly
without compulsion or restraint from her husband and for the purpose
therein contained.Express witness for the County.Thos H.Burton .Clk.
At office this 3rd day of October 1836.--T.H.Burton-Clk.

State of Tennessee, Benton County,Personally appeared before me Thos
H.Barton.Clerk of the County Court of said County.Sarah & William
Beard,with whom I am personally acquainted who acknowledged that they signed the within deed of conveyance for the purpose therein contained given
under my hand at office.the 7th day of February 1837. Thos H.Burton.Clk.

State of Tennessee, Benton County,Clerks office 6th March 1837.There was
the within deed of bargain & sale from David A.Askew and Caleb Atkin
to John Askew for 160 acres in this county produced in my office only
authenicated from the clerk of the County of Stewart County and sate
aforesaid.The state tax being paid so let it be registered.

State of Tennessee, Benton County,Clerks office this day Daniel Still
produced in my office a deed of bargain and sale of one hundred and
twenty five acres of land in this county duly acknowledged and certified by
the clerk of the circuit court, of Davidson County and the State tax
thereon being paid ,witness certified for registration,given under my hand
at office this 3rd of April 1837.Thos H.Burton -Clk.

State of Tennessee, Benton County,April 10th 1837.There was a deed of
bargain & sale of 80 acres of land from James Lee to Simon Pope produced
at my office duly proven and certified.By the clerk of Humphries County.
and the state tax thereon being paid.So let it be registered.

Page 78

State of Tennessee, Benton County,There personally appearded before me
Thos H.Burton,Clerk of the County Court of said County.Thomas Lewis
who was a subscribing witness to adeed of bargain & sale of 28 acres
of land in the county from Allen Barker to Daniel Holland.And the state
tax thereon being paid.So let it be registered.Given under my hand at

Page 78

office April the 10th 1837/Thos H.Burton Clerk.

State of Tennessee, Benton County.Personally appeared before me Thos H.Bur
ton clerk of the county court of Benton County.Aaron Thornton with whom
I am personally acquainted who acknowledged that he signed and executed
a certain instrument bearing date of July 1st 1837.Said instrument being
an assignment on conveyance of the said Aarons part or claim of the
estate of Luke Thornton,Deceased.To John Jackson of Benton County.This
July 7th 1837.For the purpose therein expressed.

                         Thos H.Burton -Clerk.
                         James Herrin-Deputy Clerk.

Page 79.

State of Tennessee, Benton County,This day personally appeared before
Thos H.Burton,Clerk of the County Court of said County.John H.Williams
and Thomas Williams,with whom I am personally acquainted who
acknowledged execution of deed of conveyance to twenty acres of land.
In Benton County.To William Farmer who paid the state tax.And it was
ordered to be registered...Thos A.Burton-Clerk.

State of Tennessee,Benton County,Personally appeared before me Thos H.Burt
on clerk of the county court of Benton County.Robert Rochelle and William
H.Miller subscribing witnesses to a deed of bargain & sale of 640 acres
of land in Benton County. and made oath that they said Aaron O.Askew the
bargain assign and acknowledge the execution of a deed to Wm W.Wheatly
for 640 acres this 1st day of August 1836.Thos H.Burton .Clerk.

Page 80-

State of Tennessee,Benton County,This day personally appeared before me
Thos Burton,clerk of the County Court of said Benton County Court.
Robert H.Hamilton ,Marlton Myrick asubscribing witness to a deed of
conveyance for 100 acres of land executed by Aaron Hamilton executed of
the estate of Edward I Puckett,Deceased on the 12th day of March A.D.
1838.To John Runneon for Lewis Runneon and Martin Runneon who made oath
that they were personally acquainted with the aforesaid Amos Hanton
executed as foresaid and they saw him sign same and execute the same
for the purposes therein contained.

                         Thos H.Burton-Clerk
                         James Kerrin-Deputy Clerk.

State of Tennesse,Benton County.Personally appeared before me Thos
H.Burton,Clerk of the County Court,of said Benton County.George W.Beard
Burrae Beard,with whom I am personally acquainted who acknowledged they
executed a title bond for the conveyance for the conveyance of four lots
in the town of Camden and a part of a north lot in said town which said
bond bears date of this day to wit. April 15th 1838.

                         Thos H.Burton-Clerk.
                         James Kerrin- Deputy Clerk.

Page-81-

State of Tennessee, Benton County,Clerks office July 12th 1838.There
was a bill of sale produced in my office and proven by the oath of
Wm H.Burton subscribing witness to be the act and deed of within
bargain.Andon the day it bearing for the purposes therein contained
given under my hand at office.....Thos H.Burton-Clerk.

State of Tennessee, Benton County,Clerks Office August 4th 1838.There
was a bill of sale from Thomas Petty to Keziah Petty for one negro
woman"Cricy" and a negro girl Susan,one small horse,one gray horse,
seven head of cattle,head of hogs,three head of sheep three beads and
bead steads and furniture,one clock two tables,one dozen sitting chairs
one cupboard and furniture, and all his kitchen furniture.and farming
articles.and one wagon and gur. Test-Thos H.Burton-Clerk.

Page 82.

State of Tennessee, Benton County,Personally appeared in Clerks Office
this day the wishes deed of gift of Articles Mary Strawn to May L.Beard
duly proven in my office,by subscribing witnesses thereto and deed for the
purpose therein containedand on the day it bears date given under my hand
at office this 7th day of April 1838.Test --Thos H.Burton--Clerk. Geo
R.Kelsey,Deputy, Clerk.

State of Tennessee, Benton County,Personally appeared before me Thos H.
Burton clerk of the County Court for said County of Benton.William B.
Walker the barg ainor in the within deed of conveyance with whom I am
personally acquainted. who acknowledges they executed the within deed for
the purposes therein contained.Witness my hand at office this 3rd
day of September 1838.

                         Thos H.Burton-Clerk
                         James Herrjn-Deputy Clerk
                         Of said county of Benton..

State of Tennessee,Benton County,This day personally appeared before me
George R.Kelsey,clerk of the County Court of said County,Joseph Davenport
the within named bargainor,with whom I am personally acquainted and who
acknowledged the wishes to be his act,and deed for the purposes therein
contained.Witness my hand at office,this 6th day of September 1838.

                         George R.Kelsey-Clerk.

State of Tennessee,Benton County,Personally appeared before me George R.Kelsey
clerk of the County Court of Benton County.William B.Walker with whom I
am personally acquainted.and acknowledged that he signed the within bill
of sale for the purposes therein contained .This given under my hand at
my office.September 10th 1838.

                         Geo R.Kelsey-Clerk.

Page 83.

Know all men by these presents that I John B.Corn,that I am held and
truly bound with E.L.W.Hagber on his------assignment in the present sum
of One Hundred Dollars to the within payment ,will and truly be made
I bind myself and my heirs ,sealed with my seal,and dated 7th day of
February.1838.Condition if the above bounds John B.Corns shall well
and truly make cause to be made a good lawful deed to a certain lot of
land in the town of Camden.,in Benton County.No 40 to the said E.L.W.
Hagler or his heirs, and so as the commissioners appointed to supervise
the Public Building. in the said town of Camden,Shall obtain a grant
then the above obligation to be void otherwise,to remain in full force
and given under my hand and seal this day and date above written.

                          Berry Presont
                          William A.Hardson
                                 his   John B.Corns
                          Merritt   Pope
                                 mark.   SEAL*

Page 84.

State of Tennessee,Benton County,Personally appearded before me George
R.Kelsey,clerk for said County Court, of said County-William A.Hudson
Merritt Pope,subscribing witnesses to the within named bond.Who being first
duly sworn,dispose and say they are aqquainted with John B.Corns the
bargainor that he acknowledged the same in thier presence.to^be his act
and deed upon this day it bears date,Given under my hand,at office
this 24th day of September 1838.

                          George R.Kelsey -Clerk.

State of Tennessee,Benton County,Personally appeared before me George
R.Kelsey clerk of the County Court of said County,of Benton.The within
named Ann Coats,Administratrix as within stated who executed the within
power of attorney for the purposes therein contained,witness my hand at
office 2nd day of October 1838.

                          George R.Kelsey-Clerk.

Page 85-

State of Tennessee,Benton Cpunty,I George R.Kelsey,Clerk of the said
County,of Benton,Do hereby certify that James S.Sayles who swore
appeared and subscribed to the above certificate,was at the time of
executing the same chairman of said county court,duly elected and
qualified as such sill with and credit are due to all his official acts
as such given under my hand and present seal there being no public
seal at office,this 2nd day of October 1838.   -Geo R.Kelsey-Clerk.

Page 85-Continued.

State of Tennessee,Benton, County.Personally appeared before me George
R.Kelsey clerk of the County Court of said County of Benton,the within
named Richard Booker,who executed the within power of attorney,with whom
I am personally acquainted and who acknowledged that he executed the
within power of attorney for the purposes therein contained.Witness my
hand at office this 2nd day of October 1838.   *George R.Kelsey-Clerk.

Page 86.

State of Tennessee, Benton County,I George R.Kelsey Clerk of the County
Court of said Benton County do hereby certify that James Sayles has
named appeared,subscribed to the foregoing certificate.was at the time of
executing and subscribing the same acting chairman of the County Court
of the said County of Benton,duly elected and qualified,as such and full
faith and creditors all and all,his official as such given under my hand
and proven seal there being no public seal at office this 1st of October
in the year 1838.   *George R.Kelsey-Clerk.

State of Tennessee,Benton County,Personally appeared before me G.R.Kelsey
clerk of the County Court of said County.The within named Oliver Arman
with whom I am personally acqainted and who acknowledged that he executed
the above transfer for the purposes therein contained.Witness my hand at
officethis 11th day of October 1838. * G.R.Kelsey   -Clerk.

State of Tennessee, Benton County,Personally appeared before me G.R.
Kelsey,clerk of the County Court of said County,Chas Robinson and
William B.Robinson,subscribing witnessnes to the within named mortage
who being first sworn,do and say they are acquainted with Joshua
Pupils the bargainor,or mortager,that he acknowledged the same.Their
presents to be his act and deed upon the day it bears date given under my
hand at office,this 9th day of November 1838. * G.R.Kelsey-Clerk.

State of Tennessee, Benton County,Personally appeared before me G.R.
Kelsey Clerk of the County Court for said County,the within named John
McGill with whom I am personally acqaainted and who acknowledged that he
executed the within mortage for the purpose therein contained,witness my
hand at office,this 19th day of November 1838. *G.R.Kelsey-Clerk.

Page 87.

State of Tennessee, Benton, County.Clerks Office November 25th 1838.
There was a deed of bargain and sale from Thomas Jones,E.W.Hayler,
four acres of land in this county, was produced in my office duly proven
by Samuel H.Burton, and A.Lashlee,and the state tax thereon being paid.
So let it be registered.

State of Tennessee,Benton County,Personally appeared before me G.R.Kelsey
Clerk of the County Court of said County, the within named bargainor
with whom I am personally acquainted and who acknowledged they executed
the within deed for the purpose therein contained.Witness my hand at office

Page 87-Continued.

the third day of December 1836.So let it be registered.
                                        G.R.Kelsey-Clerk.

Page 88.

State of Tennessee, Benton County,Personally appeared before me G.R.
Kelsey,Clerk of County Court, said County, the within named bargainors
with whom I am personally acquainted and who acknowledged that they
signed the within deed for the purpose therein contained,given under
my hand at office,this 3rd day of December 1838.And the state tax being
paid so let it be registered.   *George R.Kelsey-Clerk.

State of Tennessee,Benton County,Personally* appeared before me George
R.Kelsey,Clerk of said County,P.T.Robertson and A.T.Robertson,
subscribing witnesses to the within named deed,who being first sworn
and deposes and says they are acquainted with William B.Robertson the
bargainor and that he acknowledged the same in their presence to be his
act and deed upon the day it bears date,witness my hand at office
this 3rd day of January 1839. *G.R.Kelsey-Clerk.

Page 88-Continued.

State of Tennessee,Benton County,Personally appeared before me George R.
Kelsey,clerk of the said Court of Benton County.I John Eason & Lillie
Smith subscribing witnesses to the within named deed who being first
sworn,depose and say that they are acquainted with Samuel Dickens the
bargainor,and that he acknowledged the same in presents to be his act
and deed upon the day it bears date given,under my hand at office in
Camden,this 9th day of January 1839.   *G.R.Kelsey-Clerk.

State of Tennessee,Benton,County,Personally appeared before me George
R.Kelsey,clerk of said County Court of said Benton County.The within
named bargainor,with whom I am personally acquainted and who acknowledged
that he executed the within deed for the purposes therein contained
Witness my hand at office in Camden this 18th day of January 1839.
                                        G.R.Kelsey-Clerk.

State of Tennessee,Benton County,Personally appeared before me George
R.Kelsey,clerk of the County Court of said Benton CountyA?Lashlee&Jonus
Haywood with whom I am personally acquainted and after being sworn
depose and say the within named Thomas Petty assign the above bill of
sale of a negro woman named "Cricy" age twenty one years.Also one negro
girl child named Susan,age four years,and to Kezeat Petty with warrant
to title,witness my hand at office in Camden this 22nd day of January
1839.   *G.R.Kelsey-Clerk.

Page 89

State of Tennessee,Benton County,Personally appeared before me George
R.Kelsey,Clerk of County Court,of said Benton County.Abraham Bulyen
& Joseph M.Benton,subscribing witnesses to the within named deed who
having first sworn,depose and say that they are acquainted with Margaret
Curry the bargainor and that she acknowladged the same to the presents
of her act,and deed upon day it bears date.Given under my hand at my
office in Camden the 4th day of February 1839.
                              * George R.Kelsey -Clerk.

State of Tennessee,Benton County.Personally appeared before me George
R.Kelsey,clerk of the county court of said county,of Benton.The within
named Irvin B.Carns,the bargainor with whom I am well acquainted ,and who
acknowledged that he executed the above land for the purposes therein
contained.Witness my hand at office this 28th day of February 1839.
                              *G.R.Kelsey-Clerk.

Page 90

State of Tennessee,Benton County,Personally appeared before me George
R.Kelsey,clerk of said county,of Benton.Seth Petty & Irvin B.Carns
subsribing witnesses to the within named deed.Who being first sworn
depose and say they are acquainted with Sam H.Burton the bargainor and
that he acknowledged the same in the presents to be his act and deed
upon the day it bears date,given under my hand at my office 5th day
March 1839.And the state tax being paid so let it be registered
                              *G.R.Kelsey-Clerk.

State of Tennessee,Benton County,Personally appeared before me George
R.Kelsey,clerk of the county court of said county of Benton.The within
named Thomas Jonus.With whom I am personally acquainted and who
acknowledged that he executed the within deed for the purposes therein
contained.Witness my hand in office, in Camden.the 9th day of March 1839.
The state tax being paid so let it be registered.
                              *G.R.Kelsey -Clerk.

Page 91.

State of Tennessee, Benton County,Personally appeared before me George R
Kelsey,clerk of the County Court of said County.of Benton.The within
named George H.Burton ,with whom I am personally acquainted and who
acknowledged that he executed the deed for the purposes therein contained
Witness my hand at office this 9th day of March 1839.The state tax being
paid,so let it be registered   *G.R.Kelsey- Clerk.

State of Tennessee, Benton County,Personally appeared before me George
R.Kelsey,clerk of said county court,of said county of Benton.The within
named T.Jenus   with whom I am personally acquainted and who acknowledged
that he executed the within deed for the purposes therein contained.
Witness my hand at office,this 9th day of March 1839/The state tax being
paid so let it be registered.
                              *G.R.Kelsey-Clerk.

Page 92.

State of Tennessee,Benton County.Personally appeared before me George
R.Kelsey,Clerk of said County Court,of said County of Benton.The
within named T.Jonus,with whom I am personally acquainted,and who
acknowledged that he executed the within deed for the purpose for
the purpose therein contained.Witness my hand at office this 9th day
of March 1839.State tax being paid so let it be registered.
                              *G.R.Kelsey -Clerk.

State of Tennessee,Benton County.Personally appeared before me George
R.Kelsey,clerk of the said county court of said county of Benton.W.H.
Burton & Paul Smith subscribing witnesses to the within named deed who
being first sworn depose and say they are acquainted with John Jackson
the bargainor, and he acknowledged the same in the presents to be his act
and deed upon day it bearsdate ,Witness my hand in office in Camden
this 2nd day of April 1839.State tax being paid so let it be registered.
                              *G.R.Kelsey -Clerk.

State of Tennessee, Benton County.Personally appeared before me George R.
Kelsey of said county court of Benton County.The within Ezekiel McBride
the bargainor with whom I am personally acquainted and who acknowledged that
he executed the within deed for the purpose therein contained.Witness my
hand at office,in Camden the 9th day of April 1839.

                       *G.R.Kelsey-Clerk.

Page 93.

State of Tennessee, Benton County.Personally appeared before me George
R.Kelsey,clerk of the County Court of said county of Benton.W.W.Barton
and James Haywood and first being sworn to depose subscribing witnesses
to the within deed and say they are acquainted with Samuel H.Burton
the bargainor and that he acknowledged the same in the their presence
to be his act and deed upon this day it bears date.Witness my hand at
office in Camden this 9th day of April 1839.

                       *G.R.Kelsey-Clerk.

State of Tennessee, Benton County.Clerks office May 7th 1839.There was a
deed certified in my office.Made by Thomas Jonus,Sheff Reedden Holland
for 90 acres of land

                       *G.R.Kelsey- Clerk.

State of Tennessee, Benton County.Clerks office May 7th 1839.There was a
deed certified in my office made by James Pinckston to James Allen

                       *G.R.Kelsey-- Clerk.

Page 94.

State of Tennessee,Benton County,Clerks office May 7th 1839.There was a
deed proved and certified in my office made by Solomon Copeland to
Mary Matlock for 36 acres of land. The state tax being paid so let it
be registered.   *G.R.Kelsey- Clerk.

State of Tennessee.Benton County,Clerks office May 9th 1839.There was
deed produced in my office made by Jessie Blackmon to E.T.Willis for
640 acres of land certified by the clerk of Davidson County.The state
tax being paid so let it be registered. . *G.R.Kelsey- Clerk.

State of Tennessee, Benton County. Clerks Office May 8th 1839.There was
a deed acknowledged in my office made by Wyatt Arnold to Ephriam Arnold
for 15 acres of land. State tax being paid so let it be registered.
                    * G.R.Kelsey.Clerk.

State of Tennessee, Benton County, Clerks office. May 8th 1839.
There was a deed acknowledged in my office made by the commissioners for
the town of Camden to James Gardner for two town lots number 23 and 24
The state tax being paid so let it be registered.

                    *G.R.Kelsey- Clerk.

State of Tennessee, Benton County. Clerks office May 8th 1839.There was a
deed acknowedged in my office made by commissioners for the town of Camden
to Jonus Gardner for one town lot No 63.The state tax being paid. So let
it be registered.

                    * G.R.Kelsey- Clerk.

State of Tennessee, Benton County, May 10th 1839-There was a deed of trust
acknowledged in my office made by Andrew S.Call to Andrew Lashlee for the
purposes therein contained and on the day it bears date,given under my
hand at office.this 10th day of May 1839.

                    *G.R.Kelsey- Clerk.

Page 95.

State of Tennessee, Benton County,Clerks office May 14th 1839.There was
as deed proven in my office,made by the commissioners to Anderson Lashlee
for three town lots.Signed sealed and decreeded for the purposes therein
contained and on the day it bears date,given under my hand at office
this 14th day of May 1839.

                    *G.R.Kelsey- Clerk.

Page 95- Continued.

State of Tennessee, Benton County,Clerks office June 4th 1839.There was
a deed acknowledged made in my office by Pleasant Mullinck to Reuben
Marchbanks for 82½ acres of land.Witness my hand at office this 4th day
of June 1839.

                              *G.R.Kelsey-Clerk.

State of Tennessee,Benton County, Clerks office,There was a deed
acknowledged in my office made by.,Reuben Marchbanks to Pleasant
Mullinicks for 65 acres of land .Witness my hand at office this 4th
day of June 1839 .State tax being paid so let it be registered.

                       *G.R.Kelsey-Clerk.

State of Tennessee, Benton County.Clerks office,June 4th 1839.There was a
plot of survey acknowledged in my office by Burrell Beard to Joseph
Wiseman for 299 acres of land.Witness my hand at office this day and date
above written.

                       *G.R.Kelsey-Clerk.

Page 96-

State of Tennessee, Benton County, Clerks office July 1st 1839.There was
a deed acknowledged in my office.for W.W.Wheatly,to John Nales for 100
acres of land.Witness my hand at office,this day and date above written
▾The State tax being paid so let it be registered.

                       *G.R.Kelsey- Clerk.

State of Tennessee, Benton County,Clerks Office August 5th 1839.There was
a deed acknowledged in my office from Cooper Milton to John Milton for
20 acres of land.Witness my hand at office this 5th day of August 1839.

                       *G.R.Kelsey- Clerk.

State of Tennessee, Benton County,Clerks office August 5th 1839.There was
a deed acknowledged in my office from the commissioners of Camden to
James Beard.for one town lot.Witness my hand at office this day and date
above written.

                       *G.R.Kelsey- Clerk.

State of Tennessee, Benton County.Clerks office August 6th 1839.There was a
deed acknowledged by W.H.H.Burton to Thomas H.Burton for 16½ acres of land
Witness my hand at office this day and date above written.

                       *G.R.Kelsey -Clerk.

Page 96 -Continued.

State of Tennessee.Benton County.Clerks office August 6th 1839.   There
was a deed acknowledged by Thomas H.Burton,to William H.H.Burton for a
town lot in Camden No 35. Witness my hand at office this day and date
above.

                        *G.R.Kelsey-Clerk.

State of Tennessee, Benton County.Clerks office August 6th 1839.There was
a transfer of a bond made from W.H.H.Burton to Thos H.Burton.Made from
A.Lashlee to W.H.H.Burton.Witness my hand at office this day and date
above written.

                        *G.R.Kelsey- Clerk.

Page 97

State of Tennessee, Benton County, Clerks office.September 2nd 1839.There
was a deed proven in my office.from John Askew to Peter Phifer for 60
acres of land.Witness my hand at office this day and date above written.

                        *G.R.Kelsey- Clerk.

State of Tennessee, Benton County.Clerks office there was a deed acknowledged in my office from Benjamin Hardy to Amos Bruce for 37½ acres of land
Witness my hand at office this 3rd day of September 1839.

                        G.R.Kelsey- Clerk.

State of Tennessee, Benton County, C₁erks office September 11th 1839.There
was a bill of sale acknowledged by Jonathan Fuller to Green Flowers for the
purpose therein contained.Witness my hand at office this day and date
above.

                        G.R.Kelsey-Clerk.

Page 98.

State of Tennessee, Benton County,Clerks office October 8th 1839.There was
a deed acknowledged by the commissioners for the town of Camden to A.Lash-
lee for lots No 13-14-36-37-62 & 63,for the purpose therein contained.
Witness my hand this day and date above.

                        *G.R.Kelsey- Clerk.

State of Tennessee,Benton County, Clerks Office.October 28th 1839.There was
a mortage acknowledged before me from Dane McQraig to James Lindsey for the
purpose therein contained. Witness my hand at office this day and ate
above.

                        *G.R.Kelsey- Clerk.

Page 98-Continued

State of Tennessee, Benton County, Clerks Office, October 8th 1839. There
was a deed proven from John W. Jonus to George Bill in my office for
25 acres of land, witness my hand at office this day and date above.

*G.R.Kelsey-Clerk.

State of Tennessee, Benton County, Clerks Office, October 23rd 1839.
There was a deed certified in my office for 10 acres of land made by
Abner McCarrall to Wyly Arnold. Witness my hand at office. This day and
date above.

*G.R.Kelsey-Clerk.

Sate of Tennessee, Benton County, Clerks Office, October 23rd 1839. There
was a deed certified in my office for 10 town lots from Isaac Ballard
to Christopher H. Wyly. Witness my hand at my office this date above.

*G.R.Kelsey-Clerk.

State of Tennessee, Benton County, Clerks Office, November 18th 1839
There was a deed proven in my office from George Buard to T.W.Sayles
5 small tracts of land containing 719 acres. Witness my hand at office
this day and date above.

*G.R.Kelsey-Clerk.

Page 99.

State of Tennessee, Benton County, Clerks Office-October 8th 1839.
There was a deed acknowledged by Benjamin Hardy to Allen Melton for
25 acres. Witness my hand at office. This day and date above.

*G.R.Kelsey-Clerk.

State of Tennessee, Benton County, Clerks Office, January 7th 1840.
There was a deed acknowledged by John Gassett for 50 acres of land
Witness my hand at office. This day and date above.

*G.R.Kelsey-Clerk.

Sate of Tennessee, Benton County. Clerks Office. January 7th 1840. There was
a mortgage acknowledged by Kenneth Reddick to Alexander McReddon, The day
and date above. Witness my hand at office this day and date above.

*G.R.Kelsey-Clerk.

Page 100.

State of Tennessee, Benton County, Clerks Office, January 8th 1840. There

Page 100-Continued.

was a deed acknowledged by Thomas Jones to Green Flowers for 280
acres of land.On the day and date above written.Witness my hand at
office.

*G.R.Kelsey -Clerk.

State of Tennessee,Benton County,Clerks Office,January 9th 1840.There
was a deed of gift made by Wyatt Arnold to Joseph E.S.Russell on the
day and date above.Witness my hand this day and date above.

*G.R.Kelsey-Clerk.

State of Tennessee,Benton County, Clerks Office,January 10th 1840.There
was a deed of trust made by Gesshanah Collins to Anderson Lashlee
for 91 ½ acres of landon the day and date above. Witness my hand at
office in Camden.

*G.R.Kelsey-Clerk.

State of Tennessee,Benton County, Clerks Office,January 30th 1840.There
was a deed made by Thomas Jones Sheriff to T.B.Adams for one town lot
No 35.Witness my hand at office this day and date above.

*G.R.Kelsey-Clerk.

State of Tennessee, Benton County, Clerks Office,February 27th 1840.
There was a power of attorney acknowledged by Thos F.Mulhallan to
Henry H.Marable on the day and date above.

*George R.Kelsey-Clerk.

Page 101.

State of Tennessee, BentonCounty, Clerks Office ,February 29th 1840.
There was a deed certified in my office from Joseph Wiseman for 23½
acres of land. Witness my hand at office this day and date above.

*G.R.Kelsey-Clerk.

State of Tennessee,Benton County, Clerks Office. February 29th 1840.
There was a mortgage acknowledged by Will A Hudson to A.T.Hudson
Witness my hand at office this day and date above.

*G.R.Kelsey-Clerk.

State of Tennessee,Benton County, Clerks Office.March 2nd 1840.There was
a deed of trust acknowledged by me T.B.Hanlbard to Lewis Cotton ham
for the purposes therein contained and on the date above written.

*G.R.Kelsey-Clerk.

Page 101-Continued.

State of Tennessee,Benton County,Clerks Office.March 13th 1840.There
was a deed proven made by the committeemen for the town of Camden to
Burwell Beard for two town lots 36 & 54.Witness my hand at office this
day and date above.

                    *G.R.Kelsey-Clerk.

State of Tennessee,Benton County, Clerks Office. March 18th 1840.
There was a deed made by committeeman to John T.Atkins for on twon
lot No 5.Witness my hand at office this day and date above.

                    *G.R.Kelsey-Clerk.

Page 102.

State of Tennessee, Benton County, Clerks Office.There was a deed made
certified from James Shiff of five lots in town of Camden,Danaiel Sutters
this 8th day of April 1840.

                    *G.R.Kelsey-Clerk.

State of Tennessee, Benton County, Clerks Office.There was a mortgage
proven before me from William Nance to James R.Nance.The 6th day of
April 1840.

                    *G.R.Kelsey-Clerk.

State of Tennessee,Benton County, Clerks Office.April 16th 1840.There
was a deed of trust made by William Sykes to A.Lashlee.Witness my hand
at office.This day and date above.

                    *G.R.Kelsey-Clerk.

State of Tennessee Benton County, CLerks Office.April 20th 1840.There
was a deed proven from John Cracker to J.B.Cars and duly certifiedin
my office this day and date within.

                    *G.R.Kelsey-Clerk.

Page 103.

State of Tennessee, Benton County, Clerks Office,April 23rd 1840.
There was a deed of trust made from Joseph D.Long to A.Lashlee
acknowledged in my office and duly certified on the date hereof.

                    *G.R.Kelsey-Clerk.

State of Tennessee,Benton County,Clerks Office, April 29th 1840.There
was a deed acknowledged by the committee of Camden to James Beard
for a town lot on the day and date above written. *G.R.Kelsey CLerk.

Page 103-Continued.

State of Tennessee,Benton,County.Clerks Office.May 13th 1840.There was
a bill of sale proven in my office of a negro boy by the name of Warin
from Samuel L.Nasbat,Executor to John Kagly.Proven by the oath of
S.C.Parrotts,on the day and date above.

*G.R.Kelsey-Clerk.

Stateof Tennessee, Benton County. Clerks Office.May 13th 1840.There was
a bill of sale proven in my office by the oath of S.C.Parrott of a negro
boy named Frank from Thos Banks to the Administrator of the Esate of
David Moore,Deceased to James Wyly.

*G.R.Kelsey-Clerk.

State of Tennessee,Benton County, Clerks Office. May 28th 1840.There
was a deed acknowledged by Andrew Still to T.H.Richardson for 5,000
acres of land.Witness my hand at office this day and date above.

*G.R.Kelsey-Clerk.

State of Tennessee, Benton County, Clerks Office,June 2nd 1840.
There was a deed for 107 / acres of land acknowledged in my office by
James Alexander to Samuel Mandin.Witness my hand at office this day
and date above.

State of Tennessee,Benton County, Clerks Office.May 15th 1840.There
was a mortgage for a horse acknowledged in my office by James McGill
Thos Jones witness, my hand at office this day and date above.

*G.R.Kelsey-Clerk.

Page 104.

State of Tennessee, Benton County,Clerks Office.June 6th 1840.There was
a deed acknowledged in my office from Joel Rushing to John W.Utley for
38 ½ acres of land.Witness my hand at office this day and date above.

*G.R.Kelsey-Clerk.

State of Tennessee, Benton County, Clerks Office,July 8th 1840.There
was a deed acknowledged by Solomon Carmack to William Lindsey for
45 acres of land on the day and date above.

*G.R.Kelsey-Clerk.

Page 104-Continued.

State of Tennessee, Benton County,Clerks Office,July 11th 1840.There was
a mortgage made by W.C.Holmes to Robert Holmes for property on the day
and date above written.

*G.R.Kelsey Clerk.

Page 105.

State of Tennessee, Benton County, Clerks Office,May 5th 1840.There was
a power of attorney made by William H.Nance to Andrew G.Browens of
south corner land.Witness my hand at office this day and date above.

*G.R.Kelsey-Clerk.

State of Tennessee,Benton County, Clerks Office,July 16th 1840.There
was a deed of trust acknowledged by William Lindsey to James Lindsey
for property on the day and date above.

*G.R.Kelsey-Clerk.

State of Tennessee,Benton County, Clerks Office,August 4th 1840.There
was a deed acknowledged by James M.Camp to Joshua Waggoner for thirty
five acres of land.Witness my hand at office,this day and date above.

*G.R.Kelsey-Clerk.

State of Tennessee, Benton County,Clerks Office, August 4th 1840.There
was a deed proven in my office.from David Waggoner to Jonus M.Camp
for 35 acres of land.Witness my hand at office.The day and date above.

*G.R.Kelsey-Clerk.

Page 106.

State of Tennessee,Clerks Office ,August 4th 1840. There was a deed
proven in my office from Martin Waggoner to T.P.Drummond for 42 acres
of land.Witness my hand this day and date above.

*G.R.Kelsey-Clerk.

State of Tennessee, Benton County, Clerks Office, August 8th 1840.There
was a deed proven in my office from A.Lashlee to Wyly Arnold for 2o
acres of land on the day and date above.

*G.R.Kelsey-Clerk.

State of Tennessee,Benton County, Clerks Office,August 17th 1840.There
was a deed of trust for property made by Dan McTuaga to M.Benton on the
day and date above.   *G.R.Kelsey-Clerk.

Page 106-Continued.

State of Tennessee, Benton County, Clerks Office.August 29th 1840.
There was a deed acknowledged in my office for William McGee to
Joseph Hawkins. for forty acres of land on the day and date above.

                    *G.R.Kelsey-Clerk.

State of Tennessee,Benton County,Clerks Office.11th day of September
1840.There was a bill of sale acknowledged by Thomas Jones ,Sheriff
to John P.McCutcheon for two negroes, a man named Lornos and a woman
named Maud,Silvy.Witness my hand at office this day and date above.

                    *G.R.Kelsey-Clerk.

State of Tennessee, Benton County, Clerks Office,September 9th 1840.
There was a deed acknowledged by E.Perkins to John Thompson 1/3 of
one town lot.Known on the plan as lot 69.Witness my hand at office
this day and date above.

                    *G.R.Kelsey-Clerk.

State of Tennessee, Benton County, Clerks Office,September 14th 1840.
There was apt at and certificate signed by James H$_0$gg to Hilary
Crabb for tue ascens of same.This day and date above.

                    G.R.Kelsey-Clerk.

Page 107.

State of Tennessee, Benton County, Clerks Office,September 14th 1840.
There was a mortgage acknowledged by Thos T.Floyd to Lewis W.Bro wn
this day and date above.

                    *G.R.Kelsey-Clerk.

State of Tennessee, Benton County,Clerks Office,September 17th 1840.
There was a mortgage acknowledged from David Morris to Seth Utly on
the day and date above.

                    *G.R.Kelsey-Clerk.

State of Tennessee,Benton County.Clerks Office.October 6th 1840.
A power of attorney for Unity Cole to Cullin N$_0$well was day assigned
and executed and acknowledged.by said Unity Cole.

                    *G.R.Kelsey-Clerk.

State of Tennessee, Benton County,Clerks Office,November 21st 1840.
There was a plat and certificate proven in my office for John Runneon
for 200 acres of land for Bird B.Barnett on this day and date above.

Page 107-Continued.

State of Tennessee,Benton County,Clerks Office.November 21st 1840.
There was a deed proven by R.H.Hawthorn from James Melton to Jonus Rogers
for 87 acres of land.On this day and date above.

                         *G.R.Kelsey-Clerk.

Sate of Tennessee, Benton County, Clerks Office.December 9th 1840.
There was a deed of trust acknowledged by Lewis Boswell to John D
Ward.for property on this day and date above.

                         *G.R.Kelsey-Clerk.

State of Tennessee,Benton County,Clerks Office.December 12th 1840.
There William H.Nance acknowledged as power of attorney to Anderson
G.Brannon of South Carolina to act for him in conformity to same
agreeable to law.This day and date above.

                         *G.R.Kelsey-Clerk.

Page 108.

State of Tennessee, Benton County, Clerks Office.December 19th 1840.
There was a mortgage acknowledged made from John B.Brennayor to Isaac
Bond for property on the day and date above.

                         *G.R.Kelsey-Clerk

State of Tennessee, Benton County, Clerks Office,January 11th 1841.
There was a deed acknowledged by the commissioners of the town of
Camden .Thos K.Wyly for Lot No 1 in said town this day and date above.

                         *G.R.Kelsey-Clerk.

State of Tennessee,Clerks office, January 19th 1841.Benton County.
There was a bill of sale to all of the interest of Robert McCrackeing
to all the negoroes of the Estate of B.Lashlee as acknowledged as being
conveyed to Anderson Lashlee.

                         *G.R.Kelsey-Clerk.

State of Tennesse,Benton County,Clerks Office Dec 7th 1840.There was a
deed acknowledged before me E.Burkett to E.Jordon for 94 acres of land.

                         *G.R.Kelsey-Clerk.

State of Tennessee, Benton County,Clerks Office.January 19th 1841
There was a bill of sale of all interest of William H.Miller to all the
negroes belonging to the Estate of B.Lashlee,Deceased acknowledged
to be conveyed to Anderson Lashlee* G.R.Kelsey-Clerk.

Page 108-Continued.

State of Tennessee, Benton County, Clerks Office. January 25th 1841. There
was a mortgage acknowledged by John Watson to David Watson and A.C.
Prerson. for property.

*G.R.Kelsey-Clerk.

State of Tennessee, Benton County, Clerks Office, January 22nd 1841
There was a deed acknowledged by Gordon Branton to Elisha Jackson
for sixty acres of land before me.

*G.R.Kelsey-Clerk.

Page 109.

State of Tennessee, Benton County, Clerks Office, December 25th 1840.
There was a mortgage of property acknowledged by Henry Allen to T.
McGill. before me on the day and date above.

*G.R.Kelsey-Clerk.

State of Tennesse, Benton County. Clerks Office, Clerks Office December
25th 1840. There was a mortgage of propert acknowledged, Henry Aaler to
John McGill before me on the day and date above. written

*G.R.Kelsey-Clerk.

State of Tennessee, Benton County, Clerks Office. January 27th 1841
There was a mortgage acknowledged by John Wood to W.P.Bass for
property, before me, on the day and date above.

*G.R.Kelsey-Clerk.

State of Tennessee, Benton County, Clerks Office, February 11th 1841.
There was a deed of gift acknowledged by L.W.Brewer to the heirs of
Thos L.Floyd for personal property, on the day and date above.

*G.R.Kelsey-Clerk.

State of Tennessee, Benton County, Clerks Office, February 1st 1841.
There was a deed acknowledged by Thomas Jones, Sheriff to Redden
Hallowell two hundred and forty acres of land, on the day and ate above.

*G.R.Kelsey-Clerk.

State of Tennessee, Benton County, Clerks Office. February 8th 1841. There
was a deed of bargain and sale of 60 acres o land in said county
acknowledged from Elisha Jackson to Gordon Branton, for the purpose
therein contained.

*G.R.Kelsey-Clerk.

Page 109 Continued.

State of Tennessee,Benton County,Clerks Office,February 16th 1841.
There was a mortgage acknowledged R.W.Allen for property to A.Lashlee.
This day and date above.

*G.R.Kelsey-Clerk.

Page 110.

State of Tennessee, Benton County, Clerks Office.March 1st 1841.
There was a bill of sale acknowledged by James Morris to A.Lashlee
fora negro man named Rince,age twenty three years.

*G.R.Kelsey-Clerk.

State of Tennessee,Benton County,Clerks Office.March 1st 1841.
There was a mortgage acknowledged by A.T.Flowers to C.K.Coyly for
a negro woman named Molly.

*G.R.Kelsey-Clerk

State of Tennessee, Benton County,Clerks Office.March 8th 1841.
There was a deed acknowledged by A.Lashlee to Dorris Still for 20 acres o
of land

*G.R.Kelsey-Clerk.

State of Tennessee, Benton County,Clerks Office.March 15th 1841.
There was a deed acknowledged by A.Lashlee.Dorris Still for 50 acres
of land.

*G.R.Kelsey-Clerk.

State of Tennessee, Benton County,Clerks Office.March 24th 1841.
There was a deed acknowledged Edward Crain to Daniel Harkniss for his
undivided part for his undivided part of the 1/3 one thousand acres.

*G.R.Kelsey-Clerk.

Page 111.

State of Tennessee,Benton County, Clerks Office.March 24th 1841There was
a deed of gift acknowledged,Jacob H.Whitehorn for negro to Thos Patty.

*G.R.Kelsey-Clerk.

State of Tennessee,Benton County,Clerks Office.April 1st 1841.There was
a deed acknowledged by T.B.Adams for a town lot No 61 to C.K WYLY.

*G.R.Kelsey-Clerk.

Page 111-Continued.

State of Tennessee,Benton County, Clerks Office,April 3rd 1841.
There was a deed acknowledged before me ELIjah M.Bush and James H.Bush
to J.D.Rushing property on the day and date above.

                         *G.R.Kelsey-Clerk.

State of Tennessee,Benton County,Clerks Office.April 3rd 1841.There
was a deed proven by the oath of E&J.Bush to J.J.Rushing for property

                         *G.R.Kelsey-Clerk.

Page 112.

State of Tennessee,Benton County, Clerks Office.May 6th 1841.
There was a deed acknowledged Willie Arnold to P.Arnold for 96
acres of land.

                         *G.R.Kelsey -Clerk.

State of Tennessee,Benton County, Clerks Office,May 9th 1841.There was
a deed acknowledged by Joseph Wiseman to A.Lashlee for 15½ acres of land.

                         *G.R.Kelsey-Clerk.

State of Tennessee,Benton,County,Clerks Office,May 10th 1841.There was
a deed proven before me from Allen Petty Attorney in fact for James
Curn for 111 acres of land

                         *G.R.Kelsey-Clerk

State of Tennessee,Benton County, Clerks Office, May 11th 1841.There was
a deed proven before me from A Petty attorney in fact of Hugh Curn for
125 acres of land.

                         *G.R.Kelsey-Clerk.

State of Tennessee,Benton County, Clerks Office,May 22nd 1841.There
was a mortgage acknowledged by Abner.Sinaubly to W.M.Sinaulby for
property.

                         *G.R.Kelsey- Clerk.

State of Tennessee,Benton County, Clerks Office,July 3rd 1841.There was
a deed for a town lot No 22 acknowledged by Jackson Rushing to James
Wyly.

                         *G.R.Kelsey-Clerk.

State of Tennessee,Benton County, Clerks Office,July 6th 1841.There was
a deed acknowledged by the county for the the town of Camden for two
town lots numbers 21 and 41.

Page 113.

State of Tennessee,Benton County, Clerks Office, July 7th 1841.There
was a deed acknowledged by Willis Rushing to Richard P.Rushing for 81
acres of land.

                    *G.R.Kelsey-Clerk.

State of Tennessee, Benton County,Clerks Office.July 7th 1841.There
was a mortgage acknowledged by Allen T.Corbit to Denis Rushing for
property.

                    *G.R.Kelsey-Clerk.

State of Tennessee,Benton County,Clerks Office,July 7th 1841.There was
a deed acknowledged by John Davis to Jackson Rushing for a town lot No
22.

                    *G.R.Kelsey-Clerk.

State of Tennessee,Benton County,Clerks Office,July 15th 1841.There was
a deed acknowledged in my office to D.Settle,Jr for 50 acres of land.

                    *G.R.Kelsey-Clerk.

State of Tennessee,Benton County,Clerks Office ,May 12th 1841.There was
a power of attorney acknowledged before me.T.C.Parot to Thomas H.Burton

                    *G.R.Kelsey-Clerk.

State of Tennessee,Benton,County,Clerks Office.July 31st 1841.There was
a mortgage acknowledged Isaac Ballard to David Morris agray mare.

                    *G.R.Kelsey-Clerk.

State of Tennessee,Benton County, Clerks Office.August 6th 1841.There
was a deed acknowledged by C.Wheatly to William C?Hall for 100 acres.

                    *G.R.Kelsey-Clerk.

State of Tennessee,Benton County,Clerks Office,August 6th 1841.There was
a deed acknowledged by W.C.Hall to John Nobles for 100 acres of land.

                    *G.R.Kelsey-Clerk.

Page 114.

State of Tennessee,Benton County.Clerks Office,August 14th 1841.There
was a deed acknowledged by Sam Settle to B.Settle for 25 acres of land.

                    *G.R.Kelsey-Clerk.

Page 114-Continued.

State of Tennessee,Benton County, Clerks Office,September 11th 1841.
There was a deed acknowledged by Sam Madden to Jonathan C.Latimer
for one hundred seven and 3/4 acres of land.

*G.R.Kelsey-Clark.

State of Tennessee,Benton County,Clerks Office,September 16th 1841.
There was a deed acknowledged by Thomas Jonus,Sheriff before me to
T.B.Attom for one town lot No 35.

*G.R.Kelsey-Clark.

State of Tennessee,Benton County, Clerks Office,September 20th 1841.
There was a power of attorney acknowledged before me,G.B.Altom to
R.M.Altom.Before me.

*G.R.Kelsey-Clark.

Page 115.

State of Tennessee,Benton County,Clerks Office,September 25th 1841
There was a deed proven before me from the committees from the town
of Camden from A.Caldwell to A.Lashlee for one lot No 4.

*G.R.Kelsey-Clark.

State of Tennessee,Benton County,Clerks Office this December 10th 1841
There came before me Mark Hatley and Cullen W.Luper and proved the sale
of the 1/6 part of 6 negroes from Anderson Lynch and his wife Elizabeth
Lynch to James Wyly on the day and date above.

*G.R.Kelsey-Clark.

State of Tennessee,Benton County,Clerks Office December 10th 1841.There
came before me Mark Hatly one of the witnesses and proved a bargain
and sale of the sixth part of 6 negroes from from Cullin W.Luper
to Bancy Luper his wife to James Wyly the day and date above.

*G.R.Kelsey-Clark.

State of Tennessee,Benton County,Clerks Office ,December 10th 1841
There came before me Mark Hatly one of the witnesses and proved a bargain
and sale of the one thirty sixth part for Luck and Sarah Hatly to
JamesWyly.The day and date above.

*G.R.Kelsey-Clark.

State of Tennessee,Benton County,Clerks Office,January 1st 1842.There
was a deed acknowledged before me by John Cole to William Cole for 50
acres of land.The state tax being paid so let it be registered.

*G.R.Kelsey-Clark.

Page 116

State of Tennessee,Benton County, Clarks Office-January 8th 1842.There
was a deed of trust acknowledged before me #by Samuel Madden to James
S.Sayles.

G.R.Kelsey-Clark.

State of Tennessee,Benton County, Clarks Office,January 8th 1842.There
was a deed acknowledged by the sheriff of Benton County for 22 2/9 ths
acres.Also one town lot the one known and designated on the plan of
Camden as lot No 36.

G.R.Kelsey-Clark.

State of Tennessee,Benton County, Clarks Office,January 10th 1842.
There was a mortgage acknowledged before me from a Herrin to Beverly
Herrin.

G.R.Kelsey-Clark.

State of Tennessee,Benton County, Clarks Office.January 11th 1842.
There was a bargain and sale of the estate of I.Hatly acknowledged
by Mark Hatly to Solomon Hatly before me.

G.R.Kelsey-Clark.

State of Tennessee,Benton County,Clarks Office,January 11th 1842.
There was a bargain and sale of the interest of Patsy Oatsvale from
the court of Charles Oatsdale acknowledged before me of her interest
of Sherod Hatly

G.R.Kelsey-Clark.

State of Tennessee,Benton County, Clarks Office.January 27th 1842.
There was a deed acknowledged before me by Ephriam F.Jordon to Harry B.
Laurance for 46 1/4 acres of land.The state tax being paid so let it be
registered.

G.R.Kelsey-Clark.

Page 117.

State of Tennessee,Benton County, Clarks Office,March 8th 1842.There
was a deed proven in my office for B.B.Barnett to Wm Hubbs for 40
acres of land.The state tax being paid so let it be registered.

G.R.Kelsey-Clark.

State of Tennessee, Benton County, Clarks Office,March 14th 1842.
There was a deed acknowledged before me by Jonathan P.Mills as the
lawful attorney in fact of John Jackson for 22 acres to A.Lashlee.

Page 118

State of Tennessee, Benton County, Clerks Office.March 28th 1842.There
was a bill of sale proven before me from J.T.Florance to C.K.Boyly
for a negro woman named Milly.

                        G.R.Kelsey-Clark.

State of Tennessee, Benton County.Clerks Office.April 6th 1842.
There was a deed proven before me from Martin Runneon to B.B.Barnett
for 33½ acres of land

                        G.R.Kelsey-Clark.

Sate of Tennessee, Benton County, Clerks Office, April 25th 1842
There was a mortgage acknowledged from Hugh M.Brown to Sam F.Tittle
for a horse on the day and date above.

                        G.R.Kelsey-Clark.

Page 119

State of Tennessee, Benton County, Clerks Office,May 9th 1842.There
was a mortgage acknowledged before me Benjamin Holland to 3.Cowell
for one sorrell mare.

                        G.R.Kelsey-Clark.

State of Tennessee, Benton County,Clerks Office. May 10th 1842.There
was a deed proven before me of John & Lewis Runneon to B.B.Barnett
for 100 acres of land.

                        G.R.Kelsey-Clark.

State of Tennessee, Benton County,Clerks Office May 11th 1842.There
was a bill of sale acknowledged before me Green Flowers to John Wyly
for a negro boy named Reddin.age about 21 years.

                        G.R.Kelsey-Clark.

State of Tennessee, Benton County, Clerks Office, May 11th 1842.
There was a deed acknowledged before me Burrel Beard to W.P.Morris
for 22 acres of land

                        G.R.Kelsey-Clark.

State of Tennessee, Benton County, Clerks Office.May 31st 1842.
There was a power of attorney acknowledged from Theo J nes to J.T.
Florance to sign his name to a bond of twenty thousand dollars
conditioned to Burtons faithful performance according to law as entry
taken of Benton County.

                        G.R.Kelsey- Clark.

Page 119 Continued.

State of Tennessee, Benton County, Clarks Office, Juen 6th 1842.
There was a deed acknowledged before me by Ephriam Perkins to John
Fargason.

G.R.Kelsey-Clerk.

State of Tennessee, Benton County.Clerks Office.January 15th 1842.There
was a deed presented in my office for John Lyons to William Pemberton
for 90 acres of land. The state tax being paid thereon.

G.R.Kelsey-Clerk.

Page 120.

State of Tennessee, Benton County, Clerks Office.June 22nd 1842.There
was a bill of sale acknowledged before me in my office from Thos Jones
to Michael Fry for a negro woman named Fanny.

G.R.Kelsey-Clerk.

State of Tennessee, Benton County.Clerks Office.July 2nd 1842.There was
a deed acknowledged before me E.Perkins,G.Flowers,T.F.Johnson.Lewis
Brewer,Commissioners for the town of Camden to A.S.Cole for a town lot
No 6.

G.R.Kelsey-Clerk.

State of Tennessee, Benton County.Clerks Office.July 5th 1842.There
was a deed acknowledged by the commissioners for the town of Camden
to Green Flowers for 4 town lots,before me.

G.R.Kelsey-Clerk.

State of Tennessee, Benton County.Clerks Office.July 5th 1842.There was
a deed acknowledged by the commissioners to E.Perkins for two town lots
before me.

G.R.Kelsey-Clerk.

State of Tennessee, Benton County, Clerks Office.July 11th 1842.There
was a deed acknowledged in my office from S.Copeland to John Smawley for
80 acres of land.

G.R.Kelsey-Clerk.

State of Tennessee, Benton County, Clerks Office.July 25th 1842.There
was a deed of gift acknowledged by Lewis Hyar for a negro woman named
Harriett and her child Elizabeth.

G.R.Kelsey-Clerk.

Page 121.

State of Tennessee, Benton County,Clerks Office ,July 23rd 1842.
There was a deed of gift acknowledged by Lewis Hyer to R.F.Hyer
for a negro man named Harry.Age about 25 years.

G.R.Kelsey-Clerk.

State of Tennessee, Benton County.Clerks Office,July 30th 1842.There
was a bill of sale acknowledged before me by N.T.W.Wortham to Robert
Wortham for a negro boy named Nathan about eleven years of age.

G.R.Kelsey-Clerk.

PAGE 122

State of Tennessee Benton County, Clerks Office. August 1st 1842.
There was a mortgzage proven before me by the oaths of Nat Nunnery
and James Nunnery for property from Reuben Mitchell to Nathan B.Cox
to the amount of fifty five dollars, and fifty cents.

G.R.Kelsey-Clerk.

Sate of Tennessee, Benton County, Clerks Office, August 2nd 1842.
There was a bill of sale proven before me from Jas Merrick and wife
to John Beard for a negro girl named Mariah.

G.R.Kelsey-Clerk.

State of Tennessee,Benton County.Clerks Office.August 13th 1842.There
was a mortgage acknowledged by Lewis Runnby to Alexander M.S.Rea.

G.R.Kelsey-Clerk.

State of Tennessee, Benton County, Clerks Office,September 12th 1842.
There was a deed of conveyance for 15½ acres of land from Jessie
Hammond Andrew to A.T.Barnett.

G.R.Kelsey- Clerk

Page 123.

An aggregate statement of fines and forfeitures arising in the circuit
court of Benton County, and which the said court bound to collect and
account for with the trustee of said for the year ending the first day
of September 1842.To wit.

State of Tennessee			Vs	N.Brewer Fine	$ 5.00
"	"	"	"	G.Francisco	5.00
"	"	"	"	B.Holland	10.00
"	"	"	"	L.Cracker	10.00
"	"	"	"	T.Null	10.00
"	"	"	"	T.Rushing	5.00
"	"	"	"	A.Utley	2.50
"	"	"	"	T.Phifer	5.00

Page 123-Continued.

State of Tennessee	Vs	T.Johnson	$ 1.00
" " "	"	T.Jordon	2.50
" " "	"	T.Jordon	3.00
			$60.00

Clarks Commission 2½%	$1.50	
Making out acct	1.00	
Total..	$2.50	2.50
Total	-------- --------	$57.50

State of Tennessee.Benton County.Personally came before me E.Perkins
an acting Justice of the Peace for said county.D.P.Hudson clerk of the
circuit court and makes oath in due form of law that above account
contains a true statement of the fines and forfeitures by him
collected and which by law he is bound to account for,with the trustee
of his county. for the year ending September 1st 1842.
Sworn to and subscribed before me this 1st day of September 1842.
D.P.Hudson------E.Perkins,Justice of the Peace in said county.

Personally appeared before me D.P.Hudson a acting justice of the peace
in and from said county.E.Perkins and William A.Steel.Revenue Commission
ers from said county and made oath in due form of law that they have
examined the books,other evidence in the office of the clerk of the
circuit court of said county and that they beleive the foregoing act
contains a true statement of office by said clerk collected & which by
law he is bound to account for with the 12th September 1842.Sworn to
and subscribed before me this 1st day of September 1842.
                              E.Perkins.
                              W.A.Steele.
Test-D.P.Hudson-J.P.

Aggregate statement of the state tax on Revenues Comms of Benton County.
for which the clerk of the county court of said county court is bound to
collect and pay over to the treasurer of the state of Tennessee for the
year ending the first of September 1842.,as follows to wit.

Page-124.

Jack Wyly-Merchant license	$6.00
T.K.Nance Salesman	3.00
Thomas Brown-Peddling	25.00
T.Alsup-Salesman	2.50
S.H.Davidson-Station	3.00
T.W.P.Lewis-Station	3.00
T.K.Wyly-Merchant	10.00
Jacks Baker-Station	2.50
	$ 109 .00
Clarks Commission @ 2½%	7.75
" " making statement $5.00	$ 101.25

Page 124-Continued.

State of Tennessee,Benton County, This day George R.Kelsey,clerk of the
County Court personally appeared before me T.Perkins an acting Justice
of the Peace in and for said county and made oath in due form of law that
the above is a full and true statement of Revenues or state tax that he
by law was bound to collect and account for with the treasurer of the
state of Tennessee for the year ending September 1st 1842.Sworn to and
subscribed before me this 1st day of September 1842.

T.Perkins. J.P. for Benton Co.   G.R.Kelsey-Clerk.

Page 125.

State of Tennessee, Benton County,This day came before me D.P.Hudson an
acting Justice of the Peace in and for said County. T.Perkins and
William A.Steele,Revenue Commissioners for said County and makes oath
in due form of law that they have examined the records in the office
of the clerk of said county. And they beleive the   writing to contain
a true statement of the state tax which the clerk is allowed by law
to collect and pay over to the Treasurer of the State for the year
ending the 1st of September 1842.Sworn to and subscribed this 1st day
of September 1842.
Test-D.P.Hudson-J.P. Benton County.   T.Perkins
                                                       W.A.Steele
An aggregate statement of the county tax or revenue of Benton County
for which the clerk of the county court of said county is bound to
collect. and pay over to the trustee of this county for the year ending
the 1st of September(to wit)

Page 126.

C.K.Wyly.	Merchant License	$60.00
T.K.Nance	Station License	3.00
James Brown	Paddlers License	25.00
T?Alsup	Station License	2.50
S.H.Davidson	Station License	3.00
T.W.P.Lewis	Station License	3.00
Y.K.Wyly	Merchant License	10.00
Zack Brown	Station License	2.50
		129 .00
	Credit.	12 .73
		106 .27

Credit by 2½% commission   .72½
Credit for entering set Circuit Clerk   1.00
Credit 42 Road over 12½%   5.00
Redinsive order 7 at 25   1.75
By paupers order 3 at 50¢ each   1.50
By the venirs faced   1.50
Credit for entering City,Claim.   1.00
                                                $12.72

Page 126-

State of Tennessee, Benton County. This day George R. Kelsey Clerk of the
County Court for Benton County, personally appeared before me T. Perkins
an acting Justice of Peace in and for said county and made oath in due
form of law that the above is a true statement of all the revenue or tax
that he by law is bound to collect and account for with the trustee of
said county. for the year ending September 1st 1842. Sworn to and
subscribed before me this 1st day of September 1842.

Test-E. Perkins-J.P.   G. R. Kelsey-Clerk.

State of Tennessee, Benton County, This day came before me D. P. Hudson
Justice of the peace in and for said T. Perkins & W. A. Steele revenue
commissioners for the county, approved and made oath in due form of law
that they had examined the records in the office of the clerk of that
county. court, and they beleive the within to contain a true statement of county tax which the said clerk is bound by law to collect
and account for with the trustee of his county. For the year ending
September 1st 1842. Sworn to and subscribed before me this 1st day of
September 1842.

Test-D. P. Hudson-J.P.   T. Perkins
                                         W. A. Steele.

Page 127.

State of Tennessee, Benton County, We the undersigned revenue commissioners
for said county have this day proceeded to make settlement with Amos
Bruce former trustee of said county in accordance with an order at the
last term thereof and by law to report as follows to wit First we find the
Trustee charged at the last settlement with the sum of $72.00 and 98¢
remaining in his hands. $72.98

Second we find with six dollars and twenty five cents on account of
fines collected, bastardy by T. Alsup Esquire..   6.25

Third we find him charged with the sum of three hundred with
Three Hundred Eight dollars and 70cents. $308.70

Page 128.

Twenty Seven dollars and sixty five cents which is still remaining
in sheriffs hands.

Fourth, we find him charged with the sum of fourhundred and seventy one
dollars and thirty four cents. on account of tax for year $471.34

Fifth we find him charged with the sum of Ninety Three dollars
and fifty two cents. $ 93.52

Page 128--Continued.

Sixth,We found him charged with the sum of Thirty Four dollars
and Eighty Four Cents. Of tax collected from county court $34.84
clerk.

We find him charged with one hundred thirty two dollars and 77
cents $132.77

Making the sum of Eleven Hundred twenty two dollars and
37 cents.   1122.37
We also find he should have the following credits.

First.The sum of five hundred eight dollars and 99 cents
Not paid from sheriff   508.99
second.Part of the bill of cost in the state vs Redden
and others.Letter A. No 24.   .180.27
Third.On account of money paid to paupers.   99.62½

Page 129.

Fourth.On account of money paid to C.Channes   62.81¼

Fifth .To money paid jurors   268.00

Sixth.For trustees comments on 9962 @ 2½ % of $511.   28.00

Making in all the sum of ----   1147.73¾

Paid the sum of twenty five dollars that the trustee apid
the state   25.36¾

Thus he has received which showed he refunded the first
money paid in to the treasurer.

State of Tennessee, Benton County.Personally came before me D.P.Hudson
acting as Justice of the Peace for the said county-W.Perkins and
William A.Steele.Revenue Commissioners,for said county made oath in
due form that the above settlement is correct,agreeable their papers
presented to us.Sworn to and subscribed this 16th day of April 1842.
                                        W.Perkins-R.C.
Test- D.P.Hudson-J.P.   William A.Steele.

Page 129-Continued.

State of Tennessee,Benton County,May 20th 1843.This day came T.F.Wills
Trustee of said county and made settlement with W.P.Mowis clerk of
the county court for said county,according to an act of the General
Assembly that case made and provided making it the duty of each trustee
to make settlement with the clerk of the county court respectively
showing the receipts and disbursements of the common school funds in
his hands which settlement I find to be as follows
Total amount of funds that came to the trustees hands for the
year 1843--- PAGE 130   ---------   --------$901.76
Which being distributed to the several districts as follows....

1st Dis.	109.00
2nd Dis	106.44
3rd Dis	67.73
4th Dis	92.51
5th Dis	147.00
6th Dis	114.68
7th Dis	80.47
8th Dis	88.07
9th Dis	91.87
Commission 1%	9.73
Total..........	$901.78

All of which is respectfully submitted. W.P.Mowis-Clark.

Trustee Bound-Office of the Superintendent,Nashville,July 17th
appointment of the common schools fund.Average the several counties
in the state district,Benton, County,District.

Page 131

		Dollars-Cents	
No 1	206	96	82
No 2	205	96	35
No 3	182	85	54
No 4	172	80	84
No 5	345	162	15
No 6	237	111	39
No 7	156	73	32
No 8	182	85	54
No 9	188	88	36
	1873	880	31

Scott Terry Supt

Page 131.

A list of the scholastic population of the first civil district in
Benton County for the year ending the last day of June 1843.

James Shirley	1	James Walker	4
Thurston Camp	5	Perry Massey	5
James Camp	2	Benjamin Harrison	1
James Latin	5	James Massey	1
Sam Dancer	9	James Bell	5
Sam Bright	5	John McIlwain	5
Edward Hatly	6	Page 132	
Charlie Oatsvale	4		
Sarah Hatly	8	Jess Hammonds	3
Pleasant Mulling	7	Smith Walker	2
John Gassett	5	P.Adams	7
M.Harrison	5	John Ignite	3
Jessie Dillon	2	John Hubbs	1
Wm Fargason	5	TOTAL....................... 233	
Wm Malin	1		
Priscilla Harrison	1		
James Cooper	6		
E.Conly	5		
Wm Whittington	2		
F.Whittington	4		
Elijah Wood	6		
William Haygood	2		
Daniel Barnett	2		
Michael Fry	4		
Bird B.Barnett	4		
J.R.Matthews	2		
Hillory Crabb	1		
James Crabb	1		
James Henry	4		
Elizabeth Brissom	3		
Mansfield Massey	3		
William Benton	2		
Thos H.Burton	4		
Henry Sparks	2		
Peggy Sloan	1		
Robert Prosk	1		
Aaron Victory	5		
Alford Lewis	1		
Whitfield Tippett	3		
Richard Sawrey	7		
Ezekial Duncan	3		
Henry Wood	1		
Henry Walker	1		
JamesWhite	4		
Mathews McDaniel	7		

Page 132-Continued.

Nathan Williams	3	Thomas Osburn	5
James Merrick	3	Gilliford I Sanders	1
William Smith	2	William Hall	1
Isaac Smith	3	Blake Fornhard	3
Shadnick Smith	1	Henry Gassett	4
Isiah Bright	7	Amos Bruce	3
Diza Smith	3	Jesse Bruce	1
Colin Nowell	5	Randle Jordon	1
John Baggett	7	C.Burgess	1
John Prince	6	Elizabeth Sawrey	1

Page 133

Sam Alford	5	D.Tempola	3
Alford Harris	7	Redden Hallowell	6
John Robertson	5	Jeremiah Hale	3
Hillsman King	2	Jesse King/Hale	2
Allen Gassett	4	Irvin Jordon	2
Randle Forhand	1	John Kelly	1
I.W.Lewis	1	James Evans	4
Jesse Newman	3	Richard Nordon	4
Willis Bridges	4	Frances Beaton	5
M.Junking	3	Herbert Hains	1
David Burkett	1	Wyly Ellis	2
Joshua Waggoner	3	Orpheus Kirk	1
Thos P.Drummond	5	S.T.Anksman	3
I.Perry	5	Peter Self	3
Hilliard Crabb	2	J.Goldburt	1
Young Adams	3	Dolly Kirk	5
James Hagg	5	Thomas Curtis	3
M.Eston	6	B.Beard	1
J.J.Jordon	4		

TOTAL...183----

We the commissioners of said district do certify this to be Axnt report
of the scholastic report for the year ending,July 1st 1843.

                        Jessie Bruce.
                        John Rilly.   Commissioners.

Page 134..

And also state that there was three schools thought amount received
                                                        $106.44
Amount expended..$100.96
Balance unexpended...$ 5.48

No 3.District Chalk Level.State of Tennessee, Benton County.We the
commissioners for the said district have taken the school population
and report to the clerk of the said county court.

Page 134-Continued.

The number of children and names of the parents and guardians over six under twleve over.

William Barnes	6	W.C.Anderson	1
Henry Barnes	3	William Ballew	7
R.H.Hathorn	4	Joel Taddor	4
J.B.Cox	4	Nancy Dalton	4
D.W.Barnes	-3	Jesse Barney	1
John Barnes	2	Eli P.Ballew	6
R.Nunnery	2	Wm H.Camp	4
Rebecca Nunnery	1	T.H.Burton	4
D.Barnes	4	Andrew Lynch	4
John Anderson	3	C.Leeper	4

Page 135..

Wm Sevindle	8	Elijah Higgins	4
N.Nunnery	2	Levi Smith	3
Asa Sevindle	8	J.Miller	1
T. Sevindle	1	H.Z.Tittle.	5
Wm Cole	5	A.Bunn	4
H.Kee	1	Jas Wyly	5
I.Hicks	3	G.Thomson	7
Thos Hale	1	S.Davidson	5
John Waltross	4	Mary Combs	7
William Halve	5	A.Harris	1
N.Sevindle	1	S.S.Sayes	1
Mary Cox	4	S.Marchbank	1
J.Mullinck	1	Seth Utly	7
O.Harden	6	W.Marchbank	6
B.Utly	4	T.Anthershead	5
A.Powell	2	J.Marchbank	3
Frances Williams	2	John Cravens	1

Page 136.

Thos Cole	3	John Davenport	5
E.W.Lynch	8	J.F.Johnson	6
L.Pearce	5	Giles Marchbank	8
Utly Cole	7	J.McAuley	2
May Townsoms	3	May Gray	2
Stephen Garnet	2	Wm Moore	2
John Garnett	4	Nancy Walker	4
Thos Homison	1	David Baker	1

TOTAL.. ...200

Page 136-Continued.

We the commissioners of the third district do hereby certify that we
employed A.B.Wilson,a school teacher for the term of weeks for the
sum of...   .... $31.37
Also employed W.H.Barnes to teach for a term of weeks   30.00
Amount drawn from Trustees.........   .... $62.75

Page 137-

We the commissioners of the 4th district do certify that we received
from the trustee of Benton County,October 3rd 1842 the same. $91.58
One school taught at Sandy 2 months   30.00
One at Shay Grave.The amount expended   29.44
One at Cotton Creek   30.00
                                                              $89.44

Which leaves in the hands of the Commissioners the saving of $1.50

Page 138.

A Scholastic Enumeration of the Fifth District of Benton County for
the year ending the 30th of June 1843-Giving the names of Parents.
Or persons with whom they reside.

W.A.Steele	1	J.R.Thorno	1
B.Redden	2	H.Durdin	2
T.Perkins	5	Thos McGill	4
A.Lashlee	6	P.Capps	6
T.Jones	5	T.Wiseman	3
N.McCarroll	4	J.Wiseman	5
J.B.Carnes	3	B.Hardy	2
Ann Carnes	1	D.Holland	6
WM.Surrett	3	C.Williams	3
Jas Hudson	3	B.Turner	3
J.S.Wright	3	M.P.Ford	2
Wm H.Hudson	3	N.Stricklin	1
John Hudson	3	W.Farrow	5
J.B.Bridges	1	V.Odin	8
John Davis	2	S.Poe	4 -
Jas Stepp	2	P.Thompson	6
Wm Sykes	7	L.Thompson	1
Mary Lashlee	7	A.Utly	7
D.L.Settle	2	Wm Walker	1
A.G.Holt	3	W.H.Rushing	3
H.Johnson	2	John Patty	3
S.Surrett	4	R.C.Patty	4
John Cole	2	A.Ballard	2
William Cole	3	J.T.Flance	3
J.Hollingsworth	2	M.S.Corbett	2
S.Boswell	3	D.Morris	4
W.R.Aden	1	Jancy Bell	7

Page 138-Continued.

B.Holland	1	James Hansel	4
D.B.Williams	5	P.Rushing	2
D.Rushing	4	E.House	1
A.Smalley	6	R.Beasley	3
Willis Rushing	4	Spartin Bruce	3
Louisa Herron	3	John Pearce	2
Elizabeth Browning	6	George Bruce	2
F.A.Cuff	1	D.P.Hudson	3
F.A.Cuff	8	W.H.Hudson	1
R.Holmes	2	J.Hudson	1
M.Hifnu	1	J.Johnston	4
C.Mittu	2	J.Alston	3
J.P.Arnold	1	P.Milton	1
John Arnold	3	J.Allson	4
Willie Arnold	1	E.Arnold	7
F.Arnold	2	Widow Honey	4
Wyatt Arnold	1	Jas Presson	8
F.Farrow	4	S.Higbin	4
Jonus Milton	4	S.Maden	6
B.W.Wheatly	2	E.F.Wills	3
W.Markham	1	G.R.Kelsey	5
E.A.Crowley	4	Jas Gordon	1
A.S.Cole	3	H.M.Brown	1

Making in all...   332
from 6 to 21 years of age

Page 139

The commissioners of the fifth district reports the following school
which was taught in said district commencing and ending in the year
1842.One was   taught by J.T.Flowers,commenicing in August 11th a term
of 50 days at 70¢ per day
61 students taught $35.40
Numbers of males   37
Numbers of females   .24
One by S.V.Aden commencing August 1st 1842, aterm of 25 days at 70¢
amounts to   17.50

Males taught   33
Females taught   24
                                          ——
                                          57

Page 139-Continued.

A list of the scholastic population of the 6th school district in Benton County.

Prozy Bealer	1	Benjamin Greer	4
Cynthia Pickler	1	Freeman Presson	6
Lewis Cross	3	T.Presson	1
Henry Allen	3	Robert Ward	4
Mary Swift	4	Hardy Rushing	5
Nancy Brand	1	David Watson	5
Thomas Craig	4	Jesse McGill	1
Eli Crowell	3	Matthew Presson	5
Jackson Peeples	1	John Presson	12
Nancy Cath	2	Marcellus Cain	1

Page 140

Jemima Thrasher	3	Henry Stagall	2
Elizabeth Hutchinson	4	Thos Presson	4
John Elmon "	7	John T.Presson	5
John Elmon	6	Elizabeth Holmes	4
William H.Nance	3	H.Greer	3
Louis Cottingham	4	John McGill	4
Lewis Rosenville	5	John McGill,Senior	3
Mrs Wiseman	1	James Crossnoe	6
William D.Wiseman	4	H.C.Presson	4
Oliver Armor	6	William Bond	5
John H.Williams	4	Joseph Pickler	8
William Greer	7	Hudson Taylor	6
John Watson	4	John Guntill	1
Sam Presson	4	John D.Rushing	2
A.A.Berryhill	2	Hamilton Pinkston	1
Asa Rushing	2	L.D.Pearce	3
John Pearson Sr	2	W.Cunneyham	4
William Rowe	2	George Franciso	3
Thos Ward	5	James R.Nance	8
Elizabeth Rushing	3	John P.Greer	5
William Ward	5	K.S.Ward	1
James Block	2	John Pearce	4
John Tice	6	Mary Bain	6
B.Pearson	3	W.Addington	3
E.Bush	3	W.Bloodworth	1
J.J.Rushing	1	R. Spivens	5
Jonus Greer	3	George Greer	3
James Webb	1	Total.....................264	

Received of the trustees one hundred thirteen dollars and fifty three cents for the term of three months each.All the money expended.
                    A.C.Presson-Clerk.

Page 140-Continued.

District No 7.The following shose the scholastic population of Civil
District No 7.The County of Benton for the Year ending July 1st 1843.

William Barry	6	A.Roling	3
Thos Hollomon	1	J.Ballvue	1
James Holloman	8	Percy Milton	1
W.C.Cole	3	John P.Barton	4
Jacob Cuff	5	David Benton	2
James Garner	8	S.Milton	2
Charlie Wheatly	6	Elizabeth Halland	1

Page 141

R.Parker	4	A.B.Winchester	1
George Phifer	1	James B.Hill	1
Matthew Williams	3	Joseph Beaton	1
Mary Pully	3	I.Farmer	1
Mitty Nabbs	3	James Pipin	2
Martha Middleton	1	John Phifer	2
Henry Cherry	1	Jesse Webb	6
Calvin Hall	1	H.Remps	1
W.McCatham	3	A.Davidson	7
Martha Hall	5	S.Benton	7
Susana Holland	1	W.W.H.Holland	2
N.B.Parker	2	Geo W.Farmer	3
W.H.Coooley	2	Sussana Hill	5
John Cooley	1	T.Milton	1
John Milton	3	William Pafford	7
John Pafford	9	Wm Holland	8
John Myers	5	C.Pafford	1
Lewis Holland	4	Wm Smith	3
I Weal	1	Calvin Parker	5
J.W.Milton	7	Barry Vester	5
Wm Parker	1	D.W.Benton	1
Jessie Bates	1	Total.................	188

Page 142

I-G.W. Farmer do certify the foregoing to be correct.G.W.Farmer Clerk
money received $80.47-Dr expended $93.00 .No school taught.No money
received or otherwise no money expended but for teaching.

G.W.Farmer.

A list of the Scholastic Population of District No 8 in Benton County.

W.M.Taylor	1	Henry Milton	1
Isham Jones	1	John Rayshall	4
John G.Allen	1	Hugh Alsup	2
Lewis Brewer	3	I.P.Smalley	1
John F.Milton	2	C.N.Herron	5

Page 142 -Continued.

| L.N.French | 3 | B.Herron | 5 |

Page 143.

Neal McNeal	5	Thos L.Floyd	3
Herman Pearce	4	John W.Jones	1
Robt Raidwell	3	L.W.Brewer	1
Mary Melton	4	Elizabeth Phillips	1
A.McRea	4	Henry Robertson	5
Wm J.Given	1	Sarah Rushing	2
Thos Smith	7	Stephen W.Barnes	5
Mary McRanger	3	S.Alsup	1
Daniel Brewer	1	Elbert Waggell	3
William Bill	1	Matilda Shilley	1
Elizabeth Bill	1	James Greer	3
William Holland	4	George Greer	3
Samuel Wilson	2	Robert Rushing	3
Nicholas Brewer	1	Judith Cole	2
Ezekiel McBride	5	Daniel Buchanan	1
T.Reddick	5	William McGee	3
Charles Barnes	4	Barrett Bell	4
William Womack	2	James Taylor	4
William Cottingham	3	Mary Wilson	4
S.Wheatly	3	William Manners	2
K.Redick	4	C.B.Redick	1
D.Smith	3	W.C.Cole	3
Wm Hernlow	2	Elizabeth Hernlow	1
Jesse Rarburg	1	Elias Phifer	2
William Jones	3	William Waters	6
John Phifer	1	Total..	188

Total amount of children of scholastic age in Civil District No 8 is
188.

Signed.
John Phifer
D.J.Buchanan
David Brewer.

Test.V.D.Brewer-Clerk.

Page 144

A list of children in the 9th district on the last day of June 1843
over six and under 21 years of age.

John Rawls	5	Wm Right	7
Harriett Townsend	5	Dennis Stagdale	2
Uriah Cheatham	3	L.Beatin	5
William Rowe	4	M.Beatin	5
Netty Showers	5	L.Allen	4
Charlie Robbins	7	John W.Cooper	7
G.W.Daniel	3	Nancy Buchanan	2

Page 144-Continued.

William Vuorn	1	M.Mannor	1
John Greer	1	A.James	3
D.A.Askew	2	John Buchannan	1
Robert Holmes	3	B.Culpeper	6
John Christopher	5	David Ross	1
John Bonds	1	- John W.Bromager	2
Wyly Davis	1	D.W.Guays	2
B.George	1	John W.Whiterson	1
Harty Robbins	1	John Thomas	1
John McGlohon	6	Solomon Carmack	8
Thos Andrews	6	L.Grissom	1
Elizabeth Wynn	4	J.C.Milton	1
Henry Hansel	4	John Graham	2
Unton Mizell	1	William Nash	1
A.Pitt	3	Aaron Clement	2
Martha Graham	4	S.Nicholas	6
James Daniel	5	Daniel Graham	5
Sam Redey	1	Noah Wyatt	2
Effey Buchanan	1	John Stagner	2
William Wynn	1	Ann Myrick	5

Page 145.

Nathan Styner.	2	Edward Lindsey	7
Lewis Adom	1	Rebecca Smith	2
J.D.Hall	1	B.Gros	4
A.W.C.Mitboney	8	William Acres	1
Lewis Ayor	2	James Lynsa	5
William Lindsey	1	John A.Fain	1
		TOTAL.............261	

Amount received $91.87½
Unexpended   1.57
No schools taught
All male 4

No 1.	$109.84 2/7
No 2	85.80
No 3	93.84 2/7
No 4	94.28 2/7
No 5	152.27 2/7
No 6	124.45 2/7
No 7	88.63 2/7
No 8	88.62 2/7
No 9	94.75 5/7
	932.01 5/7 For the year 1844.

Treasurers office Nashville,July 15th 1844.Due Benton County and to each
district as follows.

Page 145-Continued

State of Tennessee,Benton County,This day being the 14th day of August
1844.E.S.Wills former trustee of Benton County made application to
make settlement with me, T.W.Morris,Clerk of the County Court of
Common School fund which came into his hands as such trustee for the
year 1843.According to an act of the general assembly.In such case made
and approved which said settlement I find to be as follows.I find
such Trustee wholly charged with money received from superintendent
of Public Instruction the sum of $880.31

Page 146   VOUCHERS AS FOLLOWS.

No 1.	Receipt from Treasurer of First District.	$95.85
No 2.	" " " " " Second "	95.38
No 3.	" " " " " Third "	84.68
No 4.	" " " " " Fourth "	80.03
No 5.	" " " W.A.Steele	100.00
Also from D.F.McElrod and Jas Gordon		60.00
No 6	Receipt from Treasurer of sixth District	110.27
No 7	" " " " " Seventh "	72.57
No 8	" " " " " Eight "	84.26
No 9	" " " " " Ninth "	88.24
Trustee's Commission		8.80
	TOTAL.........	808.52

Which shows the trustee has twenty one cents cents over and above
the amount which he was charged .   W.P.Morris-Clerk.

Page 147.

Commissioners report 1844.Commissioners annual report to the Clerk
for the First Civil District.July 1st 1844.

W.M.Bridges.	4	James Cooper	7
Wm Malin	2	Mary Fullerton	1
John Stanly	1	Pleasant Mullinx	7
William Fulty.	3	Jimmie Dilion	2
Matthew McDaniel	7	John Gassett	6
JamesWhite	6	Mae Harrison	4
James Walker	5	Eli W.Conley	6
Ezekiel Tippett	2	Sarah Hatly	2
Whitfield Tippett	2	Samuel Duncan	7
Henry Woods	1	James Laton	3
Charley Duncan	3	James Shirley	1
Garrett Massey	6	T.Camp	6
Ben Harrison	1	Charlie Oatsvale	4
Wm S.Walker	1	Edward Hatly	7
John McElsoaim	5	Samuel Bright	3
James Myreck	1	William Whittington	4
Jessie Hammond	6	Elijah Wood	6

Page 147-Continued.

Frances Whittington	4	John Johnson	4
Mary Barnett	1	M.Barnett	3
Thos McGill	4	Henry Parks	2
Mary Matlock	2	Henry Allison	4

Page 148.

Mansfield Massey	3	William Waygard	3
J.R.Matthews	2	M.Fry	4
James Crabb	1	H.Crabb	1
B.B.Barnett	5	Aaron Victory	5
William Hubbs	4	Martha Barnett	2
Elizabeth Grisson	2	James Henry	3
Rhoda Benton	2	John J.Gnate	3
William Mailin	1	TOTAL.	202

Commissioners Report.

Number of teachers 3,Number of schools 3,Pupils enrolled 60, pupils
in average attendance 45,

Amount of money received by trustee,	$95.95
Amount of money paid to teachers	148.00
Balance of funds wa expended	14.00

Length of time schoolis taught 11 months.
Number of school houses built   1

Signed--
Alford Tippett
W.M.Johnson
Pleasant Mullinix.
Commissioners.

To the clerk of the County Court of Benton County.The Report of
Scholastic Population-District No 2 1844

Bray Hist	1	D.M.Burkett	2
Redden Hallowell	7	Thos Osbon	5
Sarah Turner	1	Milton Myrick	3
Richard Norden	5	R.M.Jordon	1
Willie Ellis	2	John Sanders	4
Dolly Kirk	4	J.S.Sanders	1
Peter Self	3	T.Burkett	2
Jas Hogg	5	Daniel Waggoner	1
Thomas Curtis	4	B.Beard	3
Morning Alston	4	Hilliard Crabb	3
T.Kirk	1	Canney Burges	1
Joseph Talbott	1	ELI Hatly	1
James Ervins	5	Jerry Perry	5
Jannie Hale	2	J.M.Camp	3
John Kelly	1	Henry Gassett	5
Francis Beavers	5	Richard Jerill	7
Jackson Jordon	2	Isiah Smith	4

Page 148 Continued.

Evans Jordon	1	Jacob Bright	1
Young Adams	3	Sela Smith	1
Jessie Bruce	5	Cullen Nowell	7
Willie Bridges	5	James Merrick	3
Wyatt James	4	John Bagette	8
John Dillon	3	Alford Harris	7
John Robertson	5	John Newman	4
John Prince	6	Samuel Oxford	5
James Taylor	2	Deza Smith	3
William Smith	3	Hiriam Smith	1
Nathan Williams	3	H.King	3

TOTAL...187

Page 149.

All the public money coming to the district expended.

Wm Smith
McAney Osbion
Redden Holloway. Commissioners.

REPORT CF DISTRICT NO-3.

William Marchbanks.	5	Thos Martinshed.	5
William Ballew	8	Colman Brear	3
Henry Barnes	3	Samuel Bright	6
William Barnes	6	James Sayles	1
John Barnes	2	Marion Sayles	1
Dennis Barnes	2	S.H.Davidson	5
D.W.Barnes	3	John Gillion	6
Jackson Cox	5	William England	1

Page 150.

Cinch Nunnery	2	A.Powell	2
Martin Ford	3	Gregory Thomason	7
Nath Swindell	1	Obdesh Harding	6
Thomas Swindell	2	John Walthrop	4
Catvin Halve.	5	Seth Utly	6
Holloway Kee	1	Burrell Utly.	5
Jefferson Hicks	4	James Wyly	5
Wm Cole	6	Mary Combs	6
John Anderson	6	James Marchbanks	3
William Swindell	3	L.D.Combs	7
Asa Sweindell	6	Berry Harris	1
N.Nunnery	2	Horatio Tuttle	5
Isaac Anderson	1	Alford Burn	5
A.B.Wilson	1	Joseph Blanks	2
R.H.Hathhorn	1	Amos Boluna	1
Ben Michie	2	John M.Croninins	1
Stephen Marchbank	2	Thomas R.Turner	3
E.P.Ballew	6	Cullen Lupor	4
William Camp	4	Thos H.Burton.	4

Page 150 Continued.

Elijah Huggins	3	James Hillis	1
Anderson Lynch	1	Jessie Barnes	1
Je sie Barnes	1	Joel Teddor	4
Nancy Dobson	4		

TOTAL... 208

Amount received from the trustee all expended $84.50
Except.   .40
And ten cents of that being paid for pepper.

                                    Stephen Marchbank
                                    John Cravins
                                    Joel Teddor-Commissioners.

Commissioners report.The report of the Commissioners of 4th district
of Benton County.-----   1844.

Names	No	Names	No
Ervin Earp.	7	U.Thomason	2
Neehan Short	5	Rubin Mitchell	9
Gillis Marchbank	3	Mark Hatly	2
William Fowler	4	John W.Davidson	2
Wm Kirchbeth	2	James Holland	5
William Ray	8	Joshua Howe	5
John Sanders	4	L.B.Pierce	3
Mary Denis	5	Granville Dyers	1

Page 151.

Names	No	Names	No
Abraham Sanders.	6	Benton Bridges	7
Shadrock Romey	5	Barnett Holland	2
Henry Abbott	5	John L.Holland	2
James Allen	5	Wesly Davenport	2
David Foster	4	Johnathan	3
Dolly Morris	3	Z.Barker	3
Gruen Flowers	5	L.Crocker	1
Isaac Ray	4	Edward Cowell	2
Jonas Thomason	2	Bennett Morgan	1
Thos W.Walker	2	Matthew Williams	2
Nelson Pierce	1	Samuel Pierce	2
John Douglas	6	F.W.Pierce	3
Frances Williams	2	Moses Jordon	4
Sarah Pace	4	Charlie Cowell	1
Sanders Harden	2	Joseph Cowell	1
A.J.Peoples	1	Elizabeth Hutchinson	4
William Moore	2	Thomas Harrison	1
Nancy Walker	3	John Garrett	4
Mary Pray	2	Letty Davis	3
John McAuley	2	May Townon	3

Page 152.

Name	No	Name	No
Unity Cole.	1	Thomas Cole	1
Green Adams	5	Edward Lynch	8
John F.Johnson	8	Willis Cole	1
Julous Cole.	5	John Davenport	5
Latum Pearce	5	Mary Williams	4
John Cole	6	Gillin Smothers	1
Denpe Sanders	1		
Total............................... .... .237			

Amount received from Trustee $80.84 and all expended

L.Crocker.
J.J.Cole.
L.H.Pope.
Commissioners.

A Scholastic Record Enumerating which children of the 5th district for Benton County over six and under twenty one for the year ending the 30th of June 1844.With the names of precincts or persons with whom they reside annexed.

Names	No	Name	No
D.P.Hudson	2	M.S.Corbett	3
G.W.L.Hudson	1	James Wright	3
P.B.Hubbard	1	R.Murphy	4
Willis Rushing	4	L.B.Wheatly	2
A.J.Hudson	1	January Hudson	3
Sparton Bruce	3	U.Hepner	1
Robert Holmes	2	James Milton	2
Alford Ballard	3	William Markham	1
John H.Hudson	3	E.Hansel	1
Wm H.Hudson	3	Daniel Latnor	1
Geo W.Bruce	2	Cooper Milton	2
Balard Rushing	2	W.M.Pafford	8
James Hanes	4	Simeon Higdon	3
R.Berky	3	Brown Bridges	1
George Hallmark	3	Joseph Allison	5
John McGill	1	Wm A.Stute	1
Elizabeth Browning	3	Wm Sykes	8
Lanisa Herron	3	E.F.Wills	3
James Bill	5	L.Thompson	1
Elizabeth Honey	5	Thos Jonus	5
F.Thompson	5	James Presson	8
Daniel Holland	6	N.McCorrale.	4
Timothy Barnes	1	A.S.Cole	3
Mary Lashlee	6	I.B.Carnis	3
Mary Capps	5	H.M.Brown	2
A.G.Holt	2	Joseph Wisdom	5
Z.Callis	5	E.Wisdom	2
John Petty	3	G.R.Kelsey	5
Robert Petty	3	J.N.Jones.	4

Page 153.

Name	No	Name	No
William Cole	3	C.A.Crawley	4
Irvy Akers	3	A.Lashlee	6
J.Cole	2	E.Perkins	5
Wm Surratt	2	S.Madden	6
Henry Durdin	2	N.Stricklin	5
J.R.Thomas	1	B.Hardy	3
John Arnold	4	J.T.Flance	3
Isaac Worrell	2	Wm Farrows	5
Joseph Surratt	3	Jas Bussell	1
Stephen Boswell	3	D.Patterson	2
Daniel Settles	3	D.Morris	5
Willie Arnold	1	D.Cuff	2
E.Arnold	5	S.V.Adams	8
L.B.Williams	4	P.Mitton	2
William Walker	2	John Cole	3
Jonus Gordon	2	B.N.Farrow.	4
A.Utly	8	A.Carnes	1
Charlie Williams	4	W.H.Rushing	4
B.Turner	3	John Jones	1
Isiah Cates	2	John Pearce	2
		TOTAL..................	322

Page 154.

We the commissioners beg leave to report that there was three schools
taught said district-----1843 and that the portion including Camden
had no school then in remaining four for said district.Including Camden

Unexpended sums of....	$76.00
Aid for Beaverdam School House.........	6.00
The sum of	82.00

All of which is submitted......

       G.W.L.Hudson.
       James Gordon.
       C.F.McElyra   -----Commissioners.

Page 155.

A list of Scholastic Population of the School Districts No 6 in
Benton County. for 1844.

Name	No	Name	No.
Matthew Presson	4	A.C.Presson	5
Wm D.Wiseman	4	John Presson	10
James Wiseman	1	Hezekiel Greer	4
John H.Williams	4	M.Cain	1
Oliver Arnor	5	James Presson	7
Wm Greer	6	James Greer	4

Page 155 Continued.

Name.	No	Name	No
Samuel Presson	5	John Tice	6
Freeman Presson	6	John D.Rushing	4
John Watson	2	John Sims	6
Benjamain Greer	3	Asa D.Rushing	2
Eli Craig	3	R.S.Ward	3
J.J.Rushing	2	Thos Ward	6
Thos Presson	4	J.K.Nance	8
David Watson	6	I.Pearce, Jr	6
T.Presson	1	E.Rushing	3
Hardy Rushing	5	W.Bloodworth	1
J.P.Greer	5	A.Lewis	1
John Thornton	1	E.Bush	3
John McGill,Jr	4	Maury Bain	6
John McGill Jr	1	W.B.Addington	3
James Crassons	5	Wm Ward	5
Robert Ward	4	James Beck	2
L.D.Pearce	3	John Pearce,Jr	3
W.D.Markham	1	F.M.Rushing	2
Wm Cottingham	2	Louis Rosvale	5
Synthia Pickler	2	Wm Bond	3
Louis Cross	8	Eli Crowell	5

Page 156.

	No		No
L.Cottingham	5	Mary Swift	3
Nancy Brand	1	Thomas Craig	5
Hudson Taylor	6	John Elmore	5
W.H.Nance	4	Richard Nance	1
John M.Elmore	1	Wm Cunningham	3
George Francis	4	total	252

Of all districts No 6 in Benton County. as to me by school
commissioners of said district for the year 1844/

A.C.Presson-Clerk.

Amount received from Trustee. $110.27
All expended.
I certify the within is a true list of all the scholastic population.

Commissioners Report.
The following shows the scholastic population and report   of the 9th
district for the year 1844.

Name.	No	Name	No
Sussana Holland	1	Wm H.Holland	3
N.B.Parker	3	E.Melton	1
R.F.Cole	2	George W.Farmer	3

Page 156 Continued.

Name	No	Name	No.
Mead J.H.Coley	2	Joseph Bilinger	4
James Pipin	2	Samuel Beaton	2
Susa Hill	5	William Holland	8
J.W.Hill	3	D.W.Benton	1
John Phifer	1	John Mitton	3
Nancy Taylor	2	John Pafford	7
Joseph Bealer	1	William Smith	3
Nancy Wheatly	3	Jonus Faremer	8
Jacob Tevi	1	Peter Phifor	1
John Myors	3	C.J.Wheatly	6
William Berry	9	Beo Phifer	3
Jonus Holoman	9	Obidiah Bullock	7
Thos Holomon	1	Martha Middleton	1
W.C.Cole	3	Thos W.Pulley	3
Jacob Cuff	7	Berry Vester	5
John Turner	1	Lewis Holland	3
Abrham Davidson	6	James Pafford	2
H.C.Camp	3	John W.Milton	8
American Vicks	1	Jackson Farmer	1
S.Milton	2	Conrad Milton	.2
David Benton	2	J.B.Winchester	1
John L.Benton	5	Perry Milton	1
William Parker	1	Jim Bates	1
Henry Cherry	1	Calvin Parker	6
Calvin Hall	2	Katherine Parker	3
Wm W.Wheatly	3	TOTAL	192

Page 157.

Amount received of trustee the sum of.............................$72.56
Amount expended in said district   52.00
All of which is respectfully submitted..Benton County,July 1st 1844.

George W.Farmer-Clerk

COMMISSIONERS REPORT
A list of children the eighth district of Benton County.................

Name	No	Name	No
A.McRae	4	Lewis W.Brewer	2
Mary Milton	3	Burrell Bell	4
Nancy McKenzie	3	Henry Robors	6
Elizabeth Bell	2	Thos L.Floyd	4
Wm Bell	1	Edward Waggle	4
Thos Smith	8	S.W.Bons	6

Page 158-

Page 158-

Name	No	Name	No
Robert Birdwell	3	James Calvin	4
Herman Pearce	4	A.B.Herron	5
W.J.Greer	1	B.Herron	3
Charlie Barnes	6	E.Alsop	4
Wm Holland	5	Samuel Alsop	1
Jacob Block	6	Hugh Alsup	4
Thos Colman	2	John Ragsdale	3
Neil McNeal	5	H.Bird	1
Ezekiel McBride	5	J.Cole	2
Lewis Brewer	2	Elizabeth Felph	1
Isham Jones	2	J.W.Utly	1
William Warmick	4	Sarah Rushing	4
Nicholas Brewer	1	John Smaley	2
A.Clement	1	William McPor	4
Edward Brwer	1	Geo Greer	3
J.T.Allen	2	Elisha Herron	1
Robert Rushing	4	James Greer	3
Matilad Shelling	1	William Cottingham	2
David Smith	4	William Martin	1
E.Herndon	1	William Herndon	2

Page 159.

Name	No	Name	No
Mary Willson	4	Kenneth Reddic	5
C.B.Riddick	6	Martin Milton	1
John Phifer	3	Jessie Rosebury	2
John Roseberry	1	TOTAL	188.

We the undersigned do certify the foregoing is a true list of the
Scholastic population of the 8th district.,in Benton County.Ending the
30th day of June 1844.

L.W.Brewer
John Phifer
D.Brewer Carns.

Page 159-Continued.

A list of children in the 9th district on the last day of June 1844
Over six and under twenty one years of age.

Name	No	Name	No
R.Holmes	3	B.Grass	4
J.D.Hall	1	Lewis Hyor	2
Mary Rodds	1	Simison Nickols	6
Harriett Townsend	5	Wm Acres	2
Daniel Leighnip	5	Noah Wyatt	3
John Rolls	5	M.Frince	1
Geo M.Daniel	2	Lewis Adam	1
John Christopher	2	Robert Wynn	3
Bert George	2	Rebecca Adam	1
Nancy Cummings	3-	Burrell Wynn	1
Wm Reeves	4	Jonus Lindsey	2
Neely Shires	2	Jonath Holmes	5
Charlie Robins	7	William Lindsey	2
Charlie Adam	2	L.B.Allen	4-
Drewe Askew	2	Aron Clement	2
John Greer	2	Martha Graham	4
Cawthon Cheatham	3	Daniel Graham	6
John Barnes	1	John Graham	2
John McClavin	6	Daniel Buchanan	1
A.W.CMithanna	4	L.Beaton	5
James Daniel	5	M.Beaton	6
James Stager	2	William Nash	1
Nathan Stayner	1	Chris Beaton	2
Ann Myrick	5	Effa Buchanan	1

Page 160.

Name	No	Name	No
Nancy Buchanan	1	Arthur Pitts	3
David Ross	2	J.W.Bromager	4
John Buchanan	1	M.Mannon	1
Wm Wright	8	J.W.Cooper	6
B.Culpepper	7	J.W.Whitaker	4
J.M.Keaf	2	Wm Measzels	2
Wm Stockdale	1	Sal Cramack	3
Henry Hassell	4	Theo Andrews	6
L.H.Grissom	2	Edward Lindsey	5
		TOTAL........	210

Wm Wright
Drewe H.Askew
James Staynor------Commissioners.

Page 160-Continued.

Amount received from Trustee $87.48
Amount paid teacher   87.48

We the undersigned commissioners for 9th district,certify the above
report is true to the best of our knowledge and beleif.Given under our
hands July 12th 1844.

Apportionment for common school fund for the county of Benton for the
year 1845.

District.	Population.	Dollars.	Cents.
1	202	$93.	.93
2	189	$86	.95½
3	208	$96	.72
4	234	$110	.20½
5	322	$149	.73
6	252	$117	.18
7	192	$89	.28
8	188	$87	.42
9	210	$97	.65
TOTAL..	$1998	$929	.07

M.Nelson-Treasurer of Tennessee.

Page 161.

State of Tennessee Benton County,April 9th 1845.
Amos Bruce ,Trustee of Benton County and made settlement with me with
me W.P.Morris,Clerk of the County Court of Benton County.In accordance
with an act of the General Assembly. In each case made and provided
showing the respective disbursement of the common school fund for the
year 1844.which I find to be as follows.

Amount of money received from
Treasuer of Tennessee.........$932.01¾
Received from C.W.Coyly due
1843......... .... 19.37½
Also M.A.Steele   17.50
Total...................... 968.89¼

Trustees commission... ... $ 9.68¾
No 1 Paid   108.30
No 2 Paid   84.94
No 3 Paid   61.00
No 4 Paid   93.35
No 5 Paid   185.99
No 6 Paid   76.62½
No 7 Paid   68.54

Page 162.

No 8 Paid... .. $ 81.90
No 9 Paid   84.00
Expended.. ....$844.64½
Commission... 9.68¾
                                                        854.33¾

Which leaves in the hands of the Trustee unexpended for the year
1844 the sum of $114.54.All of which is respectfully submitted.

                                        W.P.Morris -Clerk

District No-1-Commissioners report- 1845.

Name	No	Name	No
Elizabeth Wood	6	MarthaBarnett	1
George Lewis	3	Edward Hatly	7
Henry Allison	4	Marchia Harrison	5
Mansfield Massey	3	Sarah Hatly	2
John Johnson	3	Samuel Dancer	6
Mansfield Barnett	4	Whitfield Tippett	4
Mary Barnett	1	Charlie Duncan	3

Page 163.

William Whittington	3	J.R.Mathews	2
F.S.Whitington	4	James Merrick	1
Henry Parkes	3	James Walker	6
Ezra Bishop	1	James White	6
Benjamin Dillon	2	Mather McDaniel	7
Thos Matill	3	Charlie Oatsvale	4
Mary Matlock	1	Jimmie Dillon	3
B.B.Barnett	6	Henry Walker	1
Michael Fry	4	Evans Jordon	2
William Hubbs	4	Jessie Hall	2
Jane Henry	3	William Malin	2
John H.gnile	4	Anthony Teffle	6
Aron Victory	6	Martha Malin	2
Elijah Lissham	1	Synthia Harrison	1
William F.Crifton	1	A.I.Fulks	4
Hilloey Crabb	1	Martin Douglass	4
John Willis	1	Garrett Massey	4

Which leaves in the hands of the trustee unexpended for the year 1844
the sum of $114.54.
All of which is respectdully submitted............. .. ...
                                        W.P.Morris-Clerk.

Ayly Ratliff	4	Yancy Bohannan	2
Calvin Spence	3	Theresa Camp	4
Jessie Bruce	5	Mary Fulerton	1
John Gassett	6	James Shirley	2
John Stanly	2	TOTAL................ 192.

Page 164-

We the commissioners of the first civil district certify that the above is a true return of the scholastic population of said district for the year 1845.

COMMISSIONERS REPORT FOR YEAR 1845

Amount expended for year 1844........   ....$81.13

Also.   31.25

Signed.

L.R.Teppett

Eligah Wood--Commissioners.

State of Tennessee- Benton County.School District No 2

DISTRICT NO 2

Name	No	Name	No
Dolly Kirk	4	Jeremiah Perry	6
Peter Self	3	Jimmie Newman	3
James Hogg	7	Richard Jowell	6
Thos Curtis	5	David Rainey	5
Morring Acesting	3	Henry Gassett	4
Theophilis Kirk	2	James Myrick	1
Green Flowers	5	Milton Myrick	3
Jonus Eavins	4	Young Adam	4
Milie Ellis	3	David Burchett	2
Richard Nordin	5	John Sanders	4
Starks Moore	1	Willie Bridges	5
Redden Hallowell	7	Wyatt Jenkins	4
Edward Jordon	2	Gilford Sanders	2
Frances Barber	6	James Camp	4
Hayrain Haynes	1	Burville Beard	3
Charlie Haynes	1	E.W.Conley	6
Wm F.Doherty	7	Samuel Bright	1
John Talbot	1	Wm Smith	3
J.S.Raper	3	C.Smith	1
Thos Osborn	4	James Taylor	1
Jessie Bruce	5	Hillsman King	3
Amos Bruce	2	Elizabeth McCord	2
Herman Smith	2	John Baggett	7
John Dillion	3	Jonus Myrick	4
Cullen Norvell	6	Alford Harris	8
J.B.Pettigrew	6	John Prince	7
John Robertson	5	Sam Oxford	6
		TOTAL................	201

All the money was expended except $8.94.I B.Beard hereby certify that the foregoing is a true report of the Scholastic Population of District No 2 as was handed me by the commissioners.

B.Beard- Clerk.

Page 165

COMMISSIONERS REPORT DISTRICT NO 3

We the commissioners of the 3rd Civil District of Benton County
State of Tennessee have taken scholastic population of said
district,which is as follows.

Name	No	Name	No
James Hillis	2	Ben Michie	2
E.Higgins	3	George Thornton	7
Cullen Leeper	6	Samuel Davidson	4
Levy Smith	5	Samuel Bagal	2
Elisha Teddor	1	Washington Adams	1
Manly Dalton	5	Stephen Marchbank	2
Jesse Barns	1	Henry Burrus	4
Joel Teddor	3	John Andserson	2
Mary Combs	6	William Seville	3
James Wyly	5	Isaac Anderson	1
James Sayles	1	H.Kee	1
Warren Sayles	1	N.Nunnery	1
John Waltnip	5	B.Stiers	4
Seth Utly	6	Asa Swindle	6
Martin Ford	3	William Cole	5
J.Gilland	6	Jefferson Hicks	4
O.Hardin	6	Catherine Howe	5
Burrell Utly	3	Nath Swindle	1
James Marchbanks	2	Wm Barnes	6
L.D.Combs	1	John Barnes	3
Thos Mathersheld	5	J.Cox	3
E.P.Ballard	6	Jane Barker	1
R.H.Hamthaw	1	Kincher Nunery	2
Thos Seville	3	P.Mullinx	7
Taylor	5	Alford Barnes	5
Wm Ballew	7	William H.Camp	5
Colman Brewer	2	Wm E.Taylor	1
		TOTAL...............176	

Page 166

Amount due from Trustee for 1844.........	$92.40
Amount expended.........................	61.00
Balance due..$31.40	

DISTRICT NO 4.

A list of the Scholastic Population in the 4th Civil District of Benton
County.

Name	No	Name	No
Rubin Bridges	3	Nancy Cathey	3
Bennett Holland	3	Mima Thracher	3
John T.Holland	3	J.J.Cole	8
Matthew Williams	2	John Cole	6

Page 166-Continued..

Name	No	Name	No
B.C.Morgan	1	John Garrett	5
Edwin Caldwell	2	John McAuley	3
Jackson Peoples	1	John Davenport	5
Zecheriah Barker	5	John F.Johnson	4
Allen Barker	2	Stephen Garrett	2
Masse Jordon	5	Willis Cole	4
Johnath House.	4	Thomas Cole	4
Jonus Holland	5	Latan Pearce	6
Joshon House.	4	Thomas Harrison	1
Middeson Thomason	-3	William Moore	2
John W.Davidson	3	Nancy Walker	2
Rubin Mitches	7	Green Adams	4
Mark Hatly	3	Unity Cole	1
L.B.Pearce	3	Elizabeth Hutchinson	5
S.B.Pearce	2	Mary Gray	2
F.W.Pearce	3	Mary Townsend	2
L.Crocker	2	Charlie Moore	1
Joseph Caldwell	1	Rebecca Cole	1
Benjamin Holland	2	Lewis Boswell	5
B.Stiers	4	Mary Williams	3
James Allen	4	Nelson Pearce	1
H.Foster	2	Thos Walker	2
L.H.Pope	2	John Douglass	5
Wm Fowler	4	Charles Westerman	3
William Marchbanks	4	Gill Marchbanks	3
Denesy Sanders	1	John Sanders	5

Page-167-

Name	No	Name	No
N Short	6	Cyrus Foster	1
Henry Abbott	5	Mary Deneson	7
Hurhei Sanders	6	S.Romly	5
Arnold Tomason	6	James Thomasson	3
Gillen Smothers	2	Barker	4
		TOTAL....	234

Signed
L.Crocker
Wm Fowler
J.J.Call--Commissioners.

COMMISSIONERS REPORT.

The Commissioners of the 5th Scholastic District for Benton County
Proceeded to take the enumeration of the white children in said district
from 6 years of age to 21 years of age with the names of parents or
persons   with whom they reside from the year ending the 30th day
of June 1845.

Page 167-Continued.

Name	No		Name	No
Joseph Wiseman	5		J.F.Cales	2
J.N.Steer	4		W.C.Guthrie	3
John Davis	2		Hugh H.Brown	2
J.M.Williams	3		John Atckins	1
Cooper Milton	2			

Page 168

Name	No		Name	No
J.R.Kelsey	5		F.Arnold	3
A.L.Lashlee	5		John Arnold	3
A.S.Cole	3		Jas Swett	2
Jas Gordon	2		R.Murphy	3
C.A.Crowly	5		A.G.Holt	3
J.B.Carnes	3		W.M.Surrutt	3
E.Perkins	5		J.M.Petty	3
B.Badler	3		R.C.Petty	3
Elander Wiseman	1		J.A.Kims	3
Y.Collins	5		J.H.Hudson	5
R.Thompson	6		W.M.Sykes	9
Biggs	2		Mary Lashlee	6
Robertson	3		D.L.Settle	3
W.H.Rushing	4		H.Johnson	2
J.C.Wright	4		L.B.William	5
Sleaphi Boswell	3		John Hudson	4
John Cole	3		P.D.Hubbard	1
James Russell	1		A.J.Hudson	1
Timothy Reeves	2		Sparton Bruce	4
E.F.Wells	4		George Hallmark	1
W.C.Thompson	1		Robert Holmes	2
John Pearce	4		Willis Rushing	4
G.W.L.Hudson	3		Isaac Casig	3
Elga Browning	3		Dennis Rushing	3
A.Ballard	3		J.C.Latimer	1
J.B.Bridges	1		Harty Hansell	4
John McGill	2		James Bell	4
R.S.Beasly	4		Eliza Hansell	1
D.Holland	6		Eliza Herron	3
N.Strickard	2		J.F.Flance	3
E.Arnold	6		D.Morris	4
R.Rushing	-3		W.S.Corbitt	5
W.M.Hudson	4		Henry Allen	4
Eliza Haney	6		B.Wheatly	2
James Addison	6		W.Smith	2
Wm Walker	3		James Alston	4
J.F.Arnold	1		D.Cuff	8
R.N.Farrow	6		Isaac Ward	3
Jacob Capp	4		Willie Arnold	1
S.Madden	7		S.Higdon	1
A.Utly	6		S.V.Aden	7

Page 169--

Page 169.

Name	No	Name	No
Charles Williams	4	Benson Turner	3
Lem Thompson	2	A.Smalley	6
William Pafford	1	J.K.Thomas	1
James Presson	7	David Patterson	1
C.K.Coyly	1	A.T.Corbett	1
R.P.Rushing	1	Jesse Stafford	1
H.Darden	3	D.F.McClyde	1
Babb	3	B.Burton	4
D.Darden	2	William Sullen	2
		TOTAL.......	372

The balance of money in favor of district for trustee the same.$13.50
Signed.G.W.L.Hudson
D.F.McClyea
James Gordon.

Page 170.

COMMISSIONERS REPORT.

Name	No	Name	No	Name	No
E.W.Lynch	8	Benn Greer	2	James Greer	4
L.Hall	4	Frances Presson(6)		John Tice	6
Narcissa McCord	5	D.Watson	5	E.Rushing	2
Lewis Cross	4	Thos Presson	4	E.Bush	3
W.M.Stewart	1	Thos Presson 1(Jr)		Mary Bone	6
Wm Bando	4	Hardy Rushing	4	Thos Ward	6
Eli Craig	3	J.P.Greer	5	R.S.Ward	2
Thos Craig	5	Robt Ward	4	Alford Lewis	2
Provy Beeler	1	A.Harris	1	W.B.Eadington	3
Hudson Taylor	7	John Thomas	1	J.D.Rushing	5
L.Cottingham	6	John McGill	2	J.Pearce,Jr	4
Richard Pace	4	Jane Crosnoe	5	J.McGill Jr	4
Joseph Pickler	3	H.Greer	4	W.W.Crews	2
Eli Crowell	4	P.Hednis	4	H.Nisler	1
Richard Nance	1	E.Hong	5	M.Crossno	1
John Elmore	7	J.T.Presson	4	J.Webb	2
Mary Swift	3	Wm Presson	1	J.Conly	1
Nancy Eran	1	Z.Armour	5	J. Bennett	5
J.Presson	7	W.Armour	1	H.Francesca	1
Mathew Presson	5	M.Cain	1	G.Francesca	4
W.D.Wiseman	4	J.Presson	11	J.R.Nance	7
J.H.Williams	4	Jas Block	3	D.Pearce	4
Wm Greer	6	W.Markham	1	Sarah Spires	5
S.Presson	4	L.Word	1	Jas Crews	3
John Watson	2	L.D.Pearce	3	W.Ward	6
Asa Rushing	3	Cottingham	1	F.Rushing	1
				TOTAL	288

I certify the foregoing is a true list of the Scholastic Population of the
of the 6th district of Benton County. for the year 1848.As reported to
me by the commissioners of said district.Amt remaining in hand of trustee

Page 170-Continued.
Forty dollars.
        A.C.Presson-Clerk of the board.

Page 171.

Commissioners Report 1845- The following is the Scholastic Population in the School District No Seven in the County of Benton for the year 1845.

David Benton	2	Obidiah Bullock	1	Abraham Davidson	7
Wm H.Holland	9	Wm H.Wheatly	4	Joseph Benton	2
John Melton	3	George Phifer	3	W.H.Cooley	3
John Pafford	8	Charlie J.Wheatly	7	Eli Parker	3
Wm Pafford	7	Thomas Smith	7	Richard J.Cole	2
Jackson Farmer	1	Wm Berry	7	Susanah Holland	1
James Pafford	5	James Garner	7	John Phifer	2
Berry Vester	5	J.Holloman	8	George W?Farmer	3
John W.Milton	8	Catherine Parker	3	Nancy Wheatly	3
S.Milton	2	James Cooley	1	William Smith	3
Conrad Milton	2	Andrew Bethel	3	Samuel Hayward	1
Ethelred Milton	1	John Myers	4	John W.Hill	3
P.Benton	2	Elenezer Reddick	4	Jane Pepples	1
John P.Milton	4	Matthew William	1	Age Hall	1
Perry Milton	1	Wm H.Holland	3	A.Belew	3
Cortin Parker	7	P.Milton	2	Jchobod Farmer	1
Berry W.Wheatly	3	Nancy Taylor	4	Mary Pulley	1
Susanah Hill	5	Henry Cherry	2	Henry C.Camp	1
				TOTAL.........	184-

A six months school has be taught 192 Persons have been taught $87.74 in the hands of the trustee of Benton County.$72.00 have him paid. for teaching.Only $31.00 has been drawn from last year from the trustee No money received from any other source.

                                        George W.Farmer-Clerk of

Page 172...   said district.

            COMMISSIONERS REPORT* 1845..

Bennett Bush	1	L.W.Brewer	3
William Waters	7	Burrell Bell	4
William Jonus	4	J.A.Cole	1
Elias Phifer	2	Sarah Rushing	1
Peter Phifer	1	Robert Rushing	3
John Phifer	2	Elbert Waggel	4
Mary Williams	3	A.R.Herrin	1
William Herndon	2	Beverly Herrin	2
E.M.Bush	1	John Smalley	1
C.B.Reddick	1	Elisha Herrin	1
D.A.Smith	4	W.McGee	3
John Carter	1	James Colier	4

Page 172- Continued...

Henry Allen	4	S.S.Barnes	4
Merritt Melton	1	Elizabeth Alsup	3
Melton Smith	1	Henry Roburn	5
Henry Milton	2	J.G.Taylor	1
John Taylor	2	Sam Alsup	1
Wm Taylor	1	Hugh Alsup	4
L.D.Grissans	3	John Ragsdale	4
Jacob Tice	1	Matilda Shilling	1
Kenneth Reddick	6	Haggard Bird	1
J.R.Childors	1	W.B.Cole	1
James Lickhart	1	J.W.Utly	2
James Click	6	Lewis Holland	4
Robert Birdwell	2	Lewis Brewer	1
Hyram Pearce	4	L.W.Brewer	3
W.C.Cole	3	M.Cherry	2
William Warmack	2	N.Brewer, Jr	2
Isom Jones	1	W.W.Holland	5
Nicholas Brewer	1	Samuel Brewer	2

Page 173..

Neal McNiel	5	Nancy Brewer	2-
E.McBride	4	Bell	2
D.Brewer	1	Nancy McKenzie	2
A.McRae	2.	TOTAL................	183

We the undersinged do certify the within is a true list of the scholastic population in the 8th civil district of Benton County for the year....1845.

J.Phifer
L.W.Brewer.
D.Brewer.

COMMISSIONERS REPORT 1845........

We the commissioners certify this is a true copy of the scholastic population of the ninth district in Benton County Tennessee on the 1st day of July 1845 .Over six and under twenty one years of age.

Balam Culpeper	4	M.Mannon	1
John Buchanon	2	Daniel Grayham	5
J.W.Brominger	3	Katherine Beaton	2
John Leagan	1	Nancy Buchanan	1
David Ross	2	Ed Lindsey	7
J.W.Whitaker	4	Aron Clement	2
Mary Cooley	3	D.G.Buchanan	1
William Wright	8	R.Grayham	1
Dennis Stockdale	3	J.W.Cooper	7
William Stockdale	1	Martha Graham	4
Thomas Anders	5	James Cooper	7
Wm Mizell	2	Jess D.Hall	-1
Henry Hansell	4	A.W.C.Matheny	5.

Page 173-Continued..

M.Bealer	6	P.Gross	4
L.Beaton	4	Wesly Daniel	5
Ann Myneck	6	William Rowe	2
James Staynor	2	Nancy Clemmons	3
Nathan Staynor	1	Mary McDaniel	1
William Lindsey	2	Breton George	2
Simmons Nichols	6	Daniel Lightmore	3
William Akers	2	Nancy Greer	2
Noah Coyatt	3	Chrtstohper	3
Lanson Nichols	3	Harriett Townsend	4
Burrell Wynn	1	Liby Davis	2
Lewis Hyer	1	W.R.Wynn	2
Jonus L ndsey	5	John Matheny	1
Wm Waters	5	John McGlown	7
Robert Holmes	3	David Askew	1
John Rolls	5	Charlie Robins	7

Page 174...

George McDaniel	2	Mary Rhodes	2
Everett Askew	3	Eli Carmack	1
W.M.Adams	2	Elizabeth Wynn	3
James McDaniel	3	Thomas Pafford	2
		Total........... ..	214

Signed
Drew Askew -Clerk
William Wright
James Stagner-Commissioners.

The amount due the 9th district for the year 1844 is $93.70
Amount paid......   84.00
Balance due.................. $9.07

Page 175-- --

Sate of Tennessee,Treasurers Office,Nashville,Tennessee,August 15th 1846.
I certify the following is the apportionment of the school funds by me
made to the County of Benton for the year 1846.

District No1......	$87.46
Dis No2	92.46
Dis No 3	90.16
Dis No 4	107.64
Dis No 5	171.12
Dis No 6	132.48
Dis No 7	84.64
Dis No 8	83.72
Dis No 9	98.44
	$948.52

R.B.Turner-Treasurer of Tennessee.

Page 175-Continued..

The above curtail...   .... $258.75
Which leaves Benton County....   .....   689.77

Sate of Tennessee ,Benton County, This day being the 21st of September
1846.Amos Bruce Trustee of said County made application to make
settlement with me W.P.Morris ,Clerk of the said County Court.
agreeable to an act of assembly .in such case made and provided
showing receipts and disbursements of the common school fund for the
year 1845..Amount received from the treasurer for said year after
deducting the trustee's commission.

The sum of $919.78
Amount left in the hands of trustee year 1844 at last settl   114.33
Total.............   1034.11

Page 176.........

                           VOUCHERS...

District No 1   Paid. $94.97
   "   " 2   "   81.70
   "   " 3   "   118.50
   "   " 4   "   97.70
   "   " 5   "   107.75
   "   " 6   "   132.95$\frac{1}{2}$
   "   " 7   "   35.66$\frac{1}{4}$
   "   " 8   "   92.60
   "   " 9   "   87.12$\frac{1}{2}$
                    Amount ##expended..... 848.36\frac{1}{4}$

Which leaves in the hands of the trustee   the sum of 185.74\frac{3}{4}$
All of which is respectfully submitted.   W.P.Morris--Clerk

Page 177..

Commissioners Report 1846.The number of children in the first civil
district of Benton County. for the year 1846.

Martha Malin.	3	Elijah Woods	7
William Malin	3	Mary Barnett	1
Sarah Hatly	2	Mac Barnett	4
Charles Oatsvale	3	Thomas Mc Gill	3
Edward Hatly	7	Henry Parkes	3
Nancy Gaforth	3	Henry Edison	4
Jesse Dillion	3	John Ignite	3
Thivey Camp	5	Mrs Massey	3
James Shirley	2	Michael Fry	4
John Gassett	5	Hill Crab	1
Hardyman Forehand	1	James Henry	3

Page 177-Continued..

Samuel Dancer	5	E.Grisson	1
Wilson Barr	3	Squire Bishop	1
Whitfield Tippitt	5	Martha Barnett	2
James Watkins	6	George Lewes	3
H.Woods	1	B.B.Barnett	6
Mrs Walker	2	Mary Matlock	2
James White	6	Wm Hubbs	3
Francis Whitington	5	James Hillis	3
William Whitington	4	Elizabeth Ratliff	2
Aeon Victory	6	Charles Duncan	3
John Johnson	2	Jesse Hale	3
Shack Daly	3	E.Jordon	1
E.W.Conly	7	Robert Doherty	2
Peggy Talbert	1	Yancy Bohanan	1
Polly Fulterton	3	Synthia Harrison	1
Jerry Massy	4	S.Walker	2
Wm Grogan	3	Wm Steel	1
J.Crabb	1	J.Lack	1
Jesse Newson	4		

TOTAL........ ...... .184.

John Gassett
E.Woods
J.E.Mirick--Commissioners.

Page 178..

Commissioners Report 1846..A list of scholastic population with the parents and guardians name and civil district.No 2. Benton County Tennessee. 1846.

Green Flowers	5	Thos Asburn	4
James Evans	4	Samuel Bridges	6
Jack Smith	1	A.C.Harris	8
Richard Nordin	5	William Pettigrew	4
Willie Ellis	3	Jonus Myrick	4
Pete Self	3	James Taylor	2
Dolly Kirk	2	Isaac Smith	3
James Hogg	5	Isiah Bright	1
Samuel Oxford	5	William Smith	3
Robert Pettigrew	5	Nathan Williams	2
Wesly Crabb	1	Hyman Smith	2
T.Kirk	3	John Bagget	7
Thomas Curtis	-6	John Dilion	4
Cullen Nowell	5	Jeremiah Perry	6
John Robertson	4	David Raney	6
John Prince	7	Henry Gossett	4
G.Sanders	2	Hillman King	4
Amos Bruce	1	Elizabeth McCord	3
Lanner Watson	2	Young Adams	4
Milton Myrick	4	Hugh Buchanan	1

Page 178-Continued..

William Orneal	1	A.Games	4
Jesse Bruce	4	Wm F.Doherty	5
Thomas Harrison	4	James M.Camp	4
J.S.Harper	3	George Reeves	3
James Basford	3	J.R.Mathews	3
D.M.Burkett	2	Wyatt Jenkins	5
Jas B.Comitte	1	C.G.Haynes	1
J.A.Jordon	2	W.Bridges	5
Jess Newsom	4	William Crabb	6
Frances Bohn	3	Redden Hallowell	7
John Atchison	1	S.Moore	1
		TOTAL...............	234.

Commissioners Report 1846, Scholastic Report of The Third District.

Thmas Matherhead	5	E.Teddor	1
William Camp	5	Mark Hatly	3
Burrell Utly	5	Nancy Dalton	4
John Hardin	1	Joel Teddor	3
Stephen Marchbanks	1	James Hallis	2
Norman Stires	5	Jesse Barnes	1
Alfred Bunn	5	John Smith	1

Page 179.

Ben M.chie	1	William Ballew	6
Geo W.Adams	2	Jackson Hatly	1
Geo Thomason	5	John H.Hayler	1
S.Utly	6	Isaac Anderson	2
O.Harden	6	John Anderson	1
John T.Ford	2	W.C.Anderson	1
John Waldrop	5	Wm Swindle	4
Elv Sayles	1	Asa Swindle	4
L.D.Cain	4	Coty Howe	5
James Wyly	5	Arch Starr	4
John Davidson	1	Wm Cole	4
Isham Taylor	4	Thomas Swindle	3
S.H.Davidson	3	Jefferson Hicks	4
Eli P.Ballew	6	Wm Davidson	1
Levy Smith	5	Nathan Nunery	3
A.Lynch	1	Nathan Swindle	1
Cullen Looper	6	David W.Barnett	4
Wm Marchbanks	3	Mrs Gilland	6
A.B.Wilson	2	Hannah Collins	3
Henry Barnes	4	Wm Barnes	7

Page 180.

John Barnes	3	Jas Latin	4
John Dancer	1	M.Edward	2

Page 180 Continued..

J.B.Cox	4	Polly Brewer	2
Kenchu Nunnery	3	John T.Winprey	1
Pleasant Mullinix	7	H.Ree	1
		TOTAL....	208.

COMMISSIONERS OF THE FOURTH DISTRICT.

John Davidson	5	Ervin Caldwell	2
Rubin Mitchell	7	B.Turner	3
M.Thomason	3	John Davenport	4
Samuel B.Pearce	2	Thomas Peron	3
T.W.Pearce	4	John Garret	5
Jonus Holland	5	John Cole	7
John Holland	3	Charlie Moon	3
Bennett Holland	3	L.Davis	3
Benjamin Holland	1	Giles Marchbank	3
Lily Crocker	2	Thomas Harrison	1
J.Jordon	4	William Moon	2
Moss Jordon	4	Nancy Walker	1
Ruben Bridges	4	Stephen Garret	2
Jackson Peoples	2	Berry Calvell	1
M.Williams	2	Julius J.Cole	8
Allen Banks	2	Thomas Cole	3
Elizabeth Gillispie	3	Willis Cole	1
Z.Barker	4	Lewis Roswell	6
Daniel Cole	6	Taylor Pearce	6
B.C.Morgan	1	John F.Johnson	4
Nancy Thrasher	3	John McAuley	3
G.Thrasher	3	Loyd Cole	1
Little B.Pearce	3	Green Adams	4
Joshua House	4	Albert Townsend	4
John N.Stires	1	Ruben Marchbank	2
Mary Townsend	2	James Allen	4
James Thomason	4	Henry Abbott	5
Wm Kilbreath	2	Abraham Sanders	7
Mary Dennis	5	Josiah Foster	2
A.B.Aden	2	Needham Short	6
William Fowler	5	John Samuel	5

Page 181.

Hezekiah Foster	2	Shadrack Ramby	5
James Y.Barker	5	Lillian Smith	1
L.H.Pope	1	Wm Boswell	7
		TOTAL............	239

Page 181-Continued.

We the undersigned commissioners of the fourth district.Certify the
above is a true list of the scholastic population of said district
for the year 1846.

                                    Little B.Pearce
                                    James Allen
                                    John F.Johnson.

Commissioners report 1846. Has account of the scholastic population
in the five civil districts in Benton County ,over the age of six
and under the age of twenty one years.For the year 1846.

J.T.Florence	4	Wm Sykes	6
John McGill	2	Wm C.Holms	1
Berry Wheatly	2	D.L.Settles	3
A.Ballard	5	John Arnold	4
Eliza Herron	4	J.P.Arnold	3
R.P.Rushing	1	Hiriam Johnson	2

Page 182.

R.M.Browning	2	L.Burnett	1
F.Arnold	2	R.S.Beasly	4
James Bell	4	David Cuff	8
W.Rushing	3	E.Wheatly	1
Hearty Hansel	4	Elizabeth Browning	3
John Pearce	5	David Morris	3
Wm Sullins	1	W.S.Corbett	4
T.Mayberry	5	Wm M.Surratt	3
Wm Corbett	7	R.Holmes	2
Widow Farrow	4	R.T.Lashen	1
E.Arnold	-7	D.Rushing	3
John Davis	2	Abner Smally	5
Willie Arnold	1	J.C.Latiner	1
Cooper Milton	2	Thomas Glover	2
James Milton	4	Wm Carraway	1
John Williams	3	J.Shepard	3
Isaac Ward	3	J.Thornton	3
Isiah Oats	2	S.Boswell	4
A.P.Holt	3	E.T.Carnell	1
E.Haney	6	Wm P.Morris	1
George Hallmark	2	Wm Farrow	6
Spartin Bruce	4	J.M.Williams	2
G.W.L.H dson	2	Pigton Lashlee	2
P.B.Hubbard	1	Wm Thompson	1
J.G.Hudson	4	C.A.Crowley	4
J.Hudson	5	Jack Cuff	4
J.C.Wright	4	Simeon Higdon	1
B.Rodden	3	James McGill	3
T.Reeves	1	Samuel Madden	6
J.Darden	1	Wm Bridges	2
A.S.Cole	5	D.McElyed	2

Page 182-Continued.

Jane Rushing	1	W.A.Hudson	4
James Alston	5	W.C.Thompson	2
W.K.Perkins	1	C.Williams	5
B.Bridges	1	L.F.Wills	5
A?Lashlee	5	D.England	5
R.Rushing	2	B.Burton	3
L.H.Thompson	.2	J.Akins	4
B.William	5	A.Utly	2
P.Thompson	6	J.Robertson	5
William Walker	3	H.M.Brown	3
Joe Wiseman	3	F.Reeves	1
Thomas Farrow	1	J.P.Allison	6
J.U.Hudson	1	J.R.Childress	1
L.Perkins	6	Z.Collins	6
T.Jonus	4	Wm A Steele	1
D.P.Hudson	2	A.Bivens	5
Mary Capps	5	J.B.Carns	3
J.Cole	2	J.Cole	1
J.M.Petty	4	D.Holland	6
N.Strickland	3	J.K.Thomas	1
J.Surratt	3	L.Wiseman	1
C.K.Wyly	1	George	1
		TOTAL.............378	

L.H.Thompson.
Wm A Hudson.

Page 183....

COMMISSIONERS REPORT-1846.

James Presson	8	Narcissa McCarroll	5
John Presson	12	Leberry Hill	2
William Wiseman	3	Eli Craig	4
Oliver Armour	4	Edward W.Lynch	8
John T.Presson	4	John Elmore	6
M.Cain	1	W.H.Rushing	3
W.F.Presson	1	Mary Flemmings	3
John H.Williams	4	Eli Crowell	4
Wm Greer	4	C.H.Bettarg	2
Samuel Presson	4	Thos Craig	5
John Watson	3	Robert Swift	1
Benjamin Greer	7	Thomas Higon	1
J.J.Rushing	2	L.Cottingham	6
A.C.Presson	5	Nancy Brann	1
James Crossno	2	J.J.Rogers	1
Jane Wiseman	1	P.Beeler	1
Thomas Presson	5	Mary Swift	1
James Richardson	1	Joseph Pickler	3
T.Presson	2	William Stuart	2
David Watson	5	Louise Thornton	1
Hardy Rushing	4	Lewis Cross	4

Page 184.

John P.Greer	5	William Bond	5
John McGill	2	Richard Nance	1
Jane Crossno	5	James K.Nance	8
Robert Ward	5	Thomas Ward	6
Alberry Harris	2	William Ward	5
Patience Helms	4	Jonus Black	3
Joseph Collins	1	W.D.Marcum	2
Phillip J.Rushing	4	Elizabeth Rushing	1
Henry Stogall	3	F.M.Rushing	1
Freeman Presson	9	T.Pearce	5
M.Presson	5	John Pearce .Sr	2
James Greer	4	L.D.Pearce	4
Asa Rushing	3	Eleanor Bush	3
J.D.Rushing	4	Alford Lewis	2
Sarah Spain	5	Willie Eddington	4
Mary Bane	4	William Bloodworth	1
John Tice	7	John Mc Gill	5
Elizabeth	5	R.S.Ward	2
		Total	287

We hereby certify that the foregoing is a true list of th e scholastic
population of the 6th civil district of Benton County from the year
ending the 30th of June 1846.

      A.C.Presson
      Liven Cottingham
      R.S.Ward   Commissioners.

Page 185   C

     Commissioners Report 1846.

The children in the 7th civil district of Benton County for the year
1846.

George Phifer	2	John Randle	3
George Buck	1	E.Riddick	4
William Berry	7	Thos Snider	1
L.Grissom	2	Wm W.Wheatly	4
James Holloman	7	Berry Vester	6
Katherine Parks	3	Wm W.Holland	9
John Myers	4	David W.Benton	2
Calvin Myers	1	John Pafford	9
Thos Cuff	1	Wm Pafford	8
James Turner	7	John W.Melton	9
Thomas J.Floyd	5	B.Benton	2
Charles J.Wheatly	7	John P.Benton	5
William H.Williams	1	Perry Milton	1
O.Bullock	2	S.Milton	1
Mary Pulley	4	J.C.Melton	2
Henry Cherry	1	David Patterson	2
Henry Sitfoot	4	Jackson Farmer	1
James Pafford	1	Calvin Parker	7
Wm A.Benton	1	Nancy Taylor	4

Page 185-Continued.

S.Hill	5	John M.lton	3
E.Parker	3	J.J.Farmer	1
S.Holland	1	Job Tice	1
A.Hall	1	John Flowers	7

Page 186.

H.C.Camp	2	E.Milton	1
John Cooley	1	Nancy Whitly	3
V.Carter	1	P.Milton	3
G.W.Farmer	3	W.H.Holland	3
H.Belle	5	J.M.Benton	2
J.W.Hill	4	W.C.Cole	3
J.Pipin	1	A.Davidson	6
W.H.Cooly	3	Total....	204.

Wm Wheatly
E.Milton
John Pafford

COMMISSIONERS REPORT. 1846.

John Pearce	2	Kenneth Reddick	6
Nancy Brewer	3	William Herndon	2
Lawson Nicholas	5	J.Taylor	3
William Holland	5	A.Petelle	3
E.B.Reddick	2	John Phifor	2
Lewis Brewer	2	Elias Phifer	2

Page 187.

Sterling Brewer	2	Elias Phifer	2
N.Brewer Jr	2	Henry Milton	1
Samuel Brewer	2	R.P.Rushing	1
Lewis Holland	4	Merritt Milton	2
Nancy McKenzie	2	James Vester	1
A.McRae	4	Wm Waters	6
R.Murphy	5	Wm Jones	4
Mary Milton	2	John Flowers	7
Robert Birdwell	3	Henry Robinson	6
H.Pearce	5	J.G.Taylor	2
Jonus Lockhart	2	Hugh Alsup	6
Nancy Vick	4	L.W.Brewer	4
Elizabeth Barnes	6	Burrell Bell	5
William Warmack	2	Robert Rushing	3
Neil McNeil	4	John Smalley	1
E.McBride	6	Sarah Rushing	1
Robert Jonus	1	J.W.Utly	1
J.J.Lowery	1	Judith Cole	2

Page 188

Page 188

Mar Chury	2	L.Wiggle	4
N.Brewer Sr	1	B.Herron	2
D.Brewer	1	S.W.Burrus	6
J.G.Allen	2	John Ragsdale	4
William Smith	3	David Alsup	1
Wm Taylor	1	Elizabeth Alsup	4
John Taylor	3	Matilda Shilling	1
Mary Wilson	2	A.Herron	4
Grisson Herron	1	D.L.Cole	1
George Greer	4	D.G.Buchanan	2
James Greer	4	John Smalley	1
Margaret McGea	4	C.Yeats	6
O.Waters	1	J.P.Smalley	1
			226

Daniel G.Buchanan-C.M.

COMMISSIONERS REPORT 1846..

The scholastic population of the 9th district of Benton County for the year 1846.

William Stockdale	2	John Whittier	4
Jesse D.Hale	1	John McGlohon	5
Thomas Andrews	5	David Askew	1
Wm Wright	9	Hamilton Townsend	4
Dennis Stockdale	3	Drew A.Askew	3
William Mizelle	2	Daniel Gauge	1
Henry Hansel	3	James Kernel	3
J.W.Barringer	4	F.Colier	3
David Rop	3	William Lindsey	5
Lucinda Williams	3	Durrell Winn	2
John Bando	2	Noah Wyatt	4
John Christopher	7	B.Grass	5
Brittian George	-2	S.Nichols	7
Daniel Lightner	4	Wesly Daniel	4
Mary Roads	2	Ann Myrick	5
Nancy Greer	2	N.Stayner	1
Thomas Pafford	3	A.W.C.Matheny	5
James McDaniel	4	James Stayner	3
Charlie Robins	5	Wm Markham	1
George Mc Daniel	2	Lewis Lyer	1
William Adon	2	William Waters	2
John Rolls	5	Jesse Webb	3
William Akers	3	C.Beaton	3
James Story	1	Edward Lindsey	5
Henry Suter	4	Eli Castner	3
Malcolm Beaton	6	Littleton Allen	5
Latha Beaton	6	Henry A.Barnes	3
Daniel Graham	6	Arthur Pitt	7

Page 188- Continued

Robert Graham	1	Martha Grayhorn	5
John W. Cooper	7	John Wyatt	1
James Cooper	7	Green B. Rolls	1:
Aron Clement	2	Nancy Cummings	4
Mathew Hammons	2	Martha Milton	2

Total adition of original book 233

Page 189

We the Commissioners do hereby certify the foregoing to be a true amount of the Scholastic Population of the Ninth District for the year 1846.

D.A.Askew
Jake Wynn
John Wyatt

State of Tennessee)   This day being 6th day of July
Benton County   )
1847
Amas Bruce Trustee of said County made application to make settlement with me.   Wm. P. Morris Clerk of said County Court agreeable to an act of the general assembly in such case made and provided showing the Receipts and Disbursment of the common school fund received for the use of Benton County for the year 1846.

Amount received from Treasur	$ 689.77
Deduct Trustee Comission	$ 6.89
	$ 682.88

Page 190

Amount left in the Trustee hands at last settlement $185.74
Total $868.62

Expended to each District as follows

Dis	Vouchers	
1	No 1	$ 63.22
2	No 2	70.93
3	No 3	71.51
4	No 4	88.88
5	No 5	126.72
6	No 6	124.68
7	No 7	96.37
8	No 8	59.85
9	No 9	90.25
	Amount of Vouch.	$ 792.41

Page 190 Continued

Which leaves in the hands of the Trustee for the year 1846 the sum
of $ 76.21

All of which is respectfully submitted

W.P. Morris Clk.

Page 191

School Fund

Appointment to Benton County

No.	Pop.	Amt
Dis.1	184	$80.50
Dis.2	234	102.37
Dis.3	208	91.00
Dis.4	239	104.51
Dis.5	378	165.37
Dis.6	237	125.56
Dis.7	204	89.25
Dis.8	226	98.87
Dis.9	233	101.93
		$ 959.43

R.B.Turner
Treas. of Tenn.

Page 192

Commissioners Report 1847

Number of children in the 1 st District of Benton County on the
1st July 1847

Whittington, W	5	James White	6
F.Whittington	5	Gorrett Massy	3
J. Johnson	3	S.Bright	6
McBornete	4	E.W.Conley	5
E.Wood	7	H.Forehand	1
H.Allison	3	B.Dillion	2
M.Barnett	2	Wm. M.Malin	3
M.Massey	3	Marg.Fullerton	1
McDaniel	1	Elizabeth Rattoff	2
Thomas McGill	3	Martha Malin	3
T.Bishop	1	Jesse Dilion	4
M.Fry	4	Edward Hatty	6

41

41

Page 192 Continued

Name	No.	Name	No.
J.Crobb	1	Charles Outvall	3
J. Huny	2	Sarah Hatty	1
B.B. Barnett	6	Gassitt,John	5
H.Crabb	2	Nancy Gaforth	2
W.Hubbs	1	Theresa Camp	5
John Hubb	2	Smith Walker	2
G.Lewis	2	Eaver Jordon	2
J. Hillis	2	Robert Doherty	2
H.Panks	3	Sintha Harrison	1
M.Harrison	6	Jessie Hall	3
G.Evans	2	Wilson Bare	3
Mashack,Baly	3	Larking Teppitt	1
Whitfield Tippitt	6	Alford Tippitt	1
Charles Dunkin	3	Jane Walker	6
Eliza Walker	2	Henry Woods	1
	43		38
	41		41
	8 4		79
	7 9		

Total brought forward   16 3

John Gassett
Elijah Woods
Commissioners

Page 193

No 2   Commissioner's Report   1847

Name	No.	Name	No.
Redden Halloways	7	Saml Oxford	5
Francis Baker	5	Peter Seof	1
Charles Haynes	1	Mooring Austin	3
John Atchison	1	James Evans	4
W.Stewart	2	Wesly Crabb	1
Jackson Jordan	2	Dally Kirk	3
Robert Pettigrew	5	Thomas King	5
Mrs.Basford	3	James Hogg	5
Jessie Bruce	3	James Readn	3
Willis Bridges	5	Thos. Y. Crutchfield	2
Willis Thompson	2	Cullen,Nowell	6
M. Harper	3	John Robertson	4
Mr.Reeves	2	John Prince	5
David Bemkitt	2	Gilford Sanders	2
Hillory Crobb	3	Amos Bruce	1
J. Mathis Esq.	4	John Sanders	3
Thomas Harrison	4	Amas Gastin	3
James Reeder	2	Larranor Watson	3
David M. Borvill	3	Malton Menick	5
Wyatt Jenkins	5	Thos. Osborn	4
Wyley Ellis	3	A.C.Harris	7
Richard Norden	5	Wm. Pettigrew	4
Green Flowers	5	James Monick	5
	77		84

Page 193 Continued

Theofohilas Kirk	2	James Taylor	2
Thoas Curtis	5	Isaac Smith	4
Isiah Bright	4	Willson Smith	3
Nathan Williams	2	Hynans Smith	2
John Baggett	6	John Dillons	3
David Rainey	6	Henry Gassett	4
William King	3	Young Adams	3
James Mcary	5	Eli Haly	1

```
                          33                    22
                          77                    84
                         100                   10 6
                         106
        Total brought forward2 16
```

Page 194

Commissioners Report   1847

We the Commissioners of the 3rd Civil District do report the following
as the over six and under 21 years for the year 1847.

Elnder Smith	5	Jefferson Hicks	5
E.G. Ballour	5	Holloway Kee	1
William Looper	5	William Call	5
Mark Hally	4	Asa Sevindle	4
Anderson Lynch	2	William Sevindle	4
James Hillis	2	Mahala Smith	3
Joel Tedden	2	Thomas Mathushead	5
Nancy Doalton	4	Lewes Raswell	5
Elisha Tedden	2	John Anderson	2
David Barnes	5	Isaac Anderson	2
Hinny Barnes	5	Wm. C. Anderson	1
William Barnes	1	A.B. Wilson	3
J.B.Cox	5	Wm.Davidson	1
Nathan Nunrey	3	Wm.Douglass	1
Kinchan Nunery	3	Wm.Ballou	7
Dally Cox	2	Seth Utley	7
Robert McKnight	2	Bumel Utley	5
James Taylor	4	Obedeah Hardin	6
Pleasent Mullinix	6	John Hardin	1
E.A.Reeves	1	John T.Ford	1
Thomas Sevendle	1	E.W.Sayles	1
H.Berchannon	1	Manoh Copps	6
Mary Conchs	4	L.D.Conchs	2
Stephn Marchhands	2	William Marchands	4
George Thomason	5	Isha Taylor	3
E.W.Adams	1	Alford Bunn	5
S.H. Davidson	2	Wm.Camp	5

Total Addition of original book 194

```
                        Wm.Ballowe   )
                        N.Nunny      ) Comm.
                        S.H.Davidson )
```

Page 195

Commissioners Report   1847

A list of the Scholastic Population in the   4th District, Benton County.
25th June 1847

Laton Pearce	6	J.T. Hallard	3
Unity Call	1	H.Williams	1
W.H.Cole	2	B.C.Morgan	2
John Devenport	4	Irvin Carvell	3
Pensella Townsend	4	Zeck Bonker	3
John McAuly	2	Allen Barker	7
Thomas Harrison	1	Morth Jordan	8
Green Adams	5	Jackson House	3
Chores Moone	3	Jonathan Jordon	5
Wm. Moone	2	M.Thomason	3
Mary Townsend	1	J.W.Davidson	6
Lity Davis	3	Ruben Mitchel	7
Steaphr Garrett	3	L.B.Pearce	3
John Garrett	5	J.B.Pearce	2
John F. Johnson	3	Fanny H. Pearce	4
W.G.Pac	2	Lilly Cnocker	2
Henry Jordan	7	Joseph Coevell	1
Thomas Call	5	E.W.Pearce	1
J.J. Cale	7	X.Gallaspie	3
John Cole	6	Benton Turner	3
Thomas Pardan	4	Thomas Walker	3
Rubin Bridges	3	E.S. Morris	2
Benett Holland	4	Janey Allen	1
A.Sanders	6	S. Smother	2
J. Foester	2	Henry Abbat	5
J.Neighbors	4	J.Sanders	6
R.Marchbanks	6	A.Townsend	4
Irvin Earp	7	S.Morchbanks	4
N.R.Williams	3	A. Aden	2
Sam Crockett	1	J. Foster	2
May Dunnig	4	William Rillick	3
N.Short	6	L.H. Pop	1
L. H. Pop	1	Edlow Palmer	6
James Palmer	2	M.G. Ford	4

Total addition of original book   223

John F. Johnson
L.B. Pearce
Henry Abbatt
    Commissioners

Page 196

Commissioners Report 1847
Amount of the Scholastic Population of the 5th Scholastic in Benton
County for the year ending 30th 1847

L.H. Thompson	2	L. Lashlee	1
P.Thompson	6	D.C.Settle	3
Danell Holland	5	A.T.Forrow	3
Martha Barnes	6	Wm.M.Surratt	2
B.Williams	5	J. Durden	1
C.Williams	5	J.M. Petty	3
V.Strickland	3	H. Johnson	2
Alice Uttey	8	Willie Arnald	1
Darice Ingland	5	John Davis	2
Jane Bussel	1	A.Bruce	2
E.F.Mills	5	J.R.Thomas	1
Jane Aden	1	John Thornton	3
Wm. Cole	1	H.Derdeh	4
John Cole	1	O.Atkins	3
Jr.Wiseman	5	A.G. Holt	4
J.B.Carns	3	J.M.Williams	3
Wm.Forrow	6	W.C.Holmes	1
Wm.Walker	4	R.Holmes	2
Ed Weiseman	1	Wm. P,Morris	2
William Syks	7	R.H. Lightfoot	1
S.Basewell	4	D.F.McKnight	2
Jr.Sarrett	3	S.M.Barnett	1
C.Craigherd	4	R.T.Rushing	2
H.C.Camp	2	B.Stofford	1
A.Lashlee	5	A.Hayie	2
Jane McGowen	2	A.Smally	5
C.K.Wyly	1	W.S.Corbitt	4
S.C.Pavatt	1	D.P. Hudson	2
John H. Bristo	2	Eliza Honey	6
Mary Ronto	4	J. H. Hudson	6
M.F.Doherty	5	M.B. Biggs	2
Thomas Hall	1	James Alston	5

Page 197

W.F.Prewett	1	B.Redden	3
H.S.Call	3	Wm. A. Hudson	5
H. M. Brown	5	Sarah Atkison	3
James Gordon	2	J.W.Utty	1
C.A.Cranley	4	Z.Settlins	1
D.Coff	8	S.Bruce	4
F.Arnald	3	J.C.Wright	5
H.Collins	3	J.G.Hudson	4
E.Arnald	7	R.N.Wood	1
J.P.Arnald	2	N.Collins	6
W.Rushing	4	S.George	1
A.Ballard	5	J. Melton	5
Mrs. Bell	4	C. Melton	2
J. Laximine	2	E.Farrow	5
D.Rushing	3	R.Rushing	2
D, Morris	4	R.P. Rushing	1

Page 197

E.Browning	3	Jesse Rashong	3
Harty Hansel	3	J.M. Browning	1
J.Stafford	1	R.S.Peasly	4
Ida Love	1	O.G.Combs	2
Tom Sullins	3	John McGill	2

Page 198

C.Cravins	2	J.T.Flarnce	5
I.B.Hubboard	2	T.Joins	4
S.Madlin	6	T.Reaves	2
Mabury	7	Wm.Corbett	7
Thos,Higdon	1	A.J.Hudson	1
P.W.L. Hudson	3	J.B.Bridges	1
James Robertson	3	E.Perkins	4

Total addition of original book 379

Wm. A. Hudson
R.Rushing
Commissioners

Commissioners Report 1847.
A Report of the Scholastic Population of the 6th District Civil for the year 1847

Foreman Pressar	8	Narcisa McCarrall	4
Ben Green	3	Eli Crowell	5
John Watson	3	A.J. Peeples	2
Samuel Presson	5	J.J.Rodgers	2
Thomas Presson	5	Wm.Wisemans	4
David Watson	4	Milton Wisemans	2
William Bond	6	Jane Wiseman	1
John H.Williams	4	James Presson	8
Wm.Green	6	James Watson	1
John Pressor	12	John McGill Sr.	2

Page 198

Hezekell Green	6	James Crassno	4
Racheie Rushing	4	Lucenda Nisler	1
John P.Green	6	James Crassno	2
John T. Presson	5	Hardy Rushing	4
Johnathan Holms	5	Nancy Cathy	3
Robert Ward	6	Albury Harris	3
A.C.Pressor	5	John McGill Jr.	6
Nancy Boran	1	David Warmack	9
Thoms Crairy	5	Joseph Collins	1
W.H.Rushing	3	Theophelas Pressor	2
Robert Swift	1	Elizabeth Honey	7
C.H. Bethay	1	C.H. Thompson	1

Page 198   Continued

Commissioners Report 1847

Eli Craig	3	Alvin Taylor	1
E.W.Lynch	8	Lewis Cross	5
Lean Cattingham	6	Froogy Beeler	1
Hyromm Dawson	4	Joseph Pickles	5

Total Addition of Original Book 296

We the Commissioners of the 6th School District of Benton County do hereby
certify that the above is a correct report of the Scholastic Population of
said District. August 1st,1847

Robt. L. Ward
Leno Cattingham
A.C.Pressor
By A.C.Pressor Clerk

Page 199

Commissioners Report 1847
A list of the Scholastic Population of the 7 Civil District from the year
1847

William Pafford	8	Jacob Teer	3
John Pafford	8	Wm. W.H. Holland	4
Jackson Farmer	1	Pindgene Milton	3
Garner Hatchett	2	George W.Farmer	3
David Pafford	1	Susaiah Hill	5
James Farmer	1	John W.Hill	5
James Pippins	1	W.C.Cole	3
Wm.H. Holland	10	John Phifor	2
Marth Crutchfield	2	David W.Benton	3
Wm. Beny	9	Abraham Davidson	6
John Milton	1	W.J. H. Cooley	3
Perry Milton	2	E.Parker	4
Calvin Parker	7	R.I. Cole	2
Sophia Bell	3	Adge Hall	1
John P. Benton	5	Levera Carter	2
W.C.Benton	1	Susanah Holland	2
John Myers	4	I. N. Hill	1
David Benton	2	Benj. Anderson	5
Etheland Milton	2	Jacob Cupp	4
Berry Vister	6	John Garner	1
J.W.Milton	8	James Garner	7
Conrad Milton	3	C.J.Wheatley	6
Sion Milton	3	Nathaniel Parker	2
James Hollonson	6	George Phifer	3
George W.Brack	1	Obedish Bullock	3
John Wynn	3	Henry Cheery	1
Calvin Hall	2	Ebenezer Reddrick	4
		Peter S. Schnider	2

Page 200

T.G. Snider	2	Wm. W. Wheatley	5
Thomas L. Flay	6		
Total Addition of original book	202	John Pafford	
		Wm. W. Wheatley, Commissioners	

Commissioners Report   1847

A true List of Scholastic Population of District No. 8 for the year
1847

John Peafce	3	Wm. Warmack	2
Lewis Holland	4	Rebeccah McBride	7
Wm. R. Pearce	1	Robert James	3
A. W. Brewer	3	Ledia James	1
William Hallard	5	John Lowery	1
N. Brewer Jr.	2	Manervy Cheery	2

Page 200

D. Brewer	1	N. Brewer Sr.	1
N. McKenzie	2	John G. Allen	3
John McGlohon	5	Felia Calins	5
Hugh Alsap	8	Thomas Collier	1
Lewis Brewer	1	Henry Melton	1
Matilda Herndon	1	Bucham Past	89
Nancy Brewer	3	Phifor Past	89
C. B. Reddrick	2	Sterling Brewer	3
Samuel Brewer	3	Alexander McRae	5
Mary Melton	2	Robert Birdwell	4
Hyarm Pearce	5	James Lockhart	2
Nancy Click	2	Elizabeth Barnes	5

Total addition of original book 246

John Phifor

D. G. Berchanon

Commissioners

Page 201

Commissioners Report 1847
Scholastic Report of the Commissioners of District No. 9, for 1847

James McDaniel	4	John Bonds	2
David Askew	2	Wm.Wright	8
Daniel Lightner	3	B.P.Simmons	4
Brit George	2	Mary Doolin	2
Drew A. Askew	4	Daniel McGage	1
Thomas Pafford	5	Jesse D. Hall	4
Nancy Comming	3	James Kernel	3
Charles Robbins	6	Wiley Shores	1
George McDaniel	2	Henry A.Barnes	4
Mary Redes	1	J.W.Bromagor	4
Nancy Green	2	John Legall	2
Wm.Odan	3	John Christopher	2
John Ralls	4	Lucinda Williams	3
Harrit Townsend	3	Moses McCerd	1
Dennies Stackdall	5	John Crook	1
Thomas Andrews	5	Lewis Hyer	1
John Whitekir	4	Wm.Akins	3
Willie Dockeys	3	Wm. H. Williams	1
William Mizell	2	Sarah Jackson	2
Wm. Stackdall	2	Robert Jackson	1
Henry Harnsee	3	Noah Wyatt	4
Henry Cooper	1	Mosley Daim	3

Page 202

Calvin Bamen	2	A.W.C. Matheny	5
B.Grass	6	Cathrin Beaton	6
Nathan Stayner	1	Mary Mette	2
James Stayner	3	Marthe Grayham	5
Barres Wynn	2	L.B. Allen	6
W.R. Wynn	2	Josha West	2
James Lindsey	5	Daniel Graham	6
William Lindsay	2	Mathis Mannon	2
Joseph Weathers	2	Eli Castell	4
Joseph Garner	4	Jas. F. Cooper	6
Wm.Wilson	2	Marcan Beaton	7
Semms Nicholas	6	Loftin Beaton	5
Thomas Bush	2	John W. Cooper	7
Robert Graham	3	Wm. Culpper	1
Johonah Hampton	5	Arthor Pitt	1
John Wyatt	2	Abran Clemment	5
Rice King	2	Henry Milton	1
Neil McNeil	5		

Total addition of original book   252

We certify the above to be correct

Davis H. Askew
John Wyatt
Wm.Akins

Page 202 Continued

State of Tennessee)   This day being the 6 day June, 1848.
Benton County   )   Amas Bruce Trustee formally of said County made
application to make settlement with me, Wm. P. Morris clerk of said County
Court agreeable to an act of the general assembly in such case made and to
be as follows showeing the Receipts and Disbursments of the common Schools
fund for the year of 1847. Amount recieved for the treasure for same year

1847.		$959.43
Deducted Trustee Commissions		9.59
		$947.84
Amount remaining for the year 1846		76.21
Expended to each District as follows';		$1026.05

Page 203

District	Voucher	Amount
1	No.1	$ 41.20
2	No.2	101.34
3	No.3	89.60
4	No.4	99.87½
5	No.5	148.20
6	No.6	123.65
7	No.7	90.68
8	No.8	81.17½
9	No.9	102.93
Total Amt. Voucher		$ 878.05

Total addition of original book
which learison the hands of the trustee the sum of $148.00
All of which is respectfully   Submitted
                    Wm. P. Morris Clk.

Scholastic Population for Benton County for 1848

District	Population	Amount
No. 1	166	$69.30½
2	213	88.92 3/4
4	223	93.10¼
Page 204		
5	379	158.23
6	296	123.58
7	202	84.33½
8	246	102.70½
9	252	105.21
	2171	$ 906.39

        Total Pop.
By order of the Board of Commissioners

                    A. Dibrell
                        Sec.

Page 204 Continued

Scholastic Report of District No. 1st 1848

John Gessett	6	Maron Barr	1
Heardeman Forehand	1	Wm.Wallace	1
William Pace	4	John Johnson	1
James Sherley	2	Meredith Johnson	1
Theracy Camp	4	William Whittingbon	4
Sarah Hally	1	Smith Walker	3
Jesse Dillon	4	A.J.Barnett	1
Edward Hally	6	Thomas McGill	1
Martha Malie	3	M.C.Barnett	4
Cynthia Harrison	1	Henry Parks	3Charl
Charles Oatsvall	3	Sonare Bright	5

Page 205

George Lewis	1	James Crabbs	2
William Malie	4	Squire Bishop	1
Eli W. Conley	6	John W. Mattock	1
Wilson Barr	4	William Henry	2
Pleanet Mullinix	4	Jane Henry	1
James Cox	2	Henry Atisson	2
Wms.Walker	2	Mansfield Massy	3
Jesse Hall	2	J.C. McDaine	1
John Hubbs	2	Michale Fry	5
Stark Hogg	1	Eligh Woods	8
Green Hatty	1	George Evans	2
James Smith	1	Hilliard Crabb	2
Henry Wesson	1	John Crabb	2
Willie B.Steer	1	William Hubbs	1
Martha Barnett	2	Samuel Bishop	3
James Hillis	3	James White	6
Elijah Walker	3	James Walker	6
Whitfield Pippitt	6	Charles Dunckan	3
Larkin Tippitt	1	Henry Woods	1
Garnett Massey	3	J.S. Peacock	1

Total addition of original book   163

John Gassett

Elijah Woods

Commissioners

Scholastic Report District No 2,1848

Jesse Bruce	3	Thomas Harrison	6
Jesse Newman	5	Francis Barbor	5
David Buckett	3	C.G. Haynes	1
Willis Bridges	6	Elizabeth McCrary	1
Young Adams	3	Martha Basford	1
Eli Hally	3	Margaret Basford	1
Thomas Osburn	3	Jot Davis	1
Randol Jordan	1	Ridden Holland	7

Page 206

John Summers	2	Richard Nordon	5
Guilford Sardins	3	Wiley Ellis	4
Amas Bruce	1	James Evans	4
Henry Gassett	5	Dolly Kirk	3
John Robinsoh	3	Green Flowers	5
James M. Camp	5	T.Crutchfield	1
Wyatt Jenkins	5	Thomas King	5
Siky Morick	5	Theophilas Kirk	3
Amas Gaskin	3	Wesly Crabb	1
George Reeves	2	Elizabeth Austin	3
James S. Harper	3	Daniel Reedor	1
Hillard Crabb	4	John Atchison	1
John Dillion	3	Isaac Smith	5
J.R. Mathews	3	William Smith	3
Wm.Steward	3	James Taylor	3
J.A.Jordon	3	Nathan Williams	1
Margarete Jordon	3	James Morick	5
C.Nawells	6	Sarah Boygett	4
Hillsman King	5	Thomas Curtis	6
John Prince	5	James Hogg	4
Samuel Oxford	6	Alford Harris	7

Total addition of original book 202

We the undersigned Commissioners do certify that the above is a true list
of the Scholastic Population of Dis. No. 2,Benton County.
Sept. 19th,1848

J.A.Jordon
John Atchison
J.M.Basford
Commissioners

Scholastic Report District No. 3,1844

Asa Sevendler	3	Asacc Anderson	3
John Anderson	3	Wm.Douglass	1
Jefferson Hicks	5	Mahely Smith	2
William Cole	5	George Thomason	4
J.B. Cox	6	E.W. Adams	1
D.W.Barnes	4	Warren Sayles	2
Wm. Barnes	6	Mary Comas	4
R.H. Hawthorn	5	Burk Utty	5
Seth Uttey	5	Maude Hally	5

Page 207

Kinchion Nunry	4	Isacc Davidson	1
E.A. Reevs	3	Wm. H. Camp	5
M.G.Ford	4	John Smith	2

Page 207 Continued

James Nunery	1	James Luter	4
Cathance How	3	James Hillis	2
Eragald How	2	Anderson Lynch	2
Holloway Kee Sr.	1	Malachiah Harrison	4
Henry Barnes	5	Cullen Cooper	5
Wm. H. Tyner	1	E.P. Ballowe	5
Mary Brewer	4	Elisha Tedder	2
Samuel B. Robertson	3	Isaac Hollingworth	1
Nathaniel Nunnery	4	Joe S. Hatty	1
Nathan Sevendle	1	Jos. Tedder	2
Wm. E. Sevendle	5	Nancy Callon	4
Alford Lewis	3	Elender Smith	5
Charlie Kee	1	Samuel Davidson	3
Alford Bunn	5	James Wyly	4
Thomas Mathewshead	5	Obediah Harden	5
John Harden	1	Wm. Marchbucks	2
Thomas Swendle	4	Meredith Edward	1
Allen Duke	5		

Total addition of original book 194

We certify that the within is a true report of the Scholastic Population
of the 3 rd District for the year 1848

> N.Nunry
> Plea Mullinik
> Z. B. Haw
>   Commissioners

Scholastic Report District No. 4 1848
A List of the Scholastic Population of the 4 District of the County
of Benton for the year 1848.

W.C. Cole	2	S.B. Pearce	1
John F. Johnston	2	F.W. Pearce	5
Laton Pearce	7	J.T. Holland	3
Edward Palmer	5	Bennett Hallard	4
James Palmer	3	L. Cracker	2
Anna Palmer	4	Jonatha Jordon	5
Thomas Cole	4	Rubin Bridges	3

Page 208

Henry Jordan	1	Wm. Kilbriatt	3
Thomas Veach	1	Henry Abbatt	5
John McAuley	3	Thomas Walker	3
John Cole	7	Mathew Williams	2
Julions J. Cole	8	Allen Barker	1
Thoma Harrison	1	Z. Barker	3
Charlie Moore	2	B.C. Morgan	2
Steaph Garritt	3	L.B. Pearce	3
Nancy Walker	1	T.H. Lyron	4

Page 208 Continued

John Garrett	5	Edwin Cowell	2
James Tate	1	Hilory Lewis	1
Lewis Roswell	5	Starlie Adams	1
J.W. Davidson	5	Jashon House	3
Mary Townsend	1	W. Shelly	1
Rubin Mitchel	5	Martha Jordan	3
M. Thomason	3	Wm. Winn	1
James Cowell	1	N. I. Williams	3
Soloman Dill	4	A.B. Aden	2
Allen Townsend	4	John Sanders	6
Joesailla Townsend	4	John Neighbors	4
Ervin Earp	6	Berry Hinant	5
N. Shunt	7	Green Adams	5
R. Marchbuks	6	Giles Marchburks	5
L. N. Pope	2	Josioh Forrester	3
James Allen	1	Mary Dennis	5
Abram Sanders	2	Gillion Smith	1

Total addition of original book 235

J/ F. Johnston
L. B. Pearce
Josiah Ford
Commissioners

Page 209

Scholastic Population District 5,1848
A list of children in the 5 District of Benton County.

C. K. Wyly	1	Widow Beriers	5
A. Lashlee	6	Charles Williams	5
Wm. P. Morris	2	A. Uttey	4
W. F. Previte	1	E.W. Hudson	3
A.S. Cole	2	Berry Williams	5
Bike Lightfort	1	L.D. Comes	3
H. C. Camp	2	H. Loevther	1
H. M. Brown	3	W.C. Privette	1
James Jordan	3	Widow Martin	2
D.F. McElyrd	2	M. Neely	1
J.B. Carnes	2	James Pressor	1
J. Wisman	5	J. F. Pressor	1
J. P. Lowory	3	Thomas Jones	3
N. Strickland	4	Wm. Walker	5
J. L. Duvall	4	J. T. Flarnce	5
John Hudson	6	Wm. Corbitt	6
J.C. Wright	5	D. P. Hudson	2
W. C. Thompson	3	Wm. A. Hudson	5
L. Thompson	3	M. Biggs	3
P. Thompson	4	C. Clerry	6

Page 209 Continued

W. F. Dogherty	3	S. Bruce	5
Daniel Holland	5	H. Conles	2
W. R. Aden	2	P. Lashell	1
Rushing	2	R. Beasly	4
J. Rushing	3	A. Higgin	2
A. Ballard	4	W. Farrow	7
Ira Love	1	J. M. Williams	4
B. Stafford	1	J. R. Thomas	2
R. Rushing Jr.	3	E. Arnald	7
H. Hansel	3	Jr. Sorrett	3
D. Morris	3	Willie Arnold	1
J. Henderson	1	J. P. Arnald	3
R. Alston	5	J. Arnald	3
J. Staffard	1	D. Cuff	8
I. Staffard	2	Z. Collins	6
D. Rushing	3	S. Madden	6
J. C. Latimer	2	J. Russell	1
E. Perkins	4	Widow England	4
B. Whitley	2	E.F. Wills	5
A. Smally	5	Wm. Syks	6
J. Rushing	5	E. L. Wills	1
W. Rushing	2	Wm. Hounes	2
J. Bell	4	A. S. Holt	4
S. M. Corbitt	5	J. M. Petty	4
F. Coraway	2	J. Thornton	3
Z. Sullins	1	S. Boswell	3
W. Sullins	3	F. Maherry	6
Hamilton	6	B. Lashlee	3
H. Derden	4	I. Akins	3
Wm. Sorrett	2	D. L. Settle	4
W. Browning	3	R. Honues	1
J. Davis	2	R. N. Word	2

Page 210

H. Johnson	3	T. Forrow	5
J/ L. Morgan	5	Widdow Forrow	4
J. Frederick	1	F. Arnald	5
J. Cole	3	W. Cole	1
W. T. Coraett	1	C. Milton	2
W. P. Lashlee	1	Squire George	1
W. Arnold	1	J. McKelvy	1
J. Milton	5		

Total addition of original book 386

We the Commissioners of the 5th Civil District of Benton County do certify
that this is a true copy of the Scholastic Population in said District.
This July 3, 1848.

Daniel L. Settles
Thomas Jones   (Commissioners)
A. Higgin

Page 210 Continued

Scholastic Population Dis. No. 6,1848
Scholastic Population of the 6 District for year 1848

Levne Cattingham	5	Mathew Pressor	5
James Cattingham	1	A. L. Wisamon	1
Thomas Craig	5	Samuel Wisman	2
Wm. H. Rushing	3	Narcisa McCannall	3
Nancy Braun	1	Milton Woseman	2
Griffin Holtsbrook	6	James Wiseman	4
Wm. Bard	5	Eleanor Wiseman	1

Page 211

Eli Craig	3	M. S. Caps	5
Alvin Taylor	1	John Pressor	10
Herams Davidson	5	James M. Wisman	1
A. J. Peoples	3	James Wisman Sr.	1
Nancy Cathey	3	Wm. Armor	1
Trooy Beeler	1	David Watson	5
Albrarg Harris	3	Elizabeth Rushing	4
Lewis Cross	5	John P. Green	5
John Duglass	6	Robert Word	6
E. W. Lynch	7	Samuel Pressor	4
John Elmore	6	Wm. Green	7
J. J. Royers	1	John Watson	5
B. Redden	3	Ben Green	4
Charles Bethany	2	Thomas Pressor	6
J. D. Baker	1	Mary Ann Betha	1
James Pressor	7	Rebecca McGill	2
A. D. Crossno	1	Joseph Green	1
John D. Rushing	5	A. D. Rushing	5
Patience Holmes	5	J. J. Borns	1
W. D. Markham	2	W. C. Anderson	2
R. S. Nance	1	E. Bush	2

Page 212

R. S. Ward	3	George Green	2
Jas. A. Breen	2	Thos. Word	6
Jas. R. Nance	8	Robert Spires	1
Mary Barrer	4	Wm. Word	6
James McGill	4	J. C. Crews	4
W. B. Eddington	4	Wm. Crews	3
G. W. Rushing	1	John Estes	1
F. M. Rushing	1	James Black	4
H. Green	6	John Tice	7
Mary Spares	4	Elizabeth Ward	5
O. Armor	3	Mary Watson	1
Melton Smith	3		

Total addition of original book 319
We the Commissioners of the 6th District do certify that the foregoing list
of the Scholastors wittence 21 & 6 years old is a truth to the best of our
knowe ye this Aug. 2,1848.

John N. Williams J/ J/ Rogers
J. D. Rushing (Commissioners)

Page 212 Continued

Scholastic Population Dis. No. 7,1848

B. Vester	6	J. J. Farmer	2
J.W. Melton	9	Calvin Parker	6
Sion Melton	2	W.C. Cole	3
Coonnod Melton	2	Martha Crutchfield	2
J. H. Bristo	2	David Pafford	1
J. M. Melton	4	James Tippen	1
Abram Ballowe	5	Jackson Farmer	1

Page 213

B. Givens	3	Wm. Berry	8
J.W. Hill	3	John T. Benton	5
Karnel Nobles	2	Alford Farrow	1
John Phifer	3	Terry Neston	1
David W. Benton	2	Jane Farmer	6
A. Davidson	5	Calvin Hall	1
Sopha Bell	4	Obediah Bullack	3
Age Hall	1	John Stanley	1
W. I. Baley	4	C. I. Wheatley	7
E.W. Warmur	3	Mary Hallamon	1
W. W. Hallard	4	George Phife	4
E. Melton	2	Henry Cheery	1
Elizabeth Parker	4	Catharine Parker	2
America Vicks	1	Jacob Capp	4
Sasanoh Hill	5	John Garmor	1
Wm. Benton	2	Storleig Brewan	3
James Poffard	1	Martha Middleton	2
E.G. Hatchell	1	Susan Halland	2

Scholastic Population Dis. No. 7,1848

Joah Terv

Total   1 / 169

Wm.Berry
E. Melton
James Gorner
    Commissioners

Scholastic Population Dis No. 8,1848

Nicholas Brennon Jr.	3	J.F. L. Melton	1
John McGlohn	5	Ribecca McBride	6
Lewis Hallard	5	Hyram Pearce	5
Samuel Brennon	4	Robert Bordswell	4

Page 214

Wm. Hillard	6	Nancy Click	5
Hugh A. L. Sop	7	Louiza Click	1
John Laeverg	2	Finly Caler	4
Lewis Brennan	2	Zickinoh Childris	1

Page 214

John Price	3	James Lockhart	2
Wm. R. Pierce	1	Elizabeth Banns	5
Wm. McKinzie	1	Wm. Wammack	2
Nancy Brewn	4	Robert James	3
Nancy McKinzie	2	Lidid James	2
A. McRae	5	J. S. Allen	3
Henry Milton	1	D. Brown	1
Mary Melton	1	M. Cherry	2
Alford Brewan	4	Wm. Yarbrough	1
C. R. Riddick	2	James McNeil	5
Wilson Makers	3	B. Morton	1
L.W. Brewan	4	T. G. Smally	1
G. G. Buchanan	2	Joshoa Hill	1
James Alsup	1	Robert Rushing	2
Henry Roberson	7	Tudd Coal	2
Calvin Myers	1	Charlotte Yates	7
J. G. Taylor	3	John Bird	1
Wm. Cole	1	J. R. Childers	2
Buervill Bell	5	Sarah Rushing	1
Neil McNeil	4	John Taylor	2
Elijh Alsup	5	Kennith Reddner	6
John Raysdall	4	Mary Wilson	1
D. N. Shilley	1	Wm. James	5
Elbert Wright	5	Thomas Bush	2
S. W. Bynn	6	M. Milton	4
B. Herron	3	Wm. Herndon	3
Abenmalic Hinnon	4	James Taylor	3
John Smally	1	A. Wilson	1
James Greer	5	John Carter	1
Elinor Armor	4	Cornell Pafford	1
Joseph Greer	1	Wm. Watts	6
J. W. Uttey	1	Anicholas	2
John McGill	3	Elias Phifer	3
Jarrett Taylor	5	James Pickler	5
Mary Wilson	1	James Pickles	5
A. Paghell	4	Thomas Highlon	2
E. Phifor	1	George Moore	7
James Vester	1		

Total Addition of original book 280

Scholastic Population Dis. No. 9,1848

John Berchardn	3	Thomas Wymns	1
Henry Borrus	5	James Renal	5
John W. Bramager	4	Thomas Holcomas	1
John Banes	4	Samual Cole	1
Anderson Powell	5	B. Wynns	2
Charles Rolins	6	Iasioh Semomius	2
John Rolls	4	B. C. Mathis	1
John Odom	7	Lemica Hall	2
Wm. Odom	3	Thomas Andrews	5

Page 215

John Whitaker	5	Wm. Wright	7
Nancy Commeings	3	Wm. Stockdale	3
Thomas Poffard	2	Henry Hansel	3
Mary Dooling	2	B. T. Simmons	4
Wiley Piekins	3	David A. Askew	4
Demis Stockdale	4	Wm. Mizell	3
Daniel Lightner	4	George McDaniel	3
Moses McCloen	1	Mary Roads	1
Bretta George	3	James Rolls	1
John Christopher	2	Wiley Lamkford	2
Lucy Williams	3	R. Robertson	1
Wyly Davis	3	Edward Lindsey	6
Harritt Townsend	3	R.M. Graham	4
G. B. Rolls	1	Wm. Nash	3
David A. Askew	2	Rice King	6
James McDaniel	4	L. Beaton	5
A. Pitt	1	A. W. C. Matheny	6
J. W. Cooper	7	George Stayner	2
J. F. Cooper	8	R. Gross	7
E. Castell	5	S. Nichol	7
M. Beaton	7	W. S. Hasmon	3
C. Beaton	2	R. T. Rushing	1
L. B. Allen	6	W. F. Daniel	2

Total addition of original book   275

M. Mammon	3
D. Graham	6
John Wyatt	1
N. McKenzie	2
Mary Melton	2

Page 216

John West	1
Roovrall	5
Wm. Culpepper	1
Sarah Jackson	2
L. Hyon	1
Wm. Akins	3
R. Jackson	2
Noah Wyatt	5
B. Wynn	2
W. R. Wynn	2
Jones Lindsey	5
Wm. Lindsey	2
Joseph Weathley	2
James Staymor	

We the undersigned certify the foregoing to be a true correct list of the Scholastic Population of Dis. No. 9 for year 1848

D. Graham   (Commissioners)
W. M. Akins
W. G. McDaniel

Page 217

Scholastic Population
Apportionment to Benton County for year 1849

District	Scholastacs'	Amount
No 1	163	$ 66.40
2	202	82.31
3	194	79.05
4	235	95.76
5	386	157.29
6	319	129.99
7	169	68.86
8	280	114.10
9	275	112.06
	2223	$ 905.87

W. C. Dibrell Secr. of the Board of Commissioners

State of Tennessee)   This day before the 11 th of May 1849
Benton County   )
Merritt Melton Trustee of said county made application to make settlement
with me, Wm. P. Morris clerk of the County Court agreeable to an act of the
general assembly in such case, made and provided touching the receipts and
disbursments of the Common School funds for the year 1848 which said settlement I find to be as follows. I find in the hands of said Trustee as received from Amas Bruce $ 148.00
Apportionment for   1848   906.39
                                                $ 1054 39
Trustee Commission   10.54
Balance to be distributed $ 1043.85

Expended as follows

District	Vouchers	Amount
1	No 1	$ 84.71
2	No 2	88.83
3	No 3	55.82
4	No 4	84.60
5	No 5	185.98
6	No 6	121.80
7	No 7	58.00
8	No 8	105.00
9	No 9	103.28
		$881.02

Total Amt. Expended
Which leans in the hands of the said Trustee, the sum of $155.83
All of which is Respectfully Submitted
                        Wm. P. Morris Clk.
Acendemy funds for 1849 $230.76

Scholastic Population Dis. No. 1, 1849

Alison Henry	1	Hatty Edward	6
Ausburn Corne	2	Henry William	1
Barnett, A. J.	1	Hatty	1
Barnett, M. C.	4	James Jones	4
Bishop Squire	1	Jordan Jackson	3
Bishop R.	4	Johnson John	1
Britt, Samuel	5	Johnson, Meredith	1
Baley Meshack	2	Jornld Calvin	1
Barr Wm.	2	Lewis George	1
Barr, F. M.	4	Lewis, Calvin	1
Crobb Hillory	3	Malin William	4
Crobb John	1	Mullinicks Pleasent	5
Cox James	1	McClevain Henry	1
Conley, Eli W.	7	McGea, Thomas	1
Camp, Thursday	3	McGill, Thomas	1
Dillion, Jess	4	McGill, John	3
Duncan, Charles	3	McDaniel J. C.	1
Ivy, Micheal	5	Massy Jarrad	4
Gassett, John	5	Massy Mansfield	4
Gassett, Abram	2	Malie Martha	4
Grogan, William	4	Michie Carr	1
Harrison, James	1	Patsvall Charles	1
Hubbs, Williams	1	Peacock, J. S.	2
Hubbs, John	2	Panks, James	2
Hubbs, Elijah	1	Pace William	6

Page 219

Pratt, Richard	6	Stiers Allen	1
Sherly, James	3	Smith James	1
Tippett, Larkin	1	Teppett, Ezichie	1
Teppett, Whitfield	6	Wood, Thomas	2
Wood, Thomas	2	Wals, Mary	1
Wesson, Hubbard	1	Walker, James	7
Walker, Eliza	3	White, James	5
Wood, Henry	2	Woods, Elijah	7
Whittington	3		

Total addition of original Bk. 179

M. C. Barnett (Clerk)

Scholastic Population Dis. No. 2, 1849

A list of Scholastic Population of Dis. No 2 of Benton County
July 1 th, 1849

Jrand Pritchell	6	Morring Austin	1
Mary Rogers	3	Redden Hallaway	7
Thomas Homisde	6	Jop Davis	1
C. G. Haynes	1	Daniel Readers	1

Page 220

J. P. Laurance	1	T. T. Crutchfield	1
L. B. Laurance	3	Robert Dates	4
Tom Woods	1	John Atchison	2
J. S. Harper	2	A. C. Harris	6
Amas Bones	1	William Crobb	1
Jesse Bruce	4	James Morrick	5
Amas Gustin	3	Cullen Nowell	6
Gilford Sanders	2	John Smith	1
Wyatt, Jenkins	6	J. B. Smith	6
John Sanders	2	James Taylor	3
Thomas Osborn	3	William Smith	3
Eli Hatty	2	Sarah Baygett	4
D. M. Burkett	4	Nathan Williams	3
Elizabeth Richison	2	Samuel Oxford	5
Hilliard Crobb	7	James Hogg	5
Masis McCrary	5	Thomas Cortis	5
Jesse Newsum	5	Dolly Kirk	2
George Reeves	2	Peter Selph	1
James M. Camp	6	John Prince	5
Hyram Smith	4	Wissner Kirk	1
A. J. Nowell	1	Sealy Merrick	5
Wm. Stewart	3	Frances Bohen	5
Edward Jordan	4	John Robertson	4
Dance Waygoner	1	Rebecca McDarlin	1
Willis Bridges	5	R. M. Hordan	1

Total addition of original book 227

We the commissioners certify that the within a true list of the Scholastic
Population of the District No 2 for the year 1849

John Pasford
John Atchison
John Prince

The Scholastic Population of the 3 District of Benton County taken July
1st 1849

John Dillion	4	Jefferson Hicks	6
Malchaa Harrison	4	Nancy Lewis	4
Anderson Lynch	3	Dreuburg White	6
Cullen Looper	6	James Wyley	2
Joe Tedder	2	Ennzala Howe	3
Wm. H. Camp	5	Cath. Annie Howe	3
E. P. Ballowe	5	Nathan Sevendle	1
Nancy Dalton	4	J. Sarah Bright	1

Page 221

James Sherly	2	Alford Bunn	5
Elender Smith	3	E. W. Sayes	2

Page 221 Continued

Elisha Tedder	3	Wm. Marchanks	2
Mary Combs	4	S. H. Davidson	1
Isaac Davidson	1	Wm. Walker	5
G. W. Adams	2	Obediah Hardan	6
E. G. Reeves	3	Burnie Utley	5
B. Hinnant	7	Mark Hatty	5
Isaac Anderson	4	John Harden	2
Wm. Cole	5	John T. Ford	1
George Thomason	5	M. G. Ford	4
L. D. Combs	3	Sarah Hicks	3
Thomas Mathishead	6	I. J. Tuttle	1
N. Nunery	4	Thomas Robertson	3
Asa Swindle	3	Lewis Roswell	4
Thomas Swindle	5	Wm. Barnes	6
Henry Barnes	4	D. W.Babnes	4
Wm. H. Tyner	2	J. B. Cox	6
Kincher Nunry	4	Seth Utley	5
Mary Bruven	3	Taylor	2
W. C. Anderson	2	Wm. Sevendle	5
John Anderson	2	Charles Kee	1

Total addition of original book 216

Z. B. Howe
Nathe Nunry
P. Mulleniks
Commissioners

Page 222

Scholastic Population of District No. 4.
Scholastict Report from Dis. No. 4,1849

L. B. Pearce	3	Ben Hallard	2
B. Mitchel	5	M.Williams	1
M. Thomason	4	N. Short	6
S. B. Pearce	3	A. B. Adens	2
F. W. Pearce	4	Irvan Earp	5
John T. Halland	4	John Sanders	6
Bennett Hollard	4	John Sanders	5
			97
L. Crack	2		
J. Jordon	6	Mary Veach	4
R. Bridges	3	Letiled Davis	4
Allen Barker	1	H. Abbatt	5
Z. Barker	3	W. Kilbreatt	3
H. Lewis	1	T. Walker	4
Starkey Adams	2	H. R. Forrest	3
Josuha Home	2	Wm. McAuley	3
Martha Jordon	3	Jas. Allen Sr.	1
Jos. Cowell	1	B. J. Allen	2
R. H. Hawthorn	5	Jno. Neighbors	5

Page 222

Joseph Cowell Jr.	1	R. Marchbarks	4
Edward Cowell	3	Mary Townsend	1
Wm. Lathen	4	Mary Barker	1
Henry Jordon	2	G. Smith	3
Nancy Kathey	2	Jas Forrest	7
B. C. Morgan	2	N. R. Williams	3
E. W. Lynch	7	David Pickler	1
L. H. Pope	1	S. Crockett	1
J. W. Sanders	1	I. A. Baker	1
J. F. Johnston	2	Laytor Pearce	7
John McAuey	3	W. H. Cole	3
Thos. Cole	4	John Cole	6

Page 223

J. J. Cole	8	T. R. Veach	1
Thomas Harrison	1	Thomas Horton	4
Stephe Garrett	3	Nancy Walker	3
C. H. Bethany	1	B. Eason	6

Total addition of original book   223

L. B. Pearce
John F. Johnston
Josiah Forrest
Commissioners

Scholastic Population Dis. No 5

A list of the Scholastic Population of the 5 Civil District for the year 1849

J. T. Flarnce	5	Willis Rushing	2
Wm. Corbitt	6	Jane Bell	4
Andy Hudson	5	S. W. Corbett	5
E. W. L. Hudson	6	Frances Caraway	2
E. Honey	6	F. Mabury	

Page 224

Spartin Bruce	5	Rubin Beasley	4
A. G. Camps	2	Peter Evans	5
Richard Rushing	2	Wm. Mitchel	6
Jess Rasberry	3	H. Harris	5
A. Ballard	4	A. Haggie	2
Martha Love	1	John Pafford	7
R. Rushing	2	Wm. Pafford	10
Harty Hansel	3	J. C. Wright	5
David Morris	3	John Hudson	6
A. J. Hudson	1	J. T. Pressor	5
Rebecca Alston	5	Henry Stegall	4
John Stafford	2	W. A. Steel	1
Dennis Rushing	1	Edward Cowell	4
J. C. Latirmor	2	Wm. Bustle	1

Page 224

E. Pirkins	4	Noah Strickland	4
B. W. Whitley	2	Berry Williams	4
A. Surley	5	Charles Williams	4
John Rasberry	5	Mathews Williams	2
B. C. Morgan	2	C. K. Wyly	1
Thos. Farrow	3	J. W. Davidson	5
Dance Hollard	5	A. Lashlee	5
J. L. Duvall	7	J. Thornton	2
Thos. James	4	H. W. Luther	2
Perry Thomson	5	W. Farrow	7
Lena Thompson	3	R. N. Wood	2
Wm. C. Thompson	3	Wm. Serratt	2
Elender Bevins	4	E. Browning	3
Mrs. Hooper	3	J. Arnold	4
Abee Utty	4	D. Coff	7
Joseph Wiseman	7	E. Farrow	4
W. C. Prewitt	2	S. England	4
H. M. Brown	4	J. Akins	3
James Gordon	4	A. Corbitt	2
A. S. Cole	3	P. S. Lashlee	2
H. C. Camp	3	J. Milton	4
John M. Murty	1	Wood	1
S. C. Patte	2	Joseph Sarrett	3
J. T. Lowery	2	W. Arrow	1
C. A. Crawley	5	J. Feddinick	2
J. B. Carnes	2	W. Syks	4
M. B. Biggs	3	W. Holmes	1
J. G. Sims	1	W. HOllard	7
Wm. P. Morris	3	J. Davis	2
D. F. McElyrd	2	J. McCreevis	1
S. Boswell	3	W. Cole	1
J. Cole	3	J. R. Thomas	2
S. Madden	6	J. Williams	4
E. Arnold	7	H. Johnson	2

Page 225

J. P. Arnold	2	C. Melton	2
A. P. Hall	4	Z. Wilkeis	1
H. Durdenn	4	D. L. Settle	4
D. L. Settle	4	Z. Collins	6
Esquire George	1	H. Hollingsworth	1
F. R. Reeves	1		
	402		

Total addition od original book

Thomas James
A. Higgis
D. L. Settle
  Commissioners

Page 225 Continued

Scholastic Population Dis No. 6,1849
The following is a list of the Scholastic Population for Dis. No. 6 for
the year 1849

Thomas Bush	2	Joseph Bane	1
Elender Bush	2	Joseph Greer	1
James Bush	1	James McGill	5
Jas. K. Nance	6	Peter G. Herron	1

Page 226

Thomas Ward	7	Wm. Ward	6
James Webb	3	H. Green	6
Cornee Green	2	David Warmick	6
James Black	4	W. D. Marcom	3
Enock Holden	6	Jon T. Pressor	6
John Tice	7	Patience Helms	5
Elizabeth Ward	6	J. S. Hill	1
Jno. D. Rushing	5	J. A. Collins	1
Geo. W. Rushing	2	Thomas Pressor	6
Sarah Spires	3	David Watson	6
John Spires	1	Theo. Pressor	2
J. P. Dorris	1	Elizabeth Rushing	4
F. M. Rushing	1	Jos. Watson	2
R. S. Word	3	Mrs. McGill	2
Wiley B. Ellington	4	James Crossno	4
George Green	4	A. D. Crossno	1
Jas. H. Green	1	Martha McGill	5
Mary Bane	4	John T. Green	7
Asa D. Rushing	4	Robert Ward	6
Mrs. Burton	1	Berry Harris	2
A. C. Presson	5	Jas. Cattinghan	1
J. J. Rushing	4	Mathews Presson	6
Ben Green	4	Griffin Holesbrook	5
Jno. Watson	4	Freeman Presson	6
Sam Presson	4	Eli Craig	4
Wm. Green	8	J. J. Rayes	2

Page 227

M. S. Copps	4	Mrs. M. C. Carroll	3
J. H. Williams	5	J. Ronton	1
S. Wiseman	1	John Presson	8
Jane Wiseman	4	James Presson	7
Milton Wiseman	4	Elender Wiseman	1
John Elmore	5	B. Rodden	4
Provy Beeler	1	Lewis Cross	5
Lewis Cross	5	John Duglass	5
Hyman Davison	4	Wm. Douglass	2
Alvin Taylor	2	Wm. Bell Bell	2
Wm. Bond	4	Levin Cottinghan	5
W. Rushing	4	Thomas Craig	2

Total addition of original book 307

Scholastic Population Dis. No. 7 - 1849
Scholastic Report Dis. No. 7, 1849

John P. Benton	6	C. Ronnly	1
J. H. Bristo	2	Nancy Wheatley	1
Perry Milton	3	H. Nobles	2
Jas. J. Farmer	2	John Phefer	3
James Pippen	1	Wm. Herndon	3
Jackson Farmer	1	A. Davidson	5
Garner Hatchell	2	S. Hallard	2
David Pafford	1	Age Hall	2
J. W. Melton	1	A. Vicks	2
Calvin Parker	6	C. Parker	5
Wm. Berry	8	W. J. H. Cooley	3
Sopha Bell	3	G. W. Farmer	3
Jacob Tery	1	W. W. Hallard	5
Jackson Farmer Jr.	1	E. Milton	3
Berry Vester	4	D. W. Benton	3
David Vester	1	Mary Benton	2
J. W. Milton	8	Wm. Hamblton	6
Sara Milton	3	Thomas Neely	1
J. C. Melton	2	James M. Halloman	1
John Myers	4	James Parmer	6
A. Ballowe	6	C. J. Wheatley	7
Jchabod Farmer	1	J. S. Cherry	2
J. W. Hill	3	George Phefor	4
Susan Hill	3	James Wilson	2
Susanah Holland	2	Wilson Mathing	3
Joseph Pickler	5	Wm. H. Williams	1
Mary Hollomans	5	W. A. Wheatly	1
M. C. Cole	3	Jacob Capp	4

Page 228

James Reddicks	2	Wm. W. Wheatley	5
Wm. W. Wheatley	5	O. Bullock	4
Calvin Hall	2	R. J. Cole	3
Wm. D. Hyer	1	John Garner	1
A. Wilson	1	S. Brewer	3
H. B. Snider	1	Martha Meddleton	11

Total addition of original book   194

Wm. Berry
E. Melton
James Green
Commissioners

Page 229

John Smally	1	Elias Phefor	4
J. Green	5	Hyram Brooks	1
A. Armor	3	William Taylor	1
Joseph Green	2	E. Phifor	2
John W. Uttey	2	Thomas Higdon	2
John Duddey	1	John Herndon	1
Joseph Baker	2	Lauson Nicholas	2
R. Rushing	2	James Alsup	1

Page 230

M. McGee	5	T. Borfoat	1
Jude Cole	1	J. R. Childers	2
R. H. Parkerson	1	James T. Smally	1
Carroll Pafford	1	John Carter	1
John Carter	1	Wm. Wates	6
Wm. James	5	Andrews Bethel	4
Harrett Taylor	5	Kenneth Reddick	5
Mary Wilson	2	James Taylor	3
George Moore	7	Merritt Melton	4
H. Cook	1	R. Bosh	1

Total addition of original book 261

John G. Allen
Elias Phifor
Nicholas Brewen
Commissioners

Commissioners Report Dis No. 9,1849

Sarah Jackson	3	John W. Cooper	7
Wm Akins	5	Loflin Beaton	5
R. Jackson	3	L. B. Allen	6
Noah Wyatt	5	Wm. Nash	2
B. Wynn	3	R. Delmore	5
Wm. R. Wynn	3	Joseph Culpepper	3
James Lindsey	4	D. Graham	4
Wm. Lindsey	3	Henry Melton	1
Wm. S. Morsnnon	4	Artha Pitt	2
J. J.Wheatley	1	E. Leindesy	7

Page 230

Wm. B. Allen	1	John West	1
R. T. Rushing	2	Wm. Culpepper	1
James Stayner	3	R. C. Mathews	2
A. W. C. Mathey	6	H. A. Barnes	5
John J.Cole	4	J. W. Cooper	1
B. Gross	6	J. W. Bromagor	4
S. Nicholas	7	Allen Powell	5

145

Page 230 Continued

Lewis Hyer	1	John B. Bones	3
Hohn Lindsey	1	Louisa Hall	1
R. S. Nance	1	John Buchannon	1
M. Hammon	4	Dalam Culpepper	4
J. F. Cooper	9	Wm. Odom	3
Mary Castell	6	Nancy Cummins	4
Catharen Beaton	2	Samuel Slanter	1
Malcom Beaton	7	Charles Robins	5
Danil McGuaig	1	Danie Lightnor	5
Stephen Halcom	1	Wifey Davis	3
Thos. Andrews	6	Nancy Gerrnan	3
Wm. Mizell	3	Thomas Wynn	2
Denis Stockdale	3	Joseph Huggins	1
Ben Wynn	1	E. M. McDaniel	1
R. P. Simmonas	4	John Rolls	4
Jones McDaniel	4	James Cornel	4
B. F. Akens	1	Henry Habsel	3
Wm. Wright	7	James Dennom	4

Page 231

James McNeil	6	Daniel A. Askew	3
J. T. R. Legate	1	John Christepher	2
John Hudgen	4	Thomas Pafford	3
Mary Dooty	2	Briton George	3
Nancy Whitaker	5	Harritt Townsend	2
P. H. Copland	9		

Total addition of original book   294

We the commissioners hearby certify that the foregoing returns is correct

                    Daniel Grayham
                    Wm. Akers
                    G. W. McDaniel

State of Tennessee)   This day being the 17th of June 1850 ,Merrit
Benton County   )   Melton Trustee of said County appeard for the
 purpose of making settlement with me showing the receipts and disbursments
 of the common Schools funds for the year 1849 which said settlement I
 find in the hands of the said Merrit Melton Trustee from former settlement
                              $155.83
Amount received from State for 1849   905.87
                              $1061.70
Trustee Commission off of the 905.87   9.05
Net Total $1052.65

Page 232

Expended as follows

Dis.	Vouchers	Amount
1	1	$68.51

Page 232 Continued

Dis	Vouchers	Amount
2	2	83.09
3	3	103.05
4	4	107.36
5	5	165.05
6	6	104.80
7	7	76.20
8	8	117.72
Total Amount of Voucher		$ 930.48
		122.17

Which leaves in hand of trustee all of which is submitted Wm. P. Morrice Clk.

Scholastic Population Dis. No. 1st 1850

John S. Hubb	2	R. Odle	1
Wm. M. Malin	5	H. Woods	2
Wesly Hatty	2	Wm. Grogan	3
Sarah Hatty	1	R. P. Vatt	5
Stanford Hatty	1	M. Baley	4
Charles Oatsvall	1	W. Barr	2
Alford Lewis	1	G. M. Evans	4
M. A. Malice	4	James Walker	8

Page 233

Calvin Lewis	1	James White	6
W. W. Ausbum	2	Ann E. Walker	3
E. W. Conley	6	Shemwood	1
Henry McElgain	1	John Bell	2
Jesse Dillion	5	Mary Fullerton	1
S. Bright	4	J. Cox	2
Robert Doherty	1	Wm. Hubb	2
Thursy Camp	4	Presly Thornton	6
P. Mullerinks	6	Hillory Crobb	3
James Sotherland	1	M. Fry	7
James Sherly	3	J. C. McDaniel	1
Garrett Massy	4	W. Matlock	1
Jesse Hall	5	Thos. McGill	2
W. Tippett	'7	Wm. McGee	1
C. Duncan	3	S. Bishop	1
A. B. Stien	1	R. Bishop	3
L. Tippett	1	H. H. Mitchel	1

Appropention of School proved to Benton County for the year 1850

District	Population	Amount
1	179	$72.94
2	227	92.50
3	216	88.02
4	223	90.87

Page 234

5	402	163.81
6	307	125.10
7	194	79.05
8	261	106.33
9	294	119.80
	2303	$938.47

Nashville13,July 1850

A.Bibrell Trs.

T. Henry	1	M. Massey	3
M. Barnett	3	McBarnett	3
T. Johnson	1	E. Woods	6
Henry Parks	3	E. Hubbs	1

Total addition of original book   170

We certify that the within is a true statement of the Scholastic Population
of the 1st Civil District.

E. Woods
W. Tippett
W. M. Malin
Commissioners

Page 235
Scholastic Population Dis. No. 2,1850

T. A. Jordan	4	J. S. Harper	3
Edward Jordan	4	George Reeves	2
Joseph Laurance	2	D. M. Bunkett	4
Thos, B. Larance	3	Thos Osburn	2
Thos, Harrison	4	John Bill	2
Frances Baker	6	Yancy Bohanon	1
J. R. Mathews	4	Eli Hatty	3
J. M. Camp	6	J. E. Morick	1
John Prince	6	Celia Morick	5
Sarah Beggett	4	Gilford Sanders	2
Dolly Kirk	2	N. D. T. Breurer	3
Hyram Smith	4	Jesse Bruce	4
Samuel Oxford	6	Jesse Newman	6
Thos. King	3	Hillard Crabb	5
Alford Harris	7	Henry Gossett	4
M. Austin	1	Willis Bridges	5
Green Flowers	4	Widow Toues	1
John Robertson	5	James Southerland	1
Amos Bruce	1	Daniel Waggoner	1
Wyatt Jenkins	7	Willie Ellis	5
Mary McCary	1	Iseac Smith	4
E. McCary	1	Wm. Barnes	6
Theophiles Kirk	4	R. Halloevill	6
Jas. Evans	4	B. Cates	4
Richard Norden	5	D. Ruder	1

Page 235 Continued

H. McGill	2	James Merick	5
C. Nowell	7	Isaiah Bright	1
James Taylor	3	Elizabeth Smith	4

Total addition of original book 209

Scholastic Population Dis. No. 3,1850

David Barnes	5	Nathan Sevindle	1
Henry Barnes	6	E. P. Ballowe	4
Perry Hinnant	8	Wm. Crobb	3
Isaac Anderson	5	Elender Smith	3
Wm. Cole	5	Lathan	4
Taylor	2	Joe Tedder	1

Page 236

Wm. Tyner	2	E. Tedder	3
Wm. W. Davidson	1	A. Lynch	3
M. Dunn	3	M. Harrison	4
G. S. Gully	4	C. Looper	5
Wm. Sevendel	5	Wm. Mayer	2
N. Nunery	4	Mark Hatty	5
G. C. Sevendle	2	A. Bernn	5
Drewry White	6	W. C. Anderson	3
J. B. Cox	5	Burrel Utly	5
Thomas Winfry	2	Obesiah Harlin	5
Mary Barnes	2	John Ford	2
Kinchin Nunry	4	Martin Ford	4
Katharin Howe	3	Warren Sayes	2
E. Howe	3	Wm. Marchhak	3
Thomas Sevindle	5	Wm. Walker	5
Tof Hicks	7	Mary Combs	4
Z. Bright	1	Samuel Davidson	2
Charles Kee	2	Lucy Hooper	2
Levis Bosvill	4	Geo. Thomason	5
Dickson Combs	3	John Harden	2
Timothy Reeves	1	B. Mitchel	1
Washington Adams	2	James Wyly	2

Total addition of original book 192

E. P. Ballowe
Mark Hattey
Coownis Harris
Commissioners

Scholastic Population Dis. No. 4

E. W. Lynch	7	Wm. O'Neal	2
C. H. Bethany	5	R. Mitchell	4
W. H. Cole	3	Allen Barker	1
John Cole	7	Jasham Haase	2

Page 237

J. J. Cole	8	A. Sanders	6

Thomas Cole	4	S. Rumly	6
Laton Pearce	7	R. H. Hawthorn	5
Rebecca Jordan	2	H. Kee	1
Wright Mae Jordan	1	Litata Davis	4
James Gornett	5	Mary B. Banker	1
Stephe Garrett	4	Hyram Short	1
Wm. Fowder	7	James Forrest	6
Wenna Edson	5	Josiah Forrest	2
Nancy Walker	1	F. W. Pearce	5
T. R. Veach	1	Z. D. Banker	1
John McAully	4	R. Bridges	3
T. A. Baker	1	J. Bridges	11
Mary Townsend	1	Gillum Smothers	3
R. March Marchants	5	Wm. McAuly	2
H. Lewis	1	Jon Sanders	1
L. B. Pearce	3	J. S. Childers	1
Nelson Pearce	1	H. K. Forrster	3
M. Thomason	3	Tom Walker	4
N. R. Williams	3	James Allen	1
Standard Adams	2	Henry Abbott	5
Wm. Kilbreath	2	N. Short	7
Inar Earp	5	Jno. Neighbores	4
Mary Veatch	3	James Winburg	4
L. H. Pope	2		
Total	200		

		H. Forrest	
		F. W. Pearce	
		T. W. Elmore	
T. H. Hudson	7	A. Heggie	2
J. T. Presson	6	Z. Collins	4
P. Herron	1	R. S. Beasly	4
J. S. Hill	2	A. Smally	5
J. C. Latemdn	3	A. T. Hudson	2
H. Harris	6	T. Neely	1
W. C. Pruitt	2	D. P. Hudson	4
D. Wamick	5	W. P. Eddington	4
John Presson	8	P. Helmes	4
J. T. Holland	4	T. Jones	4

Page 238

C. Cowell	1	Jas. Presson	6
Jo. Cowell Jr.	1	L. Lashlee	1
P. Jordon	3	Fed Mabury	5
B. C. Morgan	2	A. Herron	2
L. Thompson	3	Lea Moore	7
A. Utly	3	J. B. Bridges	1
C. K. Wyly	3	Bennett Hallard	4
S. C. Paratts	2	J. Jordon	6
H. C. Camp	3	E. Cowell	4
Wm. McCuttcher	2	M. Williams	1
Sam Madden	5	N. Strickland	6
W. F. Doherty	4	P. Thompson	5
Ira Love	1	E. Martin	1

Page 238 Continued

J. T. Flarmce	6	Marth Rismas	2
R. Rushing	3	C. Williams	4
D. Morris	3	Rebecca Alston	5
Wm. Bussel	1	James Aden	2
D. F. McElyrd	3	John Rasbury	5
John McGill	4	F. R. Reeves	1
T. McKeevy	1		

Total addition of original book 363

D. P. Hudson
L. Crocker
Commissioners

Scholastic Population Dis. No. 6,1850

John H. Williams	5	Samuel Wiseman	1
Samuel Presson	4	E. Rushing	1
Wm. Green	8	John Elmore	5
N. W. Presson	1	B. T. Baker	1
A. C. Presson	5	B. Rodden	4
J. J. Rushing	4	Mary Young	2
James Wiseman	3	James Rushing	2

Page 239

Melton Wiseman	4	John Douglass	5
Freeman Pressor	6	Lewis Cross	5
John Watson	4	Wm. Douglass	2
James Watson	2	Hyram Dawson	4
Jesse McGill	1	Alvin Taylor	2
Rebecca McGill	2	Nancy Catha	2
A. D. Crossno	1	Prooy Beeler	1
James Crossno	4	Wm. Bond	4
Wm. McGill	1	M. T. Presson	1
Martha McGill	5	Eli Craig	4
Sarah Cumpton	1	G. Holbrook	6
T. P. Pearce	7	Alberg Harris	2
Robert Ward	7	W. H. Rushing	4
David Watson	5	M. E. Johnson	2
Thomas Presson	7	L. Cattinghan	4
Bengan Green	5	Thomas Craig	3
Mariah Cops	3	M. Presson	5
Theophilus Pressor	2	James Cattingham	4

Page 240

N. McCarroll	3	John McGill	2
James K. Nance	3	W. H. Green	2
James Block	4	Robert Spiers	1
G. W. Rushing	2	Carroll Green	3
E. Haldenr	7	Mary Bane	4
J. A. Green	2	J. P. Dorris	1
Sarah Spires	3	R. S. Word	4

Page 240 Continued

John Speirs	1	H. H. Smith	7
Mary Watson	1	J. H. Bush	1
J. H. Bush	1	H. Greer	4
Nancy Bush	2	Joseph Green	1
A. D. Rushing	4	James McGill	5
John D. Rushing	3	John A. Nigbor	2
Thomas Ward	7	John Tice	7
E. Ward	5	William W.	6

Total addition of original book 269

John Presson
Wm. T. Turner
James Cottingham
L. C. Cottingham
Commissioners

Page 241

Report of the 7th Civil District

D. W. Benton	3	James Melton	6
Mary Benton	3	Perry Vester	7
Susan Holden	2	David Y. Vester	1
Age Hall	3	Mrs. Orton	1
Pendgen Melton	4	Wm. Bussel	1
Susan Hill	3	Calvin Parker	6
Carroll Ramly	1	Wm. Berry	6
John Phifer Jr.	2	Henry Berry	3
Wm. Mammon	1	John F. Benton	6
Harrel Nobles	3	Perry Melton	3
J. Chobod Farmer	1	John Bresto	2
A. Davidson	5	John W. Melton	1
Garrett Davidson	1	John Melton	1
A. Ballowe	5	Wm. Parker	1
Joseph H. Thetly	1	Wm. Herndon	3
Sion Melton	1	James Pippin	1
Coonrod Melton	2	Calvin Hall	2
J. W. Melton	8	John S. Cherry	2
John Myers	3	T. W. Pully	2
E. Melton	3	George Phifor	4
W. H. Halden	5	H. P. Snider	1
W. H. Cooly	4	Calvin Reddrick	3
E. Perkeirs	5	J. Copps	3
John W. Hire	3	John Garner	2
G. W. Farmer	2	James Garner	5
W. C. Cole	4	W. W. Wheatley	6
C. T. Wheatley	7	W. H. Williams	1
A. Wilson	1	W. Matheney	4
Joseph Picklers	6	James M. Holomon	2
Marth Middleton	2	Obediah Bullock	3
Total	19		

Total addition of original book

Page 242

We certify that the forgoing is a true list of the Scholastic Population
in the 7th District for the year 1850

John Phifer Jr.
Obediah Bullock
Wm. Parker
Commissioners

Scholastic Population Dis. 8 1850

Hugh Alsap	7	Wm. Holland	6
S. W. Byrns	6	Lewis Holland	6
Joseph Bakers	2	John McGlohon	4
James Green	4	Alford Brewer	5
E. Waggle	5	M. Cherry	3
Beverly Herron	3	N. Brewson	7
J. P. Smally	2	John Pearce	4
Joseph Green	2	Saml Brewen	5

Page 243

Mary Watson	1	Wm. McKinzie	1
M. A. McGee	5	Y. Childres	1
John Smally	7	Nancy Brewen	4
Richard Parkerson	1	Nancy McKenzie	2
Robert Rushing	2	Neil McNeil	3
J. W. Dudley	1	W. J. Greer	1
Burell Bell	7	Thomas Childres	1
L. W. Brewen	5	Alexander McRae	6
W. B. Cole	2	Rebecca McBride	7
H. Roberson	8	R. M. Graham	6
J. G. Taylor	3	Henry Melton	2
S. Brewen	3	Heram Pearce	5
E. P. Bush	1	Robert Birdwill	4
D. N. Shillings	3	Rice King	5
Joseph Alsup	3	E. Alsup	5
J. F. L. Melton	2	Pheraby Cole	4
N. Brewen Jr.	5	James Lockhart	4
Louis Click	2	Wm. Taylor	1
Wm. C. Barnes	2	Wm. Weters	5
Wm. Warmack	3	Carroll Pafford	2
Robert James	3	Joab Tun	2
Liddy James	1	Bennett Rush	1
John Reynolds	1	Elias Phifer	4
Lewis Brewers	1	Eliza Phifer	2

Page 244

Analiza Floyd	6	J. G. Allen	4

Analiza Floyd	6	J. G. Allen	4
James Alsup	1	David Brewer	1
Wm. Jones	6	James Cuff	1
J. H. Cook	3	Thomas Holoman	1
Ander Pethu	4	Kenneth Reddick	4
A. Nichols	2	John Herndon	1
James Wilson	3	Hyran Brooks	2
James Taylor	5		

Total Addition of original book 256

I do hereby certify that the forgoing is a true list of the Scholastic
Population of the 8 District of Benton County for the year 1850

Joseph Alsup Clk.

Scholastic Population Dis No. 9185

John Buchanon	2	James McDaniel	5
Mathern Mannon	4	Nancy Cummings	3
Mary Castell	6	Thomas Pafford	3
J. F. Cooper	8	John Bond	2
Katharin Beaton	2	Daniel Lightner	5
Malcom Beaton	7	Britton George	3
L. Beaton	5	Charles Robins	6
John W. Cooper	6	Harritt Townsend	2
E. Lindsey	7	John Rolls	4
J. H. Ross	2	George McDaniel	1
David Dorch	1	Daniel McGuire	1
A. McDaniel	1	Louisa Hall	1
Daniel Graham	6	B. F. Akers	1
L. B. Allen	4	R. C. Mathews	2
T. Robertson	6	James Cumel	4
Wm. Nash	2	Thomas Andrews	5
John Wyatt	1	Wm. Mizell	4
N. A. Jarmon	3	E. A. Robertson	2
Jones Coffmon	2	Harry Hansel	2
Stephn Halcom	2	Wm. Stockdale	3
B. P. Simmons	5	Wm. Wright	7
Samuel Slaughter	1	D. E. Ross	4
D. Stockdale	5	Henry A. Barnes	4
D. A. Askew	5	Alison A. Powell	5
David Askew	3	John Manard	2
J. W. Bromager	4	Burrel Wynn	4
J. T. Legatt	1	James Lindsey	4
R. H. Caplinger	10	Wm. Lindsey	3
John Marburg	1	Wm. S. Hollomon	4
Nancy Whitiker	5	Wm. R. Wynn	3
Mary Dooly	2	James Stayner	3
Marth Price	1	A. W. C. Mathey	4

David Mass	1	B. Grass	6
A. Rasburg	2	Simeon Nichols	6
Wm. Akens	5	R. T. Rushing	3
Richard Gilmon	1	Lewis McDaniel	2
Lewis Hyer	2	J. H. Rushing	1
T. R. Childres	3	T. Lockhart	1
Robert Jackson	3	Noah Wyatt	6
R. T. Cole	3		

Total addition of original book 271

We the undersigned certify that the forgoing is a true statement of the
Scholastic Population of the 9 th Dis. for the year 1850

D. Graham
Wm. Akers
R. C, Mathews
Commissioners

Scholastic Population of Dis. No. 10, 1850

Wm. Mitchell	6	J. W. Davies	1
E. Farrow	4	H. Durden	5
J. P. Arnold	3	Wm. Syks	6
Hyram Johnson	4	Wm. Holland	10

Page 247

J. J. Penick	1	J. Samett	3
W. A. Cole	1	John Cole	8
Wm. Holms	3	W. H. Clark	2
Furmandus Arnold	3	B. Lashlee	2
Wm. Pafford	8	D. L. Settle	4
John Pafford	7	Wm. Sarrett	1
John Davis	1	J. R. Thomas	3
A. T. Corbitt	2	Robert Runa	1
David Cuff	7	T. Thornton	4
Jesse Rasborg	4	E. Browning	1
Willie Arnold	1	W. P. Lashlee	1
Thos. Tompkins	5	R. M. Hawley	4
A. Vicks	2	W. Cole	2
Ephram Arnold	6	G. Adams	5
John Williams	5	E. Martin	1
John Arnold	4	Jane Aden	2
David Melton	1	Samuel Aken	2
S. Basswell	1	T. Robertson	4
J. A. Federick	2	A. P. Hall	5

Total addition of original book 162

John Thornton
Jesse Martin
James Arnold (Commissioners)

Page 248

State of Tennessee)   This day being the 15th of June 1851,Merrit Melton
Benton County   )   Trustee of Benton County made application to make
settlement with me, P. W. Morris clerk of said County Court Fouching the
Receipt and Disbursments of the common School fund for the year of 1850
which said settlement I find to be as follows.

I find in the hands of said Trustee as record from State of Tennessee
$938.47

Trustee Commissions   9.38
Net Ballance $929.09

Amount left in Trustee hands at
Last Settlement   122.17
Total $1051.26

Expended as follows

District	Voucher	Amount
1	1	$45.44
2	2	62.82
3	3	99.31
4	4	76.46
5	5	45.20
6	6	110.90
7	7	84.80
8	8	135.00
9	9	117.15
10	10	50.40
Total Amount of Voucher		$ 840.48

Which Lines in the hands of the said Trustee unexpended the sum $210.78
All of which is respectfully Submitted
                                    Wm. P. Morris
                                         Clk.

Page 249

School Funds Approperation for Benton County for the year 1851
As follows

Dis	Popl	Amount
1	178	$67.15
2	209	82.55
3	192	75.84
4	200	79.00
5	363	143.38
6	269	106.25
7	193	76.23
8	256	101.12
9	271	107.05
10	162	69.99
	2293	$ 902.57

                          A. Dibrell Tres.

Page 250

State of Tennessee)   This day being the 29th of March 1852,Merritt Melton
Benton County   )   former Trustee of Benton County sent papers making
settlement with the clerk of said County Court touching the receipts and
disbursments of the Common Schools funds for the year of 1851

   As follows
Received from State of Tennessee $902.57
Trustee Commission of   9.02
Ballance $893.55
Amount left in the hands of Trustee of last settlement   210.78
Net Ballance $1104.33

Expended as follows

District   Amount
1st   46.45
2nd   50.00
3rd   79.70
4th   45.50
5th   236.77
6th   94.00
7th   54.85
8th   142.60
9th   119.85
10th   45.50
Total addition of original book $915.22

Settlement Condensed
Cash left with M. L. Travis & by him
Paid to W. P. Morris $69.30
Net Ballance $984.52
Which leaves in the hands of Merritt Melton   119.81

                              W. P. Morris Clerk

Page 251
Benton County Distributors for 1852

Dis.   Pop.   Amount
1st   197   8323.1
2nd   202   8534.2
3rd   204   8619
4rd   222   9379.2
5th   398   16815.2
6th   266   11238.2
7th   188   7943
8th   241   10182.1
9th   282   11914.2
10th   155   6548.3
                         2355 $ 99496.5
The above is the Amt.due your County County
at 42¼ Cents pr Schollar
                         A. Dibrell Tr.

Page 251

Recd.of W. P. Morris Sixty Nine Dollars & 30 cents left by Merrit Melton
former Trustee it being the same mentioned in forgoing settlement.

> July 9th,1852
> J. H. Williams C. T.

Recd of Merritt Melton former Trustee of Benton County, One hundred &
Nineteen Dollars & 81 Cts., it being the balance in ful of what was found
to be in his hands at his last settlement.

> J. H. Williams
> Trustee

Page 252

State of Tennessee)   This day being the 2nd day of April 1853
Benton County   )

John H. Williams Trustee of Benton County applied to me Wm. McAuly,clerk
of said County Court to make settlement touching the receipts and disbursments of the Common Schools Funds for the year 1852,I find that he

recd from the State Treasure	$994.76
Trustee Commissions of	9.95
	983.01
Trustee	119.82
	1104.88

I find that he recd. for the former
Net Balance

Page 253

Expended as follows

District	Amount
1st	$90.07
2nd	71.85
3 rd	82.73
4th	93.40
5th	147.35
6th	91.75
7th	62.19
8th	83.40
9th	63.35
10th	53.37
Total	$841.48

Which Leves in the hands of trustee $263.34
All of which is respectfully submitted

> Wm. McAuley,Clerk

School Funds

Benton County Distribution for 1853

Dis 1		Amt..
1	180	$ 7063
2	239	9380-3
3	200	7850

253 Continued

4	225	8831
5	355	13933.3
6	258	10126.2
7	230	9027.2
8	262	10483.2

Page 253

9	283	11107.3
10	197	7732.1
	2429	95558 ¼

Nashville 11,July 1853
The above is the Amt due your Co. for 1853 at 39½ cents for Schollar
A. Dibrell Tr.

State of Tennessee)   This being the 17 day of April 1854, John H. Williams
Benton County   )   trustee of Benton County applied to me to make
settlementtouching the recipts and disbursments of the common schools funds
for the year 1853 I find that he received from the Treasure the sum of
$ 955.58
I find he should be charged with   69.30
Recd, from W. . Morrison
I find in his hands at last settlement   263.34
$ 1288.22

Expended as follows

District		Amt.
1st		$88.00
2nd		78.00
3rd		76.00
4th		104.90
5th		152.36

Benton County Distribution funds 1854

Dis.	Pop.	Amt.
1	190	76.00
2	262	104.80
3	221	88.40
4	248	99.20
5	382	152.80
6	261	104.40
7	202	80.80
8	286	114.40
9	283	113.20
10	201	80.30
		$1 014 40

Nashville July 1854
The above is the amt due your Co. for 1854 at 40 cents pr Schollor
Settlement continued for 1853

Page 254 Continued

District	Amount
6	$122.06
7	126.00
8	118.30
9	140.35
10	115.50
Total **Paid** Amt.	$1121.47
Which leves in the hands of Trustee	166.75
Trustee Commission	9.78
Bal Due	156.97

All of which is respectfully submitted

Wm. McCarey Clk.

State of Tennessee) S. S.

Benton County   ) We the underasigned Commissioners set appart by the County Court of said County of Benton to lay off and set apart a <u>sufficicy</u> provisions to serve the widow Parker and children wife Howell W. Barker Decd., one year leaves as follows Viz.

Page 255

4½ Barrels Corn
Corn on hand

Bal. due for corn	62½
200 Lbs. Flour	4.00
300 Lbs.of Bacon	30.00
Credited by 95 pounds Bacon	9.50
Bal. Due	20.50
Sugar,Coffee,Salt,Spice and Pepper	6.12½
100 Lbs 1 Ps. of Seed Cotton	2.50
3 Pounds Wood	1.50

Seth Utley
John Gilbreath
Hugh Dorhy
S. Madden

State of Tennessee)
Benton County   )

We the Commissioners appointed by the County Court of said County do this day procede to lay off the Daiorr of one year provissions for the late widow of Thomas McGill Decd is as follows

Page 255

20 Barrels of corn	400 Lbs Bacon
200 Lbs Beef	300 Lbs Pork
200 Lbs flour	200 Lbs.Salt
50 Lbs lard	50 Lbs Picked cotton
Sugar or coffee	$8.00
Lether & shoemaking	6.00
1 Lbs Spice	1 Lbs Pepper

This given under our hands this 31th day of March 1837

E. W. Lynch
J. H. Williams
Oliver Armow

Page 255 Continued

The following named property is the whole amount sold belonging to the
Estate of Howell W. Barker Decd.

2 Sows & 5 Shoats	$12.18¾
1 Raw Hide and part of yearling skin	2,00
1 Buck theological Dictionary Bible	
Hymns Book	91¼
1 Cloth Brush & Hyms Books	45
1 Razor Strap Box and Brush	126½
1 Bolt Calico Containing 18⅔ Yrs at 44 Paid	8.14
A parsel of pepper & Slate	1.06¼
1 Ink Stan & Salt Bowel	50
1 Bottle	18¾
1 Horse 3 head of Geese not sold at sale	
Debets due the estate	25
Not yeat estimated ,other funds come to hands	20.00

The above is a true statement of the property belonging to the above
Estate   50.95½
that has come in to my hands except what the widow claimed under the act
of assembly of the State of Tennessee and her do any giving this 16th
May 1839

                                        A. B. Wilson

Page 256

A list of accounts on the books of Edward Haywood Decd. at Camden Benton
County, Tennessee due Dec. 25th, 1837 taken by Samuel D. Strayhorn and
supposed to be good

Robert Homes	$2,56	Thomas McGill	$22.14
H. B. Haywood	1.62	Amas Bruce	7.94
Jon. H. Williams	8.75	Capt. Chandler	.06
A. T. B. Hudson	7.75	C. C. Poe	9.88
T. H. Burton	95	William H. Camp	4.75
Thos. Kee	56	Oliver Armour	24.37
Seth Utley	12.46	Mrs. Cate	56
James McGill	8.06	Abraham Davidson	1.13
John H. Carns	33.26		348.20
Anderse A. McGill	3.19	Henry Allison	1.75
William Pickler	5.88	Jonathan Fuller	7.87
Irvin T. Carnes	256.70	Benj. Green	1.75
James T. Rust	8.38	John Jackson	21.83
John W. Utley	50.72	Rich N. Wood	14.13
Asa Sevendle	1.01	Johnson H. Saddlen	50
Mary Serratt	94	Charles Thompson	1.76
Thoms. H. Button	25.53	Hannah Spoon	7.75
Elizabeth Thornton	3.37	James Keenon	1.50
Tomos Haywood	38.28	Braddeck Haywood	35.51
A. H. A. Weaver	1.70	Wm. M. Asbey	50
Allen C. Presson	4.19	John Haywood	8.72

Page 256 Continued

John McGill	18	B. J. Browning	125
William Wood	37	A. B. Wilson	400
James Suttle	213	Daniel Hallard	620
William Smith	210	William Arnold	672
Nelson Pope	275	William Harrison	876
James Sayles	75	Dickson Hooper	1316
James C. Lewis	4594	Mseggs Barker	2017
Robert Davis	1072	Elisha Pope	550

Page 257

Abraham, Sanders	675	Isaac Ballard	793
Samuel Wiseman	359	Daniel Pressor	26
Joseph Wiseman	431	Lenniel Thompson	15
Rubin Harmon	150	Thomas James	1726
Isaac Anderson	125	W. H. H. Burton	3238
Morrit Pope	1836	Ansal Pearce	1520
James Alexander	418	Nelson Pearce	1367
William Pope	213	David Smith	1339
Alford Ballard	19	David Quilling	817
John Pope	675	David Watson Senor	670
	76282		
T. J. Corson	263	William Bateman	1321
Lewis B. Barker	1312	Josiah Foster	768
Eaton Haynes	619	Sarah Short	300
Thomas Cowell	358	Joel Oegier	596
Johnathan Taurda N.	38	Paul W. Haywood	15
August McLand	100	Burrel Beard	266
Henry Pierce	178	Wm. Cole	413
Riddly Jordon	38	Hiram Cox	390
James Williams	50	James Casarty	426
	$104347	Simnon Pope	513
Edward Calwell	250	John T. Pressor	856
Whitaly Haywoods	13	Freeman Pressor	112
James Barnette	81	John Quillin	2088
W. H. Brown	1938	William H. Rushing	338
George Beard	250	Samuel Prettle	43
Edward Buck	423	Little B. Williams	450
Daniel Foster	731	Mathews Williams	25
Aron Greer	369	Vincent Arnold	381
Clabourn Hicks	300	Lewis Baker	200
Massis Jordon	1018		$124424

Page 258

Ephrain F. Jordon	120	George Barnett	200
Mary Lashlee	800	G. & B. Beard	288
Sam G. Madden	1421	M. C. Barnett	144
James Pressor	743	John Davis	25
William Pearce	118	Green Flowers	385
Robert Kee & H. Strickland	101	Wire Haneys	285
James Sayles	1559	Taseah Haywood	119
William Stewart	1252	Jane Holloway	182

Page 258 Continued

Steaphen Sownsend	74	Lucinda Halloway	125
Able Utley	649		$1262 57
W. H. Burton Esq.	937	Simpson Bridges	38
John Hayd	1028		

The following Act is considered good

William Maken	16166	Garett Sevendle	488
Thomas Beavers	932	Charles M. Garratt	2241
P. S. Gilbreath	95	Wilkirs Pinketon	177
Elizabeth McBride	1825	Milton Wiseman	125
Alsalem Swift	2206	Thos. Wiseman	312
James Griffean	2857	William Harris	358
Henry Allen	1349	John Thornton	544
John M. Petty	1400	Jackson Ash	175
Atitece Sorratt	1714	John Beavors	1243
Chestam Campless	1286	A. Campbell	75
Yarguard Cambell	1083	John McGill	6141
Robert C. Petty	1097	James McGill	1617
Mat Presson	932	Thomas Pressor	1052
Mahala Sorratt	1437	John Sayles	27 38
Mary Highlon	315	Joseph Sarrett	1736
Anderson Ash	628	Neehan Short	640
James Hicks	716	John Pressor	963
Willis Thompson	2796	Daniel Watson	659
E. Jenkins	613	A. S. Cole	1405
E. W. Lynch	1325	John D. Carnes	1050
Cathline Kee	513	James Beovers	206
George R. Keeoey	385	Thomas Higdon	1244
	41620	William McGill	507
William Thornton	213	William Pressor	1137
Jesse Rasberry	118	John Runenon	711
Hardy Rushing	1720	Irvin B. Carnes	1000
Nathan R. Baker	1438	F. W. Pearce & A. Pearce	450
Baroor Dunn	1782	Wheatly Haywood	100
John Cattingham	933	John Jackson	500
Rich Hicks	1189	Do Do	500
Anderson Johnson	1768	William Pressor	500
	78693	John D. Conns	1587
John Gilbreath	606	David O. Roberson	675
Mat Presson	507	Eaton Haynes	387
Samuel Presson	520	Rubin Hall	263
John T. Presson Sr.	206	Malichie Short	387
H. Spurlin	613	William Wilson	1175
Aran Thornton	208	Smith & Hal Burton	4600
Daniel Cambell	593		25126
A. G. Holt	600	Simian Higdin	440

A list of notes due the Estate of E. Haywood Decd. that are considered doubtful

A list of notes due the Estate, E. Haywood considered doubtful

Page 259

William Parker	3216	Adas Reylan	794
Joseph Spaulding	2933	E. Jennings	1550
David Haywood	5950	T. F. Morris	2200
Do Do	6063	Henry Carless	212½
Henry Carless	89		$10905
Do Do	200		

A list of officer's receipt on one, P. S. Eulin   1816
Considered Doubtfull
Amount accounts considered doubtful $1261.57
Amount of accounts considered good   837 46
Amounts of notes considered doubtful   251.26

Amount of notes considered good   10905
Amount officer's Receipt Bal.   1816
Cash in hand   24700
                                                              $272450

State of Tennessee)   County Court June Term 1839
Benton County   )
To George W. Farmer A citzen of Benton County, it appearing to the court that
Richard Hallard has died having written will in which you are appointed
executor which has been duly proved in open court and you havin given bond
and qualified according to law and it having been ordered by the said court
that letter testamentary issue to you. These are therefore in power you
Page 260
the said George W. Farmer to enter upon the execution of said will and to
take into your possession all the property and to make to the next court a
perfect inventory thereof and make a due collection of all debts and after
paying all the just demands against the testator and settle up the business
of said Estateaccording to law. You will pay over and deliver the property
and effects that may remain in your hands and do all other things that may
be reguarded according to the law of the land.
Witness. George R. Kelsey Clerk at office this 1st day of July 1839 and
the year of American Independence the Sixty Third.

State of Tennessee)   County Court June Term 1839 to Mary Townsend a citizen
Benton County   )   of Benton County. It appearing to the County Court that
Nathaniel Townsend has died leveing a written Will which you are appointed
executor which has been duly proved in open court and you having given Bond
and qualified according to law and it having been order by the said court
Page 261
that letters Testamentary issue to you . These are therefore to empower you
the said Mary Townsend to enter upon the execution of said will and take in
to your possession all of the property and to make to the next term court a
perfect inventory thereof and due collections of all debts and after paying
all the just demands against the estate and setleing up the business of said
Estate according to law. You will pay over and deliver the property and affect
that may remain in your hands and do all other things that may be regarded
according to the provission of the said will and the laws of the land
                               Witness George R. Kelsey
Clerk of the said Court at officethis the 12th June 1839 and the year of
American Independence 63rd

Page 261

State of Tennessee)
Benton County   )   This day being the 27th day June 1839.
Samuel D. Strayhorn administrator Edmond Haywood Decd made application to
make settlement with me, George R. Kelsey, Clerk of the County Court of said
County in conformety to the act of the assembly in yhat case made and pro-
vided
Page 262

which settlement of the above named estate I beg leave to report as follows
to wit, first I find the administration charged as pr Inventory and accounts
of sale of said estate by him returned at January Term 1838
Amount to Nine Hundred and Sixty Six Dollars & eight & half cents

	$966.08½
2nd Cash in hand	77.00
Dollars in good money	
One hundred twenty dollars Brandon Nit	120.00
And fifty in counterfit Tr. S. Notes	50.00
Notes on hand condensed good	109.00
Account on hand condensed goods	837.40
Total	$2109.53½
Notes on hand considered doubtful	251.56
Accounts on hands Do Do	1261.57

One officer receipt for   18.00
I also find in the hands of the administraton the following voucher towit
12 provin accounts   from John H. Williams   5.43¾
1   Do   Do   for John Jackson No 2 for   6.12½
1   Do   Do   for John Jackson No 3   1791

Page 263

Proven account from James Pressor No. 4		100
1 Proven account for David Campbell No 5		175
One Do Do from C. C. Poe No 6		100
One Receipt County Court Clerk No. 7		500
One proven account Briggs Baker	No 8	2017
One proven receipt from H. M. Brown	No 9	1938
One proven receipt for James S. Sayles	No 10	1686
One proven Receipt for C. W. Burnett	No 11	200
One proven Do Isaac Halland	No 13	1366
One proven Do for David Cagart	No 12	426
One Do Do Do James C. Davis	No 14	4594
Irven B. Carnes Note	No 15	4977½
Onereceipt Money paid by Admst.	No 16	2037½
One Note Account set off with S. Madden	No 17	2327
Lowenys fee to J. Keenen	No 18	2135
To Pasteny Bons S. D. Strayhorn	No 19	2000
Expenses of Sale	No 20	462½
Attending sale & making inventory	No 21	1200
for expences for attending Goertal Cadus	No 22	1712½
Notes Covering S. D. Strayhorn		936 30
Accounts Covering to Do		790.00

I also allow the adminstrator for travel and expences in the management of
said estate. One hundred & seventy-five dollars $175.00

Page 263
Amounting in the whole to the sum of ten thousands two hundred & twenty
nine dollard and five cents $2229.05
                                                                2109.54
                                                                 120 51½
Page 263
Which shows that the administration has paid the sum of one hundred
Twenty dollars and fifty one half cents more that he has of' a vailabell
funds in his hands are of which is

                        Respectfully submitted
June 28th 1839
                        C. R. Kelsey Clerk

State of Tennessee)
Benton County   )
This is a true list of all of the notes and demands which comes to
knowledge belonging to A.K. & S. Estate Deceased

On note on Jose Taylor $33.00
On Note   Samuel Hayner which may be paid in cattle or
corn for   ?   5.00
One Note on Jesse Hail for   2.00
One Note David Fullerton for   1.50
One Note Wm. H. Bruce   for   11.19¾
One note John Garett for
Nineteen dollars worth of cattle   19.00
The above notes was found in the Pappers of A. Knight Decd.

264
Penelope Kight	1 Patent clock	5.00
Penelope Knight	3 beds & furniture	10.00
Milly Knight	1 Bed & furniture	5.00
Penelope Knight	Kitchey Furniture	5.00
Penelope Knight	1 Box	12½
Penelope Knight	6 Chairs	50
Penelope Knight	4 Books	13½
Penelope Knight	1 Parsel plants	12½
Jane Hallad	1 Lat Tools	3.12½
Penelope Knight	1 Lat Lumber	1.00
Sion Roger	1 Lat of tools	1.12
Franklin Kirk	1 Lay Chair	2.50
Edward Lewis	1 Broad ax	2.00
Morcil Knight	1 Saddle & Blanket	3.00
Penelope Knight	2 Club Axes	1.00
Penelope Knight	14 Geese	1.87½
Joe Taylor		2.00
Evanes, Jordon	1 Grind stone	27¾5
Edward Lewis	5 shots	4.00
Edward	5 shots	36½
Gilliams Adams	5 shots	2.75

Page 265
| Penelope Knight | 13 head of hogs | 1.00 |
| Penelope Knight | 2 head of hogs | 1.00 |

166

Page 265 Continued

Muncie G. Knight	1 Hog	75
Franklin Kirk	3 Hogs	73½
Penelope Knight	Plough & Geers	50
Abraham Knight Jr.	Plough & Geer	100
Penelope Knight	Slate	25
Muncee G. Knight	1 lot show tools	12½
Wyatt Jenkins	1 Pr.Candle Molds	12½
Jesse Hamsonus	1 Pr Sheep shers	50
Jose Tayler	1 Ink Stand	193
Penelope	1 Looky Glass	124
Jenny Adams	1 Grabbing hoe	63
Johnoth fuller	1 Gray Mare	6800
Marcee Knight	1 Bay Mare	3500
Penelope Knight	1 Bay Filly	2111
Penelope Knight	2 Cows & Calves	1500
Drewry Reeves	1 Cow & Calf	1500
Jane Hallard	1 Hefer	700
William Holland	1 Heffer	800
Franklin Kirk	1 Yoke Oxen	3800
Joe Taylor	1 Lot of planks	300
Penelope Knight	3 head of sheep	400
Eaton Hayns	2 Weedey Hoes	34
Penelope Knight	2 Bands	12½
Harley Hallard	1 Razor Strap	225
		28561

Page 266

4 four shots came to hads that was not sold. Also one repe hook not sold
The above is a true account of the property and estate of the deceased
Esqr. Knight as recorded by Jose Taylor Administrator and Penelope Knight
Admininistratrix of the above esgate this 13th of July 1837

Joel Taylor Administrators
Penelope Knight
Administratrix

Sworn to and subscribed to this
7 day of August 1837

A true list of the Notes of John Harrison Deceased and the amount of sale
on the 22nd day of June 1839
1 Note on Evins Smith & George Dodd for
Due the 11th day November 1838 for   15.00
1 Note on Asa Howel due 1th Nov. 1838 for   8.00
Cash in hand to the amount   17.75
1 Gray mare & Bridle & saddle Nancy Harrison   10.00
1 Rasp Curry Comb & harness   Nancy Harrison   6¼
1 Bay mare   Nancy Harrison   5.00
1 Occupemt Enny No   Nancy Harrison   1.00
                                                 128.81¼
                            Interest on notes   12.00
                                                 140 61¼

Page 266

Sworn to in open court before me Sept. 2nd, 1839
and ordered to be entered
G. R. Keesey Clk.

State of Tennessee)
Benton County   )   We the undersigned free holders of Benton County
after being duly sworn have provided to set apart to Elizabeth Holland
widow of Richard Holland Decd. to mount of provisions as will be sufficient
is own opinion to support her and her family one year from the death of
her said purpose the following articles (towit)

10 Barrel of corn   12 Bushel of wheat
3 middlings of Bacon and one cay of pork & flour
Hundred pounds of pork and two dollars worth of salt and Ten dollars
worth of sugar & coffee.
One dollar & fifty cents worth of pepper & spice & ginger and
White lard & soap is on hand

                              John W. Melton   (Seal)
                              Etheldrd Melton (Seal)
                              John Pafford   (Seal)

An enventory & amount of sales of the estate of Richard Hallads Decd the
sale Commenced the 24 June 1839 and the following is the ammount

2 head of sheep		Elizabeth Hallad	$1.62½
2nd Choice sheep	to	Joseph H. Bortins	2.25
23 Do Do	to	Henry Melton	2.12½
2 last choice	to	Joseph Benton	2.00
Muley Cow & Calf		Abraham Dalega	10.12½
1 Cow & yearling		Crow Edward	10.50
1 Heffer		N. B. Turner	10.00

Page 267
1 Do		John P. Benton	8.25
1 Yoke Oxen		James T. Farmer	40.25
1 Cart ox		Do Do	24.25
1 Cart Truck		Etheldred Wheatley	3.00
2 Choice hays		Peter Phefor	5.12
22 Do Do		Do Do	4.50
23 Choice Do		Do Do	1.37½
8 Head Hogs		Do Do	6.50
1 Mare & Mule		Robert Russell	60.50
1 Bell & Collar		Elizabeth Hollard	75
1 Bridle		Elizabeth Hollard	67½
Syph Cradle		Perry Melton	3.25
Grind Stone		John Peppin	4.80
Stand of Bees		Scian Melton	1.50
1 Stand of Bees		William C. Penton	1.87½
1 Pr. Gere & Chains		Anderson Berton	1.00
1 Do Do		Elizabeth Hollard	62½

Page 267 Continued

2 Horses	Elizabeth Hallard	168 3/8
2 Do	Do Do	56½

Page 268

1 Grubbing Hoe	Anderson T. Berton	100
1 Pr Founys	Peter Phefer	50
1 Plow	Samuel Penton	275
1 Do	Elizabeth Hallad	87½
2 Plows	John Pafford	113½
1 Single Tree & Clivis	Geo. W. Farrer	62½
1 Coulter	Ethelred Melton	43½
Do	Sanol Penton	62½
1 Do	Thomas James	113½
1 Rod & top	Ethelrod Melton	12
1 Drawing Knife	Eliza Hallard	25
1 Large Kettle	Do Do	343½
1 Pr. Hooks	Do Do	50
1 Pr. Cudle Mould	Do Do	31½
1 Cross Cut Saw	Peter Phifer	200
Large Auger	John Cooper	43½
1 Adgel P	Thomas P. Floyr	100
1 Clevis	John Pafford	11½
1 Saddle	John Melton	100
1 Large & round shovel	Peter Phifer	25
1 Chisel Awyer	John Fafford	62½
1 Axe	John Melton	75
1 Washing Tub	E. Hallard	62½
Do Do	Peter Phefr	100
1 Plater Dish	John Meth	50
1 Do Basoe	E. Hallard	100
1 Pail	E. Hallard	37½
1 Piggin	Do Do	25
1 Do	Do Do	32½
1 Do	Willie Walker	40
1 Do	E. Hallard	37½
1 Drowing Chain	W. W. Wheatley	31½
1 Needle	E. Hallard	37½
1 Hard Saw	W. Hallard	50
2 Chairs Sitting	W. Hallad	100
2 Sitting Chairs	E. Hallard	112½
2 Do Do	Do Do	75
2 Do Do	Rich J. Cole	131½
1 Crock	E. Hallard	12½
1 Tin Pan	Do Do	25
1 Crock	Do Do	25
1 Tea	Do Do	85½
1 Tub	Do Do	6½
1 Basket & some wood	Do Do	175
1 Cut of wood	Do Do	100
1 Pr. Seadyanes	Do Do	118½

169

Page 268

1 Sifter	Do Do	25
1 Churn	J. Hallard	25
1 Frying Pan	Joe W. Hallard	87½
1 Coffee Mill	John Cooper	31½
1 Jar	Jackson Farmer	6½
1 fire shovel	E. Hallard	25
1 Fire Toungs	Do Do	12½
1 Shaving Skillet	Do Do	31½
1 Flat Irons	Will Walker	50
Smothering Iron	E. Holland	12½
41 Pounds Bacon	Alford Ballard	410
1 Lot Trumpery	W. W. Hallad	31½

Page 269

1 Coffee Pot	Will Browdy	18
1 Do Do	E. Hallard	57½
1 Fire Pot Mitt	Do Do	12½
1 Fire Iron	Do Do	81½
1 Lat Leather	Samuel B. Herndon	125
Skillett & Lid	E. Hallard	87½
1 Skillett	Do Do	93 3/4
1 Pot Rack	Do Do	113
1 Pr. Shers	Do Do	25
1 Oven & Lid	John W. Mett	100
1 Slate	John Cooper	31½
1 Fire Pot Nitae	E. Hollard	38½
1 Fire Pot Hooks	Do Do	12½
1 Wash Bowl	John D. Walker	25
1 Pr. Sheep Shers	Joseph Benton	37½

Page 270

1 Bell	John Mett	25
1 Lot Medisend	W. W. Hallard	29
1 Carve Knife	John P. Benet	37½
1 Do Do	E. Hollard	26
1 Pr Saddle Bags	W. W. Wheatly	400
1 Mars Saddle	Sterling Wheatly	2000
1 Stann Jug	E. Hollad	132½
1 Sheet	J. W. Melton	62½
1 Canter Fine	Willie Walker	137½
1 Do Do	Thomas L. Floyd	50
1 Pr. Saddle Bags	John Cooper	56½
1 Woman's Saddle	Wherg C. Cats	103
Colvirts fine	John W. Melton	137½
Do Do	W. W. Wheatty	100
1 Bed Stead & furniture	John W. M. Melton	1050
1 Harness	E. Hallard	576
1 Chest	Sarah Reynolds	112½
1 Trunk	Will Hallard	137½
1 Looking Glass	Gasanoh Hallard	37½
1 Log Chain	James Farmer	50

Page 270 Continued

Bed Quilt	Crees Milton	25
1 Do Do	Do Do	77
1 Do Do	Nancy Hall	75
1 Clock	Peter Phifor	775
1 Table	E. Hallard	56
1 Bed Quilt	Rich J. Cats	
1 Weving Loom	E. Hallard	50
1 Bridle	John Pafford	43¾
1 Slay	E. Holland	150
1 OverCoat	Will Hallard	25
1 Axe	Samuel Benton	101
1 Bell	John Melton	36½
1 Tar Bucket	Young J. Farmer	43¾
1 Lot Oats 159 Bundles	E. Hallard	125
1 Spenning Wheel	Do Do	56¼
6 Heads Hogs	Do Do	200

Page 271

Sale on the 10 August 1839

1 Rifle Gun	Jackson Farmer	600
Umbrella	Samuel Benton	139½
1 Razor & Strap	Willie Walker	150
1 Lemee	Geo. W. Formor	169
1 Show Knife & formish	Samuel Benton	3¼

The following is the amt. of Bank Nots andReal Estate Banking Company,

Springfield City		50.00
Cornc & VaileRoad	Bank of Vexborgh	20.00
Mississippi & Alabama	Vaile Road Co.	20.00
Lake Washington & Deer Creek Vail Road Co.		10.00
Grand Gaff Vail Road & Banking Co.		10.00
Bank West Union Ohio		5.00
Souit Stock Co. of of	Coffevill	5.00
American Vail Road	Vexborgh	5.00

Merchants Operation of Rendolph		300
Do Do Do		

Alabama	Huntsville	10.00

Amount of promissory Notes & Apormth Notes

1 Note on Michael Stephed	Due July 1840	10.00
1 Do on Rich Hallard	Due January 1837	30.00
1 Note on Siron Melton & John Pippins Due Nov.1834		10.00
1 Do John King	Due the April 1836	17.50
1 Note John Peppin Due Feby 24th 1839		9.00
1 Do Do Geo. W. Farmer	Due Jany 21 1839	1.25

Page 272

1 Do Robert Cheery	Due March 14,1836	5.25
1 Do Do Do	Due 18 January 1837	2.00

Page 272 Continued

1 Do	Benjamin Carter		Due January 1836		25.00
1 Do	William Curril & Margret	Curril 15 Feby 1834			5.00
1 Do	James Lankford & Robert Rochell 1 January			1838	5.00
1 Do	Will Waters Due	24 March		1839	17.50
1 Do	John Myers Due	13 May		1839	1.50
1 Do	John P. Benton Due		18 June	1838	3.00
1 Expement	W. W. H. Halland				5.00
1 Do	John Pafford				1.75
1 Do	By Sterling Wheatly				18¾
1 Note Sterling Wheatly					8.00
Account on Alford Ballard	for				5.00
Recd. Money William Anderson Act.					5.50
Recd. from A. J. Benton on Ak.					187½

I George W. Farmer the executor of the last Will and Testament of Rich Halland Decd. do hereby certify that the wethire contents on accounts, of Sale and of Bank Notes and Promissory Notes Apemsth and accounts which I found in the Papers of said Deed and there is another personal Estate except what was set Apart & Claimed by the widow so far as have yet come to hand. I have not taken an inventory of the business of said Decd as a collecting officer and the reason is I canot until the whole of the business comes to a final class. There are some premises where on the Decd times in his lifetime which the Decd forgained and paid for amt. have not title whether bond or deed Nrda I know how many acres there are for the premises I learn it home Nembern Seraford and then one no other realestate which I have any knowledge of the within is a true Inventory so far as I can make at this time.

                                    Cog. W. Farmer

Sworn to in open court before me and ordered to be recorded.

                                    G/ R. Kelsey Clerk

State of Tennessee, Benton County. This day being the 28th day of September 1837. Edward Hally Administrator of the Estate of Hardy Hally Deceased, made application to make settlement with me, George R. Kelsey clerk of the County Court of said County of Benton in conforming to the act of assembly in that case made and provided which settlement of the above named estate I beg leve to report as follows (toWit)

Page 273

First I find the Administration charged as per Inventory and accounts of Sale of said Estate by him returned at the July Term of 1838
Amount to five hundred and fifty-two Dollars and Twenty Three Cents $552.23
Cash in hands Thirty One Dollars & forty Cents   31.50
the 3rd I find the hands of said Administration Notes to the amount of three hundred and Sixty Six dollars and sixty-twoand half   366.62½
all of which is good. I also find in the hands of the Administrator the following Vouchers to Wit:
One Note I have against the Estate for thirty two dollars & fifty cents
No. $132.50

Page 273

1	Proven	Act from	T. F. Hill	No 2	$30.34
1	Do	Act from	Burrel Beard	No 3	10.12½
1	Do	Do	Teptha Nunry	No 4	3.00
One	Do	Do	from Edward Simmons	No 5	25
One	Do	Do	from Wt.Hensis & Co.	No 6	4.65½
One	Do	Do	From George Barnett	No 7	4.65
One	Do	Do	From Edward Hally	No 8	5.25
One	Do	Do	from Joseph Wisman	No 9	5.00
One	Do	Do	From Henry Morby	No 10	10.00
One	Do	Do	From James Wyly	No 11	3.00
One	Clerks Recept	for T. H. Burton		No 12	2.00

Page 274

One Recept T. F. Johnston Borgon	No 13		1.00
One Clerk Recept from T. L. Rumons	No 14		1.00
One Proven Act from W. V. Whitehead	No 15		43¾
Amount of Vouchers A. Garsie Estate			113.11¼
One Tax Receipt Samuel Madden	No 16		1.25
One Do Do from T. James	No 17		.35
One Do Do from T. James	No 18		.67

I also allow the Administrator for his truble & expences Mannagment
of said Estate   Twenty Dollars   20.00
Clerk Fee Geo.R. Kelsey   2.00
                                                    137.38

All of which is respectfully Submitted August the 28th,1839

                    G. R. Kelsey Clerk

In the name of God Amen.
I Richard Hallard of the County of Benton and in the State of Tennessee
being of sound mind and memory,but is a lwa of State of health and well
knowing that it is appointed for man to die and not knowing how soon
it may please Almighty God to call me hence do make and publish the
followering the last Will and Testament in the followeing manners(to
wit)

Page 275
First my desire is that all of my just and honest debts should be paid.
Second,I give and bequeath to Jackson Farmer my wife,Son one certain
bay horse, the horse I bought from my Son Welmain Halland,also one
Saddle to be worth twenty Dollars and one good Bridle.
Third, my Will that my beloved wife Elizabeth shall have the followeing.
Two certain cows & calves,choice of my stock of cattle. Two beads &
steads and such furniture as belongs to themr for head of hogs,choice of
my stock of hogs on certain cerpparrd and the fernetenes them to belonging
and the residence and remainder of my own Estate with the real and personal
my last Will is that my wife Elizabeth shall have her share such as the Law
gives her and all my children to share equal and alike in ever part and
last may I appount George W. Farmer & Berry Vester my executors to this my
last Will and Testament in Testamoney whereof I have him to set my hand

Page 275 Continued

and seal this the 13th day of May Eighteen Hundred thirty Nine.
Signed Sealed in the Witness

G. W. Farmer   )   Richard Halland
Berry Veston   .   )

Page 276

A list of the Property sold on the 25th October 1839 belonging
Jefferson Murry Decd.

1 Grubbing Hoe	Isacc Wyatt	$1.25
1 Shovel Plow	Elish Harrison	3.00
1 Shan Plow & Geers	Litha Murry	2.00
1 Gig	John B. Grayhorn	12½
1 Man Saddle	Joseph Harvy	3.37½
1 Pr. Saddle Bags	Benjamin Breenen	2.25
1 Bed & Furniture	Litha Murry	10.00
1 Do Do	Do Do	10.00
Sugar Chest	Do Do	2.00

Page 277

6 Chairs	Do Do	2.50
1 Table	Do Do	2.00
1 Chest	Do Do	50
1 Lot of Castenigs	Do Do	2.00
1 Cuppard & Ware	Do Do	1.50
1 Comb	Do Do	25
1 Spuning Wheel	Do Do	50
1 Rifle Gun	John Dowdy	1.41½
1 Axe	Litha Murry	50
4 Shoats	Allen Corbitt	3.06½
2 Black Sow Pigs	Litha Murry	8.00
9 Shoats	Do Do	3.00
1 Bay Mare & Colt	Do Do	30.00
41 Choice Hogs	Sallamen Cormack	10.00
2 - 2nd Choice Hogs	William Wormack	7.00
2 Sows & Pigs	Charles Barnes	2.75
1 Saw & Pigs	Isaac Wyatt	6.12½
4 Shots	William Wormack	2.75
4 Do	William Lowerg	4.10
6 Do	Isaac Wyatt	6.00
1 Side Saddle	Litha Murry	2.00
1 Durm.Hefer	Litha Murry	8.00
1 Speckle Heifer	Litha Murry	8.00
1 Bell	Litha Murry	.25
Pided Cow	Robert Grayham	10.00

Page 278

Do Do	Joseph Alsup	7.12½
1 Durm Bull	William Paker	4.12½

Page 278 Continued

Heifer Yearling	Litha Murry	2.00
1 Steer Do	Lardner French	2.56½
1 Large Steer	Henry W. Davis	12.75
1 Bay Horse	George M. Arnett	53.25
1 Sorell Horse	John Wyatt	42.50
1 Bridle	Lithan Murry	25
1 Oats Stock	Isaac Wyatt	3.00
5 Barrels Corn	Do Do	5.25
5 Do Do	John D. Allen	5.25
5 Do Do	Nicholas Brewen	5.25
5 Do Do	Do Do	5.37½
5 Do Do	Isoch Harrison	5.50
1 Stack Fodder	Isaac Wyatt	3.00
1 Stack Fodder	Letha Murry	2.50
1 Do Do	E. Reddrick	2.18¾
1 Do Do	Lesay Hancock	3.50
1 Shat Boy	John C. Allen	50
1 Cutting Box	William Warmock	37¼
1 Pr. Harnes	E. Reddrick	18¾
4 Ewes & Weathers	Litha Murry	4.00
4 Weathers	Lewis P. Wade	6.31 1/3
1 Sythe & Cradle	William Wormock	2.50
Accounts Soloment	Nat Good Acts	
David Brewer Recept	5.50 Robert Birdwell	4.50
Richard Murry Do	20.00	$367.73¾
	$25.50	

State of Tennessee, Benton County
October 26th,1839
I William Warmack Admimistrator,Administrator of Jefferson Murry Decd.
do certify that this Inventory is just and true to the best of my knowledge
and belief given under my hand,Seal this October 26th,1839

William Warmack

State of Tennessee,Benton County
October 26th,1839

We the Undersigned for them holders of the above County and State after
being duly sworm have provided to set apart to Litha Murry,widow of
Jefferson Murry Decd. so much of crop and provisions on hand as will
be of sufficement is our oppenian 'to support her and her and her formaly
for one year from the death of her husband. We set apart to her for said
purpose the following articles towit.;
4 Choice of the Killing Hogs
8 Barrels corn to fatten pork
Page 279
Twelve Barrels Corn, Seven & half bushel of wheat. Twelve Dollars in
cash. Two Choice Shoats
                    Wm. Baker H. W. Davis
                    Lewis Brewen

Page 280

State of Tennessee)
Benton County   )
County Court October Term.1839
Whereas it appears to the Court herein Jefferson Murry of said County
entested William Wormack Abathos Murry having been justifield accord-
ing to law as admininstrators of the Estate of the said Jefferson
Murry Decd. These are therefore to authorise and impowered you the said
Wm.Warmack & Aatha Murry to enter in & upon all and singular the goods
& chattles rights & Credels of the said Decd and the same into your
Possessions take when power the same may be from a true and perfect
Inventory thereof to make and return into Unsmicy Court and all just
debt of the said deceased to pay and also well and truly to pay and
deliver the rest of residence of said Estate to those to whom it may
properly belong.
                    Witness George R. Kelsey Clerk of said Court
at office, Monday in October 1839
                         G. R. Kelsey Clerk

State of Tennessee Benton County
November Term 1839

Whereas it appears to the Court here that Malkjoh Bush of said County
died Inotestate and John D. Rushing having been quallified according to
law as the Administrator of the Estate of the said Malkejoh Bush Decd.
These are therefore to impower you the said John D. Rushing to enter
into and upon all aid singulor the goods & chattles rights & credits of
the said deceased and the same into your possession take whereto when
the same may be found and a true and perfect Inventory them of to make a
andreturned into over ensuing court and and just debts of the said
deceased to pay and also well and truly to pay and deliver the rest
and residence of said Estate to those to whom it may properly belong

Witness   G. R. Kelsey Clerk of own said Court at office the 11th
Monday in the year on over A. D. 1839
                         G. R. Kelsey Clerk

A List of the bill of Property that was sold at the late Dwelling
house of Eli Townsends Decd. by Harrett Townsend Adms. On the 26th of
Oct. 1837

Bed & Furniture	$6.00
Do Do	4.00
1 Table & Sheriff Ware	2.00
4 Chairs	1.00
1 Lot of Coopers Wars	50
1 Lot of Casting	2.00
1 Loom	3.12½
1 Lot Coopers word	50

Page 281

Wheel & cards	1.12½
1 Pr fire dogs	81¼
2 Sows & Pigs	6.00

Page 281 Continued

1 Cow & Calf & Bell	1012½
1 Heifer	762½
1 Rifle Gun	1125
1 Mare & Saddle	3687½
1 Bed & Furniture	625
1 Press	22621½
1 Clock	312½
1 Looking Glass	475
1 Cross Cut Saw	112½
1 Chesels 1 Oven 2 Barrells	
1 Grind Stone	50
1 Sorn Leine	106¼
1 Cable Rope	137½
1 Gray Filly	3825
1 Bee Hive	160
1 Bee Gun & Gig	100
1 Lot Farming Tools	287½
1 Pr. Chains & Harnes	118½
1 Grabbing Hoe	50
1 Lot Sheff Ware	75
8 Hogs	1093¾
9 Head of Hogs	1187½
1 Steer	1987
1 Cow	1231¾

Page 282

2 Side of Leather	200
4 Sheep	656½
5 Sheep	812¼
1 Hand Saw	68¼
1 Gray Horse	7161½
1 Man's Saddle	262¼
1 Canoe	262½
1 Sit Boat Gunuss	400
1 Frow	50
8 Head of Geese	125
1 Puter Dish	25
1 Treut	106¼
1 Trot Leine	150
2 Barrels	25
1 Lot Books	56½
	298.7½

I certify that the above returns is just and true and given a full account
of the Artickles that was in my possession and was sold at my house on
the 26th of Oct. 1837

                    Harrit Townsend
                    Adms. of E. Townsend
                    Decd

State of Tennessee Benton County. This day being the fourth day of
September 1839 Jonath Stullon Admr. of the Estate of Absalem Knight
Decd. made application to make settlement with me George R. Kelsey,
Clerk of the County Court of said County of Benton Conformety to the

Page 282

of the Assembly in that that case made and provided which settlement
of the above named Estate I beg leve to report as following (toWit)

First I find the Adms. charged as per inventory and amount of sale of
said Estate by Joe Taylor returned at the August Term 1837 Amount to
Two Hundred Eighty-Five Dollars & Sixty one Cents $285.61

1 Execution coming to said Estate No. 1		$35.00
1 Note on hand Johnathan Fulton	No. 2	268.56$\frac{1}{4}$
1 Note on Peneolop Knight	No. 3	64.75
1 Note on John Holland For	No. 4	3.06$\frac{1}{4}$
1 Note on William Hollowell	No. 5	8.00
1 Note on Milly Knight	No. 6	2.00
1 Note on M. G. Knight	No. 7	3.87$\frac{1}{2}$
1 Note on Henry Hollowell	No. 8	2.00

Page 283

Notes to the amount One Hundred, Eighty Seven Dollars Twenty Three
and One Fourth Cents   187.23$\frac{1}{4}$

I find in the hands of the Adms. in Cash Ninety Six Dollars 68$\frac{3}{4}$
                                             96.68$\frac{3}{4}$
                                            263.91$\frac{1}{2}$

One Note sworn off by John Garrett for Nineteen Dollars and No cents
No 10   19.00
1 Note on hand on David Eullertan   No 11   1.00
                                              20.00

The last Notes Despered

I also find in the hands of Adms. the following Vouchers (ToWit)
The Widow of Said Estate Resed her part

Thirty Five Dollars & 28 Cents		35.28
William Hubb's Report	No. 12	5.50
Note on hand	No. 13	27.50
J. Madden Recept	No. 14	6.28
Notes of Hands Principal & Interest	No. 15	8.02
1 Proven Act. from Joseph Wiseman	No. 16	5.00
1 Do Do From Alford Harris	No. 17	87$\frac{1}{2}$
1 Do Do From G. W. B. Beard	No. 18	1.75
1 Do Do From Jas. Brown	No. 19	1.00
Widow claim for Provision		21.00
Total Amt.		107 20.

Total Amount of Estate brought Over Two Hundred Eighty Five Dollars
Ninety One and Fourth Cents 285.91\frac{1}{4}$
Amt. of Voucher   107.20
                                              178.70\frac{3}{4}$

Page 284
I also allow the Adms. of or Truble & expense is the management of
said Estate .

Page 284

Ten Dollars $10.00
Clerk Fee for Settlement and Entry   2.50
                                                                12.50

Leaving the Estate worth One Hundred & Sixty Six Dollars
20¾ cents
Which is all

                                        Respectfully Submitted
Sept. the 4th 1839
Page 285   G. R. Kelsey Clerk

State of Tennessee)
Benton County   )

This day being 10th day of October 1839 Samuel S. Sagles Adms.of
the Estate of Williams Conths Decd. made application to make Settlement
with me George R. Kelsey Clerk of the County Court of said County
of Benton in comfomity to the act of assembly in that case made and
provided which settlement of the above named Estate beg leave to report
as follows (towit) first I find the Adms. charged as per Inventory
and Accounts of Sale by him Returned Jan. 2,1837 Amounting to Four
Hundred & Four Dollars & Eighty- Three and Half Cents
                                                       $404.83½
1 Note for Nine Dollars & 75 Cents   No. 1   9.75
1 Do   for Three Dollars   No. 2   3.00
1 Do   for Nine Dollars   No. 3   9.00
1 Do   for Five Dollars   No. 4   5.00
1 Do   for Twenty Dollars   No. 5   20.00
1 Office Recept for Five Dollars   No. 6   5.00
Jo Maddan Do for Thirty Dollars & 22½ Cents No 7   30.22½
T. James   Do for Twenty   No 8   20.00
Whittington   for Four & 95   No 9   4.95

Wills Recept for Thirty- Two Dollars & 46 Cents No 10 32.46
1 Proven Act from J. F. Cooper   No 11   3.00
T. James Recept   No 12   9.75
J. Wyly Recept   No 13   1.50
1 Proven Act for J. H. Davidson   No 14   4.68
1 Do   Do for Brooks Niven   No 15   2.16
1 Do   Do for Robert Niven   No 16   3.75
1 Do   Do from E. Halley   No 17   1.60
1 Recept   from E. Semoins   No 18   6.71
1 Proven Do for P. M. Mullemacks   No 19   3.50
1 Proven Do for J. V. Aden   No 20   1.75

Page 286
Proven Do   for W. Nivens   No 21   4.78
1Proven Do   for E. Hally   No 22   30
1 Judgment   for M. Fry   No 23   6.00
1 Proven Act. for W. H. Horthan   No 25   5.25
1 Recept for Sheriff   No 24   37
1 Proven Act. for John Neighbors   No 26   2.00
1 Do   Do   for Mathew Williams   No 27   3.12½

Page 286 Continued

	No 28	4.00
1 Do Do for S. West	No 28	4.00
1 Do Do for Henry Walker	No 29	3.50
1 Recept for Doctor Cole	No 30	5.00
Clerk's Recept T. H. Burton	No 31	1.50
For support of Widow & Family for one year	No 32	130.12½
The foregoing are Vouchers paid by		
James S. Sayles as Adms		$342.63¾

The Acts Considered Entirity last to said Estate were also provided
by said Adms as Vouchers towit:

1 Act on James Cantrel	No 33	37½
1 Do " Ruben Caps	No 34	62½
" Do " Milford Councel	No 36	25
" Do " Thomas Hubbs	No 37	18¾
" Do " Green Nivint	No 38	2.75
" Do " Robert Ellott	No 39	2.00
" Do " E. Hicks	No 40	2.00
" Do " Joseph P. Morris	No 41	37½
" Do " S. Swindle	No 42	25
" Do " Davic Forster	No 43	62½
		10 06½

Making an Agregation of which is to be added above to the Voucher for the
said J.S. Sayes as Adms. of the Estate also the sum of Twenty-five

Dollars	25.00
To the Said Sayles for Truble & Expences	2.75
Clerk's Fee	2.75
	380.45

Which Taken from the Artickles as returned of the sum of	404.83½
Having the Ballance of	380.45
	24 38

All of which is Respectfully Submitted to the Court

G. R. Kelsey Clerk

I Margarett Currie of the County of Benton and State of Tennessee being
weak in body, but of sound and perfect mind and memory do make and publish
this my last Will and Testament revoking and making void all other Wills
by me at any other time heretofore made and first I direct that my body
be decently entered in a christian manner. At the discretion of my Executors
and as to such to worldly estate as hath pleased God to intrust me with
dispose of the same as follows (Towit)

Page 287

1st. I gice and bequeath to my Brother Hugh Cumees Grandson by name, James
M. Reeves One feather bed & furniture, my large family Bible and Pat Book
and One Hundred & Fifty Acres of land off of the North Side of the Survey
beginning on the bank of the Tennessee River end Robert Thompson, South East

Page 288 Continued

corner running thence west to the north west corner of the track to a stake thence south with the west boundary line, thence west to the river, thence down the river with its meander to the beginning so as to make the One Hundred & Fifty Acres to have during his life time & to be at disposal to my relation by consanguinity but but not to my Person what were by affeenity, but I should haden without my child. It is my wishes that his Brother George Reeves home. It just is give and bequest to my Brother Hugh Currie the remainder part of all of my free hold estate I give and bequeath to my old Black Mamma Alsey, by name her freedom and her maintanance out of the land that I leave to Brother Hugh during her life or he may take her home with and take care of her there and as to all the rest Residence and remainder of my personal Estate of what kind and nations so I wish it sold and all the money of t the sale and all debts that may be due and ariving to be equally divided between my three namely namely Edey Reeves, Mary Clark and Sony Petty and James Reeves my brother, Grandson, aft all of my debts & funeral expences, we aid and all of the expences that may arrive Unpaid, I do hereby make ordain & appoint me esteemed neighbors & proceeds to John W. Hill and my Brother Grandson, James M. Reeves executor of this my last Will and Testament in witness whereof I Margaret Currie the said Testatrix have to this Will written on on sheet of pepper set my hands and seal this the Twenty Eight day June in the year of our Lord and Eight Hundred and Thirty-Eight.

Signed Sealed and Publish in the present of us who have subscribed in the presents of each other and the aid of the Testator

James B. Hill)
H.W. Hill) Margaret Currie Seal
Sterling Wheatley)

Page 289

Clemants Names	Amounts of Claimes Filed		Claimants Their Prorated Prorated At
Irvin B. Carm	$33.60	Ditto	$16.61
2 David Haywoods	72.76	Ditto	45.86
3 George M. Barnett	37.77	Ditto	18.68
4 S. D. Straghorn	830.30	Ditto	410.49
5 John Davis	5.56	Ditto	3.25
6 R. F. Davis	69.76	Ditto	34.48
7 James Haywood	61.08	Ditto	30.20
8 Nancy Williams	28.50	Ditto	14.09
9 Isiah Bateman	17.30	Ditto	8.56
10 Bradock Haywood	77.93	Ditto	38.52
11 E. F. Wills	18.91	Ditto	9.35
12 John Haywood	13.25	Ditto	6.55
13 G. W. & B. Beard	34.67	Ditto	17.14
14 Rebecca Autry	1.63	Ditto	88

Page 289Continued

16 Bradock Haywood	3.40	Ditto		1.68
17 E. F. Wells	37.68	Ditto		18.63
18 W. G. Vanhook	18.42	Ditto		9.11
19 Partie Haywood	2.85	Ditto		1.41
20 E. & T. Haywood	876.90	Ditto		428.43
21 Pratt & Buckley	214.59	Ditto		106.07
22 A. Lashlee	11.13	Ditto		5.50
23 S. D. Strayhorn	28.06	Ditto		13.87
24 Davis & Cargat	22.07	Ditto		11.10
25 James C. Davis	18.46	Ditto		9.12

We also find the following claims filled with the Clerk which we think
not properly Authink eated as have drect

1 A. M. Caldwell	41.83	Ditto
2 William Bateman	2.08	Ditto
3 M. D. T. Breevan	9.00	Ditto
4 H. Cayort	23.39	Ditto
5 Batsan & Cayort	30.75	Ditto

Page 290

We also find remaining in the hands of the Administrator Notes account
Judgment just in Court and exceptions as pre his creditors filed the
sum of Twelve Hundred Sixty Nine Dollars and Forty- Two Cents reported as
in Sal Vants claims of which Sum Three Hundred and One Dollars and fifty
three Cents were off suits in the hands of said administrations of said
in Sal Vants claimes the same of Neine Hundred Sixty Neine Dollars,
Ninty Neine Cents all of which we beg leve.
Submitted

W. G. Burton
J. H. Williams
D. F. Hudson
Commissioners

Page 291
A list of Notes, Acts and Executions in the hands of S. D. Strayhorn
Adms. of the of
Edward Haywood Deceased which are Insolvant

No 1 Note	E. Jennings		$15.50
No 2 Execution	Davis O. Robison		6.75
No 3 Note	T. F. Morris		22.00
No 4 "	Malachi Wheeling		7.94
No 5 Executor	Adams Wheeling		3.87½
No 6 Notes	William Parker		32.16
No 7 Notes	H. D. Carns		15.87½
No 8 Ak	Robert Davis		35.87½
No 9 Set Off	Martha Burtan		9.57
No 10Ak	Jane Halloway		1.63
No 11 Execut	John Haywoods		8.72

Page 291 Continued

No			
12	Do	Hannah Spoon	495
13	Ak	Aron Thornton	988
14	Do	Anderson Johnston	17.68
15	Do	Lucinka Halloways	1.25
16	Executor	Eaton Hayyns	6.19
17	Ak	N. R. Baker	14.38
18	Ak	Jas. Griffin	28.57
19	Ak	Andrew Ash	6.28
20	Do	Melton Wideman	1.25
21	Ak	Thomas Wiseman	3.12½
22	Do	Henry Allen	13.49
23	Ak	W. P. Thornton	2.13
24	Ak	A. H. A. Weaver	1.70
25	Ak	A. Swift	22.06½
26	Executor	Oliver Armons	24.37
27	Do	John Haywoods & Brodoe Haywoods	96.96
28	Do	Eaton Haynus	4.25
29	Do	N. Haarystom	13.00
30	Do	David Haywood	60137¼
31	Executor	David Haywood	64.09½

Page 292

32	Set Off	Joh Boyd	10.28
33	Do	Jas. Rust	8.38
34	Executor	Jas Spalding	27.50
35	Do	Wm. Steward	12.52
36	Do	Hardy Rushing	17.20
37	Do	Jno Thornton	5.44
38	Do	John Sayles	27.38
39	Do	Simon Higdon	4.40
40	Do	John McGill	61.41
41	Do	H. Sterling	6.13
42	Do	W. M. Thompson	27.96
43	Do	Wm. McGill	5.07
44	Do	Thos Veach & N. Short	7.53
45	Do	Hhws Barker	3.02
46	Do	N. Short & W. H. Barker	7.68
47	Do	John Runneous	7.11
48	Do	Hugh L. Buckham	6.75
49	Executor	Henry Barger	11.44
50	Set Off	Borllvell Beard	26.68
51	Executor	Abraham Sanders	7.75
52	Ak	P. S. Kilbreath	75
53	Judy	Aleta Sorratt	10.39
54	Do	Mahald Serratt	10.37½
55	Do	Mary Higdon	3.15
Amount Brought Farward			13
56	Ak	Whitly Haywood	3.58
57	Ak	Wm. Morris	25
58	Ak	Isaac Anderson	1.00

Page 293

59 Ak	Minnie Pope	75
60 "	A.Compbell	2088
61 "	Jas Quillin	38
62 "	Rilly Jordon	200
63 Executor	L. B. Barker	1825
64 Do	Ezekeel McBride	300
65 Do	Sarah Short	1300
66 Executor	Edward Lynch	1335
67 Do	F. B. Campbell	1053
68 County Court	Wm.Baker	16166
69 Suit, Co.Court	Irvin B. Carns	26271
70 Set off Field Office Clk.	James Haywood	3828
71 Executor	Christian Campbell	1286
72 Do	Catharin Keey	513
73 Do	Wilkin Pinckston	170
74 Executor	Joel Osecn	596
75 Do	David Watson Jr.	657
76 Do	A. S. Cole	1400
77 Do	Needham Short	640
78 Do	Thomas Beaverr	932
79 Do	Jas. Kilbreath	606
80 Set Off	G & B. Beard	288
81 Do	G. Beard	250
82 Executor	Richard Hicks	1189
83 Executor	John M. Petty	1400
84 Executor	James McCoard & N. Hampton	2137
Set off	John M. Williams	$154\frac{3}{4}$
Do	John Jackson	$1612\frac{1}{2}$

Page 294

Do	Do Do	11791
Do	James Pressan	1100
Do	Danels Campbaes	1175
Do	C. C. Pace	1100
	Brigs Barker	12017
	H. M. Brown	11938
	James S. Sayles	11686
	Geo. W. Barnett	1200
	Davis Cogart & Co.	1426
	Joe Ballard	113.66
	James C. Davis	14594
	T. B. Carnes	$14977\frac{1}{2}$
	Samuels Madden	12321

An account of the sale made of the personal Property of Margaret Currie Decd. at her late residence in Benton County after having Administration according to law this 21st December 1839

Articles of Property	Person's Names		
1 Lot Goods & Bread Trays	Jessie Bats	$	$56\frac{1}{4}$

ARNOLD (continued)
  JAMES, 15, 40,
    154
  JOHN, 82, 92,
    102, 111, 154
  P., 66
  VINCENT, 161
  W., 131
  WILLIE, 66, 82,
    92, 102, 111,
    131, 154
  WM., 161
  WYATT, 23, 40,
    54, 58, 82
  WYLY, 57, 61
ARNOR,
  OLIVER, 92
ARROW,
  W., 141
ASBEY,
  WM. M., 160
ASH,
  ANDERSON, 162
  ANDREW, 182
  JACKSON, 162
ASKEW,
  AARON O., 47
  D.A., 86, 116,
    153
  DANIEL A., 145
  DAVID, 106, 115,
    125, 153
  DAVID A., 31,
    46, 135(2)
  DAVIS H., 125
  DREW, 106
  DREW A., 115,
    125
  DREWE, 96
  DREWE H., 96
  DREWERY A., 31
  EVERETT, 106
  JOHN, 1, 4, 5,
    8, 21, 46, 56
  JOSEPH, 21
ATCHISON,
  JOHN, 109, 118,
    128(3), 138(2)
ATCKINS,
  JOHN, 102
ATISSON,
  HENRY, 127
ATKIN,
  CALEB, 46
ATKINS,
  BENJ., 14
  JOHN T., 59
  O., 121
ATKISON,
  SARAH, 121
ATTOM ?,
  T.B., 68
AUSBUM,

  W.W., 146
AUSTIN,
  ELIZABETH, 128
  M., 147
  MOORING, 118
  MORRING, 137
AUTRY,
  REBECCA, 180
AYOR,
  LEWIS, 86

          -B-

BABB,
  _____, 103
BADLER,
  B., 102
BAGAL,
  SAMUEL, 100
BAGETTE,
  JOHN, 89
BAGGET,
  JOHN, 108
BAGGETT,
  JOHN, 79, 99,
    119
BAIN,
  MARY, 83
  MAURY, 93
BAKER,
  B.T., 150
  BRIGGS, 164
  DAVID, 80
  FRANCES, 147
  FRANCIS, 118
  I.A., 140
  J.D., 132
  JACKS, 73
  JOSEPH, 144
  LEWIS, 161
  N.R., 182
  NATHAN R., 162
  T.A., 149
  THOS. H., 44
  WILLIAM, 1, 2,
    9, 44(2)
  WM., 173, 174,
    183
  ZACHARIAH, 42
BAKERS,
  JOSEPH, 152
BAKIN,
  WILLIAM, 1
BALEGA,
  ABRAHAM, 167
BALEY,
  M., 146
  MESHACK, 137
  W.I., 133
BALLARD,
  A., 23, 81, 102,
    111, 121, 131,
    140

ALFORD, 161,
  168, 171
ALFRD, 91
ALFRED, 9
  E.P., 100
  ISAAC, 10, 27,
    57, 67, 161
  J., 25, 27
  JAMES, 9
  JOE, 183
  JOHN, 22
  T., 26
BALLEW,
  E.P., 89
  ELI P., 80, 109
  WILLIAM, 80, 89,
    109
  WM., 100
BALLOU,
  WM., 119
BALLOUR,
  E.G., 119
BALLOWE,
  A., 143, 151
  ABRAM, 133
  E.P., 129, 138,
    148(2)
  WM., 119
BALY,
  MASHACK, 118
  SHACK, 108
BAMEN,
  CALVIN, 125
BANDO,
  JOHN, 115
  WM., 103
BANE,
  JOSEPH, 142
  MARY, 103, 113,
    142, 150
BANES,
  JOHN, 134
BANKER,
  MARY B., 149
  Z.D., 149
BANKS,
  ALLEN, 110
  THOS., 60
BANNS,
  ELIZABETH, 134
BARBER,
  FRANCES, 99
BARBOR,
  FRANCIS, 127
BARD,
  WM., 132
BARE,
  WILSON, 118
BARGER,
  HENRY, 182
BARKER,
  ALLEN, 46, 101,
    120, 129, 139,

  148
BRIGS, 183
BRITTON, 44
  H.W., 22(2), 182
  HOWELL W., 159,
    160
  JAMES Y., 110
  JANE, 100
  L.B., 183
  LEWIS, 39
  LEWIS B., 161
  MARY, 140
  MSEGGS ?, 161
  W.H., 182
  WIDOW, 159
  Z., 90, 110,
    129, 139
  ZECHERIAH, 101
  _____, 101
BARLIFF,
  AYLY, 98
BARNES,
  ALFORD, 100
  CHARLES, 85, 173
  CHARLIE, 95
  D., 80
  D.W., 80, 89,
    128, 139
  DAVID, 119, 148
  DENNIS, 89
  ELIZABETH, 114,
    124
  H.A., 144
  HENRY, 80, 89,
    109, 129, 139,
    148
  HENRY A., 115,
    125, 153
  HINNY, 119
  JESSE, 109
  JESSIE, 90
  JOHN, 6, 80, 89,
    96, 100, 109
  MARTHA, 121
  MARY, 148
  S.S., 105
  STEPHEN W., 85
  TIMOTHY, 91
  W.H., 81
  WILLIAM, 80, 89,
    119
  WM., 100, 109,
    128, 139, 147
  WM. C., 152
BARNETT,
  A.J., 127, 137
  A.T., 72
  B.B., 69, 70(2),
    88, 98, 108, 118

  BIRD B., 62, 78
  DANIEL, 78
  DAVID, 36

Z., 148
BRISTO,
  J.H., 133, 143
  JOHN H., 121
BRITT,
  SAMUEL, 137
BROMAGER,
  J.W., 96, 153
  JOHN W., 86
BROMAGOR,
  J.W., 125, 144
BROMINGER,
  J.W., 105
BROOKS,
  HYRAM, 144
  HYRAN, 153
BROWDY,
  WILL, 168
BROWENS,
  ANDREW G., 61
BROWN,
  ALFRED, 19
  D., 134
  DAVID, 16
  DR., 30
  H.M., 22, 27,
    82, 91, 112,
    121, 130, 141,
    164, 183
  HUGH H., 102
  HUGH M., 70
  J., 26
  JAMES, 74
  JAMES C., 11
  JAS., 177
  JOHN, 1
  LEWIS W., 62
  NICHOLAS, 3, 7,
    30, 40, 42
  NICHOLSON, 15
  STERLING, 19(2)
  THOMAS, 73
  W.H., 161
  ZACK, 74
BROWNING,
  B.J., 161
  E., 122, 141
  ELGA, 102
  ELIZABETH, 82,
    91, 111
  J.M., 122
  R.M., 111
  T., 27
  W., 131
BRUCE,
  A., 121
  AMAS, 126, 128,
    136, 160
  AMOS, 18, 39,
    56, 75, 79, 97,
    99, 107, 108,
    116, 118, 147
  GEO. W., 91

GEORGE, 82
JESSE, 79, 109,
  127, 138, 147
JESSIE, 79, 89,
  98, 99, 118
S., 121, 131
SPARTIN, 82,
  111, 140
SPARTON, 91, 102
WM. H., 165
BRUSH,
  WILLIAM, 15
BRUTON,
  GEORGE, 2
BRUVEN,
  MARY, 139
BUCHANAN,
  D.G., 105, 115
  D.J., 85
  DANIEL, 16(2),
    85, 96
  EFFA, 96
  EFFEY, 86
  G.G., 134
  HUGH, 108
  JOHN, 96
  NANCY, 85, 96,
    105
BUCHANNAN,
  JOHN, 86
BUCHANNON,
  JOHN, 145
BUCHANON,
  JOHN, 105, 153
BUCK,
  EDWARD, 161
  GEORGE, 113
BUCKETT,
  DAVID, 127
BUCKHAM,
  HUGH L., 182
BUCKLEY,
  _____, 181
BULLACK,
  OBEDIAH, 133
BULLOCK,
  O., 113, 143
  OBEDIAH, 123,
    151, 152
  OBIDIAH, 94, 104
BULYEN,
  ABRAHAM, 52
BUNKETT,
  D.M., 147
BUNN,
  A., 80
  ALFORD, 119,
    129, 138
  ALFRED, 109
BURCHETT,
  DAVID, 99
BURDEN,
  THOS. H., 5

BURGES,
  CANNEY, 88
BURGESS,
  C., 79
BURKETT,
  D.M., 88, 109,
    138
  DAVID, 79
  E., 63, 88
BURN,
  ALFORD, 89
BURNETT,
  G.W., 164
  L., 111
BURRUS,
  HENRY, 100
  S.W., 115
BURTAN,
  MARTHA, 181
BURTON,
  B., 103, 112
  GEORGE H., 52
  HAL, 162
  J., 25
  J.H., 10, 23,
    26, 27
  MRS., 142
  R.H., 22
  S.H., 11(2), 22,
    23, 27, 37
  SAM H., 52
  SAMUEL H., 50,
    53
  T.H., 22, 80,
    160, 172, 179
  T.W., 9
  THO. H., 16
  THOMAS H., 55,
    56, 67, 160
  THOS., 43
  THOS. H., 19,
    32, 42, 44, 45,
    46, 47, 48, 78,
    89
  V.W., 9
  W.G., 181
  W.H., 53, 162
  W.H.H., 55, 161
  WILLIAM H.H., 56
  WM. H., 48
  _____, 70
BUSH,
  BENNETT, 104,
    152
  E & J, 66
  E., 83, 93, 103,
    132
  E.M., 104
  E.P., 152
  ELEANOR, 113
  ELENDER, 142
  ELIJAH M., 66
  J.H., 151(2)

JAMES, 142
JAMES H., 66
MALKJOH, 175
NANCY, 151
THOMAS, 125,
  134, 142
BUSHING,
  R.P., 111
BUSSEL,
  JANE, 121
  WM., 150
BUSSELL,
  JAS., 92
BUSTLE,
  WM., 140
BUTLER,
  D., 27
  H.M., 27
BYNN,
  S.W., 134
BYRNS,
  S.W., 152

-C-

CAGART,
  DAVID, 164
CAIN,
  L.D., 109
  M., 92, 103, 112
  MARCELLUS, 83
CALDWELL,
  A., 68
  A.M., 181
  EDWIN, 101
  ERVIN, 110
  JOSEPH, 101
CALE,
  J.J., 120
CALER,
  FINLY, 133
CALES,
  J.F., 102
CALINS,
  FELIA, 124
CALL,
  ANDREW S., 54
  H.S., 121
  J.J., 101
  JOHN, 41
  THOMAS, 120
  UNITY, 120
  WILLIAM, 119
CALLIS,
  Z., 91
CALLON,
  NANCY, 129
CALVELL,
  BERRY, 110
CALVIN,
  JAMES, 95
CALWELL,
  EDWARD, 161

CAMBELL,
    DANIEL, 162
    YARGUARD, 162
CAMP,
    GEORGE, 15, 18
    H.C., 94, 114,
        121, 130, 141,
        149
    HENRY, 17, 36
    HENRY C., 15,
        104
    J.M., 88, 147
    JAMES, 78, 99
    JAMES M., 61,
        109, 128, 138
    JOEL, 15
    JONUS M., 15, 61
    T., 87
    THERACY, 127
    THERESA, 98, 118
    THIVEY, 107
    THURSDAY, 137
    THURSTON, 78
    THURSY, 146
    WILLIAM, 12, 89,
        109
    WILLIAM H., 100
    WM., 119
    WM. H., 80, 128,
        138, 160
CAMPBELL,
    A., 162
    CHRISTIAN, 183
    DAVID, 164
    F.B., 183
CAMPBLES,
    DANELS, 183
CAMPLESS,
    CHESTAM, 162
CAMPS,
    A.G., 140
CANTREL,
    JAMES, 179
CAPLINGER,
    R.H., 153
CAPP,
    JACOB, 102, 133,
        143
CAPPS,
    MARY, 91, 112
    P., 81
CAPS,
    M.S., 132
    RUBEN, 179
CARAWAY,
    FRANCES, 140
CARGAT,
    _____, 181
CARLESS,
    HENRY, 163(2)
CARM,
    IRVIN B., 180
CARMACK,

ELI, 106
SOLOMON, 60, 86
WILLIAM, 16, 21
CARNELL,
    E.T., 111
CARNES,
    A., 92
    ANN, 81
    IRVEN B., 164
    IRVIN B., 14(2),
        162
    IRVIN T., 160
    J.B., 81, 102,
        130, 141
    JOHN D., 162
    T.B., 183
CARNIS,
    I.B., 91
CARNS,
    D. BREWER, 95
    IRVIN B., 23,
        24, 52, 183
    IRVING B., 22
    J.B., 112, 121
    J.D., 181
    JOHN H., 160
    TRUON B., 22
CARRAWAY,
    WM., 111
CARROLL,
    MRS. M.C., 142
CARS,
    J.B., 59
CARSON,
    ANDERSON, 14
    J.B., 43
    JOHN B., 8
    ROB, 14
CARTER,
    BENJAMIN, 171
    JOHN, 104, 134,
        144(2)
    LEVERA, 123
    V., 114
CARTON,
    MARTIN, 5
CARVELL,
    ERVIN, 120
CARVILL,
    WILLIAM, 5
CASARTY,
    JAMES, 161
CASIG,
    ISAAC, 102
CASTELL,
    E., 135
    ELI, 125
    MARY, 145, 153
CASTIN,
    B., 4
    MARTIE, 4
CASTNER,
    ELI, 115

CASTRA,
    GEORGE, 21
CATE,
    MRS., 160
CATEMAN,
    LYNDAY, 2
CATES,
    B., 147
    ISIAH, 92
CATH,
    NANCY, 83
CATHA,
    NANCY, 150
CATHER,
    GEORGE, 19
CATHEY,
    GEORGE, 16
    NANCY, 100, 132
CATHINGHAM,
    JOHN, 43
CATHY,
    NANCY, 122
CATS,
    L., 35
    RICH J., 170
    WHERG C., 168
CATTINGHAM,
    JAMES, 132, 150
    JOHN, 162
    LEAN, 123
    LENO, 123
    LEVNE, 132
CATTINGHAN,
    JAS., 142
    L., 150
CAYORT,
    H., 181
CHANDLER,
    CAPT., 160
    JOHN W., 37
CHANNES,
    C., 76
CHEATHAM,
    CAWTHON, 96
    JOHN, 32
    THOMAS R., 31,
        34
    URIAH, 85
CHEERY,
    HENRY, 133
    MANERVY, 124
    ROBT., 170
CHEERY ?,
    HENRY, 123
CHENEY,
    ROBERT, 21
CHERRY,
    HENRY, 84, 94,
        104, 113
    J.S., 143
    JOHN S., 151
    M., 105, 134,
        152

ROBERT, 2, 5, 7,
    8
CHILDERS,
    J.R., 134, 144
    J.S., 149
CHILDORS,
    J.R., 105
CHILDRES,
    T.R., 154
    THOMAS, 152
    Y., 152
CHILDRESS,
    J.R., 112
    MITCHELL, 43
CHILDRIS,
    ZICKINOH, 133
CHRISTOPHER,
    JOHN, 86, 96,
        115, 125, 135,
        145
    _____, 106
CHURY,
    MAR, 115
CLARK,
    MARY, 180
CLEMENT,
    A., 95
    AARON, 86
    ARON, 96, 105,
        116
CLEMMENT,
    ABRAN ?, 125
CLEMMONS,
    NANCY, 106
CLERRY ?,
    C., 130
CLICK,
    JAMES, 105
    LOUIS, 152
    LOUIZA, 133
    NANCY, 124, 133
CNOCKER ?,
    LILLY, 120
COAL,
    TUDD, 134
COATS,
    ANN, 49
    ANNA, 28, 29
    BARTIN, 28
    BARTON, 29
COEVELL,
    JOSEPH, 120
COFF,
    D., 121, 141
COFFMON,
    JONES, 153
COGART,
    DAVIS, 183
COLE,
    A.S., 71, 82,
        91, 102, 111,
        130, 141, 162,
        183

D.L., 115
DANIEL, 110
DR., 179
J., 92, 95, 112,
    131, 141
J.A., 104
J.J., 91, 100,
    140, 148
JOHN, 68, 81,
    91, 92, 100,
    102, 110, 120,
    121, 129, 140,
    148
JOHN J., 144
JUDE, 144
JUDITH, 85, 114
JULIONS J., 129
JULIUS J., 110
JULOUS, 91
LOYD, 35, 110
M.C., 143
PHERABY, 152
R.F., 93
R.I., 123
R.J., 143
R.T., 154
REBECCA, 101
RICH J., 168
RICHARD J., 104
SAMUAL, 134
THOMAS, 91, 101,
    110, 129, 149
THOS., 80, 140
UNITY, 62, 91,
    101
UTLY, 80
W., 112, 131,
    141
W.A., 154
W.B., 105, 152
W.C., 84, 85,
    94, 105, 114,
    123, 129,
    133(2), 151
W.H., 120, 140,
    148
WILLIAM, 68, 81,
    92, 100, 128
WILLIS, 91, 101,
    110
WM., 80, 89,
    109, 121, 134,
    139, 148, 161
COLEY,
  MEAD J.H., 94
COLIER,
  F., 115
  JAMES, 104
COLLIER,
  THOMAS, 124
COLLIN,
  HANNAH, 109
COLLINS,

GESSHANAH, 58
H., 121
J.A., 142
JOSEPH, 113, 122
N., 121
Y., 102
Z., 112, 131,
    141, 149
COLMAN,
  THOS., 95
COMAS,
  MARY, 128
COMBS,
  DICKSON, 148
  L.D., 89, 100,
    139
  MARK M., 41
  MARY, 12, 13,
    80, 89, 100,
    139, 148
  O.G., 122
  WILLIAM, 12, 13
COMES,
  L.D., 130
COMITTE,
  JAS. B., 109
COMMEINGS,
  NANCY, 135
COMMING,
  NANCY, 125
COMPBELL ?,
  A., 183
CONCHS,
  L.D., 119
  MARY, 119
CONLES,
  H., 131
CONLEY,
  E.W., 99, 117,
    146
  ELI W., 87, 127,
    137
CONLY,
  E., 78
  E.W., 108
  J., 103
CONNS,
  JOHN D., 162
CONRAD,
  WILLIAM, 14
CONTH,
  WIDOW, 179
CONTHS,
  WILLIAMS, 178
COOK,
  H., 144
  J.H., 153
COOLEY,
  JAMES, 104
  JOHN, 84, 114
  MARY, 105
  W.H., 84, 104
  W.J.H., 123, 143

COOLY,
  JAMES, 1
  JAMES M., 3
  SCARABON J., 3
  W.H., 114, 151
  WOOD J., 3
COOPER,
  CULLEN, 129
  HENRY, 125
  J.F., 135, 145,
    153, 178
  J.W., 96, 105,
    135, 144
  JAMES, 12(3),
    17, 78, 87, 105,
    116
  JAS. F., 125
  JOHN, 168(4)
  JOHN W., 85,
    116, 125, 144,
    153
COPELAND,
  S., 71
  SOLOMON, 54
COPLAND,
  P.H., 145
  SOLOMON, 42
COPPS,
  J., 151
  M.S., 142
  MANOH, 119
COPS,
  MARIAH, 150
CORAETT ?,
  W.T., 131
CORAWAY,
  F., 131
CORBETT,
  A.T., 103
  M.S., 81, 91
  S.W., 140
  W.S., 111
  WM., 111, 122
CORBIT,
  ALLEN T., 67
CORBITT,
  A., 141
  A.T., 154
  ALLEN, 173
  S.M., 131
  W.S., 102, 121
  WM., 130, 140
CORMACK,
  SALLAMEN, 173
CORNE,
  AUSBURN, 137
CORNEL,
  JAMES, 145
CORNETT,
  JAMES, 149
CORNS,
  JOHN B., 49
CORSON,

T.J., 161
CORTIS,
  THOMAS, 138
COTTINGHAM,
  JAMES, 151
  L., 37, 93, 103,
    112
  L.C., 151
  LIVEN, 113
  LOUIS, 83
  WILLIAM, 85, 95
  WM., 93
  _____, 103
COTTINGHAN,
  LEVIN, 142
COTTON,
  JAMES, 5
  LEWIS, 58
COTTONHAME,
  LEVIN, 14
COUNCEL,
  MILFORD, 179
COUNCIL,
  CYRUS, 5
COWARD,
  WILLIAM C., 18
COWELL,
  C., 149
  CHARLIE, 90
  E., 70, 149
  EDWARD, 90,
    140(2)
  EDWIN, 130
  JAMES, 130
  JO., JR., 149
  JOS., 139
  JOSEPH, 90
  JOSEPH, JR., 140
  THOMAS, 161
COX,
  DALLY, 119
  HIRAM, 161
  J., 100, 146
  J.B., 80, 110,
    119, 128, 139,
    148
  JACKSON, 89
  JAMES, 127, 137
  MARY, 80
  NATHAN B., 72
COYATT,
  NOAH, 106
COYLY,
  C.K., 65, 103
  C.W., 97
CRAB,
  HILL, 107
CRABB,
  H., 88, 118
  HILARY, 62
  HILLARD, 128,
    147
  .HILLIARD, 79,

HYROMM, 123
DELMORE,
  R., 144
DENESON,
  MARY, 101
DENIS,
  MARY, 90
DENNIS,
  MARY, 110, 130
DENNOM,
  JAMES, 145
DERBY,
  H., 26
DERDEN,
  H., 121, 131
DIBRELL,
  A., 126, 155,
    156, 158
  W.C., 136
DICKENS,
  SAMUEL, 51
DILION,
  JESSE, 117
  JOHN, 108
DILL,
  SOLOMAN, 130
DILLION,
  B., 117
  JESS, 137
  JESSE, 107, 146
  JOHN, 99, 128,
    138
DILLON,
  BENJAMIN, 98
  JESSE, 127
  JESSIE, 78
  JIMMIE, 87, 98
  JOHN, 89
DILLONS,
  JOHN, 119
DOALTON,
  NANCY, 119
DOBSON,
  NANCY, 90
DOCKEYS,
  WILLIE, 125
DODD,
  GEORGE, 166
DOGHERTY,
  W.F., 131
DOHERTY,
  M.F., 121
  ROBERT, 108,
    118, 146
  W.F., 149
  WM. F., 99, 109
DOOLIN,
  MARY, 125
DOOLING,
  MARY, 135
DOOLY,
  MARY, 153
DOOTY,

MARY, 145
DORCH,
  DAVID, 153
DORHY,
  HUGH, 159
DORRIS,
  J.P., 142, 150
DOUGLAS,
  JOHN, 90
DOUGLASS,
  JOHN, 101, 150
  MARTIN, 98
  WM., 119, 128,
    142, 150
DOWDY,
  JOHN, 173
DRUMMOND,
  T.P., 61
  THOS. P., 79
DUDLEY,
  J.W., 152
  JOHN, 144
DUGLASS,
  JOHN, 132, 142
DUKE,
  ALLEN, 129
DUNCAN,
  C., 146
  CHARLES, 108,
    137
  CHARLEY, 87
  CHARLIE, 98
  EZEKIAL, 78
  SAMUEL, 87
DUNCKAN,
  CHARLES, 127
DUNKIN,
  CHARLES, 118
DUNN,
  BAROOR ?, 162
  M., 148
DUNNIG,
  MAY, 120
DURDEN,
  H., 141, 154
  J., 121
DURDIN,
  H., 81
  HENRY, 92
DUVALL,
  J.L., 130, 141
DYERS,
  GRANVILLE, 90

-E-

EADINGTON,
  W.B., 103
EARP,
  ARVIN, 90
  CROM, 42
  ERVIN, 130
  INAR, 149

IRVAN, 139
  IRVIN, 120
EASON,
  B., 140
  JOHN, 51
EAVINS,
  JONUS, 99
EBEAR,
  WILLIAM, 6
EDDINGTON,
  W., 83
  W.B., 93, 132
  W.P., 149
  WILLIE, 113
EDISON,
  HENRY, 107
EDSON,
  WENNA, 149
EDWARD,
  CROW, 167
  JACK, 11
  JACOB, 16
  M., 109
  MEREDITH, 129
  _____, 36
ELLINGTON,
  WILEY B., 142
ELLIS,
  MILIE, 99
  WILEY, 128
  WILLIE, 88, 108,
    147
  WYLEY, 118
  WYLY, 79
ELLOT,
  ROBT., 179
ELMON,
  JOHN, 83
ELMORE,
  JOHN, 14, 93,
    103, 112, 132,
    142, 150
  JOHN M., 93
  T.W., 149
ENGLAND,
  D., 112
  DAVID F., 4
  REBECCA, 3, 19,
    21
  S., 141
  WIDOW, 131
  WILLIAM, 89
ERVINS,
  JAMES, 88
ESTES,
  JOHN, 132
ESTON,
  M., 79
EULIN,
  B.S., 163
EVANES,
  JORDON, 165
EVANS,

G., 118
  G.M., 146
  GEORGE, 127
  JAMES, 36, 79,
    108, 118, 128
  JAS., 147
  PETER, 140
  SQUIRE, 14

-F-

FAIN,
  JOHN A., 86
FALKNER,
  WILLIAM, 20
FAREMER,
  JONUS, 94
FARGASON,
  JOHN, 71
  WM., 78
FARMER,
  DAVID, 4
  G.W., 84, 114,
    143, 151, 173
  GEO. W., 21, 84,
    168, 170
  GEORGE W., 5,
    93, 94, 104,
    123, 163, 171,
    172
  GEORGE W.?, 104
  I., 84
  ICHABOD, 143
  ICHOBOD, 104
  J. CHOBOD, 151
  J.J., 114,
    133(2)
  JACKSON, 94,
    104, 113, 123,
    133(2), 143,
    168, 170, 172
  JACKSON, JR.,
    143
  JAMES, 123, 168
  JAMES T., 19,
    167
  JANE, 133
  JAS. J., 143
  WILLIAM, 47
  YOUNG J., 170
FARROW,
  ALFORD, 133
  B.N., 92
  E., 121, 141,
    154
  F., 82
  R.N., 102
  THOMAS, 112
  THOS., 141
  W., 81, 131, 141
  WIDOW, 111
  WM., 111
FARROWS,

ARROWS (continued)
  WM., 92
FAULKNER,
  JOHN, 10
FEDDINICK,
  J., 141
FEDERICK,
  J.A., 154
FELPH,
  ELIZABETH, 95
FERRELL,
  PAZEY, 31
  PEOZY, 31
  SUSANAH, 31
  VEZY, 34
FLANAGAN,
  GEORGE, 28
FENCE,
  J.F., 102
  J.T., 81, 92
FLARMCE,
  J.T., 150
FLARNCE,
  J.T., 122, 130,
    140
FLAY,
  THOMAS T., 123
FLEMMINGS,
  MARY, 113
FLORENCE,
  J.T., 70(2), 111
FLOWERS,
  A.T., 65
  G., 24, 27, 71
  GREEN, 56, 58,
    70, 99, 108,
    118, 128, 147,
    161
  GRUEN, 90
  J.T., 82
  JOHN, 23, 114(2)
FLOYD,
  ANALIZA, 152,
    153
  THOMAS J., 113
  THOMAS L., 32,
    168
  THOS. L.,
    64, 85
  THOS. T.
FLOYR ?,
  THOMAS P., 168
FOESTER ?,
  J., 120
FORD,
  JOHN, 148
  JOHN T., 109,
    119, 139
  JOSIAH, 130
  M.G., 120, 128,
    139
  M.P., 81
  MARTIN, 89, 100,

148
FOREHAND,
  H., 117
  HARDYMAN, 107
  HEARDEMAN, 127
FORHAND,
  RANDLE, 79
FORMOR,
  GEO. W., 170
FORNHARD,
  BLAKE, 79
FORREST,
  H., 149
  H.R., 139
  JAMES, 149
  JAS., 140
  JOSIAH, 140, 149
FORRESTER,
  H.K., 149
  JOSIOH, 130
FORROW,
  A.T., 121
  T., 131
  WIDOW, 131
  WM., 121
FORSTER,
  DAVIE, 179
FOSTER,
  CYRUS, 101
  DANIEL, 161
  DAVID, 90
  H., 101
  HEZEKIAH, 110
  J., 120
  JOSIAH, 110, 161
FOWDER,
  WM., 149
FOWLER,
  WILLIAM, 90, 110
  WM., 101(2)
FRANCESCA,
  G., 103
  H., 103
FRANCIS,
  GEORGE, 93
FRANCISCO,
  G., 72
FRANCISO,
  GEORGE, 83
FRAY,
  MICHAEL, 98
FREDERICK,
  J., 131
FRENCH,
  LARDHNER, 174
FRINCE (PRI
  M., 96
FRY,
  LUCY, 36
  M., 88, 117,
    146, 178
  MICHAEL, 36, 71,
    78, 107

MICHALE, 127
MICHIE, 15, 36
FULERTON,
  MARY, 98
FULKS,
  A.I., 98
FULLER,
  JOHNATH, 30
  JOHNOTH, 166
  JONATHAN, 29(2),
    56, 160
FULLERTAN,
  DAVID, 177
FULLERTON,
  DAVID, 165
  MARG., 117
  MARY, 87, 146
FULTERTON,
  POLLY, 108
FULTON,
  JOHNATHAN, 177
FULTY,
  WILLIAM, 87

-G-

GAFORTH ?,
  NANCY, 118
GALLASPIE,
  E., 120
GAMES,
  A., 109
GARDNER,
  JAMES, 54
  JONUS, 54
GARENER,
  JAMES, 8
GARETT,
  JOHN, 165
GARLAND,
  ____, 39
GARMOR,
  JOHN, 133
GARNER,
  JAMES, 20(2),
    21, 84, 104,
    123, 151
  JOHN, 123, 143,
    151
  JOSEPH, 125
GARNET,
  STEPHEN, 80
GARNETT,
  JOHN, 80
GARRET,
  JOHN, 110
  STEPHEN, 110
GARRETT,
  JOHN, 90, 120,
    130, 177
  STEAPHR ?, 120
  STEPHE, 140
  STEPHEN, 101,

149
GARRISON,
  JAMES, 29
GARRITT,
  STEAPH, 129
GARSIE,
  A., 172
GASKIN,
  AMAS, 128
GASSETT,
  ABRAM, 137
  ALLEN, 79
  HENRY, 79, 88,
    99, 119, 128
  JOHN, 57, 78,
    87, 98, 107,
    108, 118, 137
GASSITT,
  JOHN, 118
GASTIN,
  AMAS, 118
GAVIN,
  JANUS, 4
GEORGE,
  B., 86
  BERT, 96
  BRETON, 106
  BRIT, 125
  BRITON, 145
  BRITTIAN, 115
  BRITTON, 7, 153
  ESQUIRE, 141
  S., 121
  SQUIRE, 131
  ____, 112
GERRNAN,
  NANCY, 145
GESSETT,
  JOHN, 127
GILBREAST,
  WILLIAM, 38
GILBREATH,
  JOHN, 159, 162
  P.S., 162
GILCLOTH,
  WILLY, 35
GILLAND,
  J., 100
  MRS., 109
GILLESPIE,
  ELIZABETH, 110
GILLION,
  JOHN, 89
GILMON,
  RICHARD, 154
GIVEN,
  WM. J., 85
GIVENS,
  B., 133
GLENN,
  JAMES E., 40
  SALLY, 40
GLOVER,

THOMAS, 111
GNATE,
　JOHN J., 88
GOFORTH (GAFORTH),
　NANCY, 107
GOLDBURT,
　J., 79
GORDON,
　JAMES, 92, 103,
　　121, 141
　JAS., 82, 87,
　　102
　JONUS, 92
GORMAN,
　JONAS, 19(2)
GORNER,
　JAMES, 133
GOSSETT,
　HENRY, 108, 147
GRAHAM,
　D., 135(2), 144,
　　154
　DANIEL, 86, 96,
　　115, 125, 153
　JOHN, 86, 96
　MARTHA, 86, 96,
　　105
　R.M., 135, 152
　ROBERT, 116, 125
GRASON,
　PATSY, 31
GRASS,
　B., 96, 115,
　　125, 154
GRAY,
　MARY, 101
　MAY, 80
GRAYHAM,
　DANIEL, 105, 145
　MARTHE, 125
　R., 105
　ROBT., 173
GRAYHORN,
　JOHN B., 173
　MARTHA, 116
GRAYON,
　JAS, 36
GREE,
　J.P., 93
GREEN,
　BEN, 122, 132,
　　142
　BENGAN, 150
　BENJ., 160
　CARROLL, 150
　CORNEE, 142
　GEORGE, 132, 142
　H., 132, 142
　HEZEKELL, 122
　J., 144
　J.A., 150
　JAMES, 143, 152
　JAS. A., 132

JAS. H., 142
JOHN P., 122,
　132
JOHN T., 142
JOSEPH, 132,
　144, 151, 152
NANCY, 125
W.H., 150
WM., 122, 132,
　142, 150
GREER,
　ARON, 161
　BENJAMIN, 83,
　　93, 112
　BENN, 103
　GEO., 95
　GEORGE, 83, 85,
　　115
　H., 83, 103, 151
　HEZEKIEL, 92
　J.P., 103
　JAMES, 85, 92,
　　95, 103, 113,
　　115, 134
　JOHN, 86, 96
　JOHN P., 83, 113
　JONUS, 83
　JOS., 10
　JOSEPH, 134, 142
　NANCY, 106, 115
　W.J., 95, 152
　WILLIAM, 83
　WM., 92, 103,
　　112
GRIFFEAN ?,
　JAMES, 162
GRIFFIN,
　JAS., 182
　JOHN, 14
　SARAH, 13
　WILLIAM B., 32
GRISSANS,
　L.D., 105
GRISSOM,
　B.R., 6
　ELIZABETH, 78
　L., 86, 113
　L.H., 96
GRISSON,
　E., 108
　ELIZABETH, 88
GROGAN,
　WILLIAM, 137
　WM., 108, 146
GROS,
　B., 86
GROSS,
　B., 106, 144
　R., 135
GUAYS,
　D.W., 86
GULLY,
　G.S., 148

GUNTILL,
　JOHN, 83
GUSTIN,
　AMAS, 138
GUTHRIE,
　W.C., 102
GUTTREY,
　JAMES C., 4

-H-

HAARYSTOM,
　N., 182
HAASE,
　JASHAM, 148
HABSEL,
　HENRY, 145
HAGBER,
　E.L.W., 49
HAGG,
　JAMES, 79
HAGGIE,
　A., 140
HAGLER,
　E.L.W., 49
HAIL,
　JESSE, 165
HAILY,
　EDWARD, 172
HAINS,
　HERBERT, 79
HALCOM,
　STEPHEN, 145,
　　153
HALDEN,
　W.H., 151
HALDENR ?,
　E., 150
HALE,
　JENNIE, 88
　JEREMIAH, 79
　JESSE, 79, 108
　JESSE D., 115
　THOS., 80
HALL,
　A., 114
　A.P., 141
　ADGE, 7, 123
　ADYE, 3, 7
　ADYR, 7
　AGE, 104, 133,
　　143, 151
　AYED, 8
　CALVIN, 84, 94,
　　123, 133, 143,
　　151
　J.D., 86, 96
　JESS D., 105
　JESSE, 127, 146
　JESSE D., 125
　JESSIE, 30, 98,
　　118
　JOHN, 1(2), 3,

4, 7(2)
JOHN W., 3, 7
L., 103
LEMICA, 134
LOUISA, 145, 153
MARTHA, 84
NANCY, 170
RUBIN, 162
THOMAS, 121
W.C., 67
WILLIAM, 79
WILLIAM C ?, 67
HALLAD,
　ELIZABETH, 167,
　　168
　JANE, 165
　RICHARD, 167
　W.W., 168
HALLAMON,
　MARY, 133
HALLAND,
　ISAAC, 164
　JOHN T., 139
　RICH, 171
　RICHARD, 173
　SUSAN, 133
　W.W.H., 171
　WELMAIN, 172
　WIDOW, 171
　WM., 166
HALLARD,
　BEN, 139
　BENNETT, 129,
　　149
　DANIEL, 161
　E., 168, 170
　ELIZA, 168
　ELIZABETH, 168,
　　172
　GASANOH, 168
　HARLEY, 166
　J.T., 120
　JANE, 166
　JOE W., 168
　LEWIS, 133
　RICH, 170
　RICHARD, 163,
　　172
　S., 143
　W., 168
　W.W., 133, 143,
　　168
　WILL, 168, 170
　WILLIAM, 124
HALLAWAY,
　REDDEN, 137
HALLEY,
　E., 178
　ELI, 18
HALLIS,
　JAMES, 109
HALLMARK,
　GEORGE, 91, 102,

H.B., 160
J., 24, 25, 26
JAMES, 53, 180,
   183
JOHN, 22(3), 23,
   24(2), 27, 160,
   180, 182
JONUS, 51
PARTIE, 181
PAUL W., 161
T., 181
TASEAH, 161
TOMOS, 160
WHEATLY, 162
WHITLY, 182
HAYWOODS,
   DAVID, 180
   JOHN, 181
   WHITALY, 161
HEDNIS,
   P., 103
HEGGIE,
   A., 149
HELMES,
   P., 149
HELMS,
   PATIENCE, 113,
      142
HENDERSON,
   J., 131
   WILLIAM, 14
HENRY,
   ALISON, 137
   DAVID, 36
   JAMES, 78, 88,
      107
   JANE, 98, 127
   T., 147
   WILLIAM, 127,
      137
HENSIS,
   W.T., 172
HEPNER,
   U., 91
HERDSON,
   WILLIAM A., 49
HERNDON,
   E., 95
   JOHN, 144, 153
   MATILDA, 124
   SAMUEL B., 168
   WILLIAM, 95,
      104, 114
   WM., 134, 143,
      151
HERNLOW,
   ELIZABETH, 85
   WM., 85
HERRIN,
   A., 69
   A.R., 104
   BEVERLY, 69, 104
   ELISHA, 104

JAMES, 48
HERRON,
   A., 115, 149
   A.B., 95
   B., 95, 115, 134
   BEVERLY, 152
   C.N., 84
   ELISHA, 95
   ELIZA, 102, 111
   GRISSON, 115
   LANISA, 91
   LOUISA, 82
   P., 149
   PETER G., 142
HEWER,
   ELISHA M., 15
HICKS,
   CLABOURN, 161
   E., 179
   I., 80
   J., 27
   JACOB, 35
   JAMES, 22, 162
   JEFFERSON, 89,
      100, 109, 119,
      128, 138
   NANCY, 34
   RICH, 162
   RICHARD, 17, 183
   SARAH, 139
   TOF, 148
   TOMAS, 22
HIFNU,
   M., 82
HIGBIN,
   S., 82
HIGDIN,
   SIMIAN, 162
HIGDON,
   MARY, 182
   S., 102
   SIMEON, 91, 111
   SIMON, 182
   THOMAS, 144, 162
   THOS., 122
HIGGIN,
   A., 131
HIGGINS,
   E., 100
   ELIJAH, 80
HIGGIS,
   A., 141
HIGHLON,
   MARY, 162
   THOMAS, 134
HIGNILE,
   JOHN, 98
HIGON,
   THOMAS, 112
HILL,
   ADGE, 4
   E.F., 172
   H.W., 180

I.N., 123
J.S., 142, 149
J.W., 94, 114,
   133, 143
JAMES B., 3, 84,
   180
JOHN, 3
JOHN W., 1, 2,
   104, 123, 180
JOSHOA, 134
LEBERRY, 112
S., 114
SASANOH, 133
SUSA, 94
SUSAIAH, 123
SUSAN, 143, 151
SUSANAH, 104
SUSSANA, 84
HILLIS,
   J., 118
   JAMES, 90, 100,
      108, 119, 127,
      129
HINANT,
   BERRY, 130
HINNANT,
   B., 139
   BERRY, 148
HINNON,
   ABENMALIC, 134
HIRE,
   JOHN W., 151
HIST,
   BRAY, 88
HOGG,
   JAMES, 62, 99,
      108, 118, 128,
      138
   JAS., 88
   STARK, 127
HOLBROOK,
   G., 150
HOLCOMAS,
   THOMAS, 134
HOLDEN,
   ENOCK, 142
   SUSAN, 151
HOLESBROOK,
   GRIFFIN, 142
HOLLAND,
   B., 72, 82
   BANJAMIN, 70
   BARNETT, 90
   BENETT, 120
   BENJAMIN, 101,
      110
   BENNETT, 100,
      110
   D., 81, 102, 112
   DANELL, 121
   DANIEL, 46, 91,
      131
   E., 168

ELIZABETH, 84,
   167
J.T., 129, 149
JAMES, 5, 7,
   8(2), 15, 19, 90
JOANAS, 8
JOHN, 1, 2, 4,
   110, 177
JOHN L., 90
JOHN T., 100
JONAS, 12
JONUS, 101, 110
LEWIS, 10, 84,
   94, 105, 114,
   124, 152
M., 2
MATHIR, 7
MERRIL, 30
MERRITT, 8
MIRRET, 31
RICHARD, 2(2),
   3, 7, 8, 167
RIDDEN, 127
S., 114
SHEFF REEDDEN,
   53
SUSAN, 4
SUSANA, 84
SUSANAH, 8, 104,
   143
SUSANEH, 123
SUSANNAH, 7, 30
SUSSANA, 93
W.H., 114
W.W., 105
W.W.H., 84
W.W.M., 19
WILLIAM, 1,
   4(2), 85, 94,
   114
WILLIAM W., 3, 9
WILLIE, 2(2), 3
WILLIE I, 2
WILLY, 1, 2, 4
WM., 84, 95,
   152, 154
WM. H., 2, 93,
   104(2), 123
WM. W., 12, 113
WM. W.H., 123
WYLY, 1
HOLLARD,
   BENNETT, 139
   DANCE, 141
   ELIZABETH, 167
   W., 141
HOLLINGSWORTH,
   H., 141
   J., 81
HOLLINGWORTH,
   ISAAC, 129
HOLLOMAN,

LASHLEE (continued)
  B., 62, 131
  L., 121, 149
  MARY, 81, 91,
    102, 161
  P.S., 141
  PIGTON, 111
  W.P., 131
LATAMORE,
  LYNDY, 2
LATEMDN ?,
  J.C., 149
LATHAN,
  _____, 148
LATHEN,
  WM., 140
LATIMER,
  J.C., 102, 131
  JONATHAN C., 68
LATIN,
  JAMES, 78
  JAS., 109
LATINER,
  J.C., 111
LATIRMOR,
  J.C., 140
LATMORE,
  SYNDID, 2
LATNOR,
  DANIEL, 91
LATON,
  JAMES, 87
LAURANCE,
  HARRY B., 69
  J.P., 138
  JOSEPH, 147
  L.B., 138
LAXIMINE,
  J., 121
LEAGAN,
  JOHN, 105
LEAIS ?,
  E., 21
LEE,
  JAMES, 46
  ROBERT G., 34
  WILLIAM, 34, 35
LEEPER,
  C., 80
  CULLEN, 100
LEGALL,
  JOHN, 125
LEGATE,
  J.T.R., 145
LEGATT,
  J.T., 153
LEHAPHER,
  JOHN, 20
LEIGHNIP,
  DANIEL, 96
LEINDESY ?,
  E., 144
LEWES,

GEORGE, 108
LEWIS,
  A., 93
  ALFORD, 78, 103,
    113, 129, 146
  ALFRED, 17
  CALVIN, 137, 146
  E., 23, 24, 26
  EDWARD, 165(2)
  G., 118
  GEORGE, 98, 127,
    137
  H., 139, 149
  HILORY, 130
  I.W., 79
  IRVIN, 27
  JAMES C., 161
  JOHN R., 22
  NANCY, 138
  P.R., 36
  T.W.P., 73, 74
  THOMAS, 46
LICKHART,
  JAMES, 105
LIGHTFOOT,
  R.H., 121
LIGHTFORT,
  BIKE, 130
LIGHTMORE,
  DANIEL, 106
LIGHTNER,
  DANIEL, 115,
    125, 135, 153
LIGHTNOR,
  DANIE, 145
LINDSEY,
  E., 153
  ED, 105
  EDWARD, 86, 96,
    115, 135
  JAMES, 56, 61,
    125, 144, 153
  JOHN, 6, 145
  JONES, 135
  JONUS, 96, 106
  WILLIAM, 60, 61,
    86, 96, 106,
    115, 125
  WM., 135, 144,
    153
LINDSY,
  WILLIAM, 6
LISSHAM,
  ELIJAH, 98
LITTLE,
  SAM, 34
LOCKHART,
  E., 154
  JAMES, 124, 134,
    152
  JONUS, 114
LOEVTHER,
  H., 130

LONG,
  JOSEPH D., 59
LOOPER,
  C., 148
  CULLEN, 109, 138
  WILLIAM, 119
LOUIS,
  EDWARD, 22
LOVE,
  IDA, 122
  IRA, 131, 149
  MARTHA, 140
LOWERG ?,
  WILLIAM, 173
LOWERY,
  ELIJAH, 43
  J.J., 114
  J.P., 130
  J.T., 141
  JOHN, 124
LOWRY,
  E.M., 43
  ELIJAH M., 43
LUCAS,
  EDWARD, 22
LUPER,
  BANCY, 68
  CULLEN W., 68
  CULLIN W., 68
LUPOR,
  CULLEN, 89
LUTER,
  JAMES, 129
LUTHER,
  H.W., 141
LYER,
  LEWIS, 115
LYNCH,
  A., 109, 148
  ANDERSON, 68,
    90, 119, 129,
    138
  ANDREW, 80
  E.W., 14, 35,
    80, 103, 123,
    132, 140, 148,
    159, 162
  EDWARD, 91, 183
  EDWARD W., 112
  ELIZABETH, 68
  ISAAC, 21,
    22(2), 23
LYNSA,
  JAMES, 86
LYONS,
  JOHN, 71
LYRON,
  T.H., 129

-M-

MABURY,
  F., 140

FED, 149
  _____, 122
McARY,
  JAMES, 119
McAUEY,
  JOHN, 140
McAULEY,
  J., 25, 26, 80
  JOHN, 23, 90,
    101, 110, 129
  W., 23
  WILLIAM, 6
  WM., 139
McAULLY,
  JOHN, 149
McAULY,
  JOHN, 120
  WM., 149, 157
McBARNETT,
  _____, 147
McBORNETE,
  _____, 117
McBRIDE,
  E., 105, 114
  ELIZABETH, 162
  EZEKEEL, 183
  EZEKIEL, 53, 85,
    95
  REBECCA, 152
  REBECCAH, 124
  RIBECCA, 133
McCANN,
  T., 27
McCARD,
  JAS., 22
McCAREY,
  WM., 159
McCARRALL,
  ABNER, 57
  NARCISA, 122,
    132
McCARROLL,
  N., 81, 150
  NARCISSA, 112
McCARY,
  E., 147
  MARY, 147
McCATHAM,
  W., 84
McCERD ?,
  MOSES, 125
McCLEVAIN,
  HENRY, 137
McCLOEN,
  MOSES, 135
McCLOWD,
  RANDINCK, 7
McCLYDE,
  D.F., 103
McCLYEA,
  D.F., 103
McCOARD,
  JAMES, 183

McCORD,
    ELIZABETH, 99,
        108
    JAMES, 23, 24
    NARCISSA, 103
    T., 27
    T.M., 23
McCORRALE,
    N., 91
McCRACKEING,
    ROBERT, 63
McCRACKEN,
    J.L., 9
    JOHN, 14
    JOHN L., 14
McCRARY,
    ELIZABETH, 127
    MASIS, 138
McCREEVIS,
    J., 141
McCUTCHEON,
    JOHN P., 62
McCUTTCHER,
    WM., 149
McDAINE,
    J.C., 127
McDANIEL,
    A., 153
    E.M., 145
    G.W., 145
    GEORGE, 6, 106,
        115, 125, 135,
        153
    J.C., 137, 146
    JAMES, 6, 106,
        115, 125, 135,
        153
    JON, 14
    JONES, 145
    LEWIS, 154
    MARY, 106
    MATHER, 98
    MATHEWS, 78
    MATTHEW, 87
    W.G., 135
    _____, 117
McDARLIN,
    REBECCA, 138
McELGAIN,
    HENRY, 146
McELROD,
    D.F., 87
McELSOAIM,
    JOHN, 87
McELYED,
    D., 111
McELYRA,
    C.F., 92
McELYRD,
    D.F., 141, 150
    D.W., 130
McGAGE,
    DANIEL, 125

McGEA,
    MARGARET, 115
    THOMAS, 137
McGEE,
    M., 144
    M.A., 152
    W., 104
    WILLIAM, 62, 85
    WM., 146
McGILL,
    ANDERSON A., 160
    H., 148
    J., JR., 103
    JAMES, 9, 37,
        60, 111, 132,
        142, 151, 160,
        162
    JESSE, 83, 150
    JOHN, 10, 37,
        50, 64, 83, 91,
        102, 103, 111,
        113(2), 122,
        134, 137,
        150(2), 161, 182

    JOHN, JR., 37,
        83, 93, 122
    JOHN, SR., 122
    JONUS, 37
    MARTHA, 142, 150
    MARY, 37
    MRS., 142
    REBECCA, 132,
        150
    T., 64
    THOMAS, 9, 37,
        38, 40, 107,
        117, 127, 137,
        159, 160
    THOS., 23, 81,
        88, 146
    WIDOW, 159
    WM., 150, 162,
        182
McGLAVIN,
    JOHN, 96
McGLOHN,
    JOHN, 133
McGLOHON,
    JOHN, 86, 115,
        124, 152
McGLOWN,
    JOHN, 106
McGOWEN,
    JANE, 121
McGUAIG,
    DANIL, 145
McGUIRE,
    DANIEL, 153
McILLWAIN,
    ABBEGAL, 46
    JOHN, 46
McILWAIN,

    JOHN, 78
McKEEVY,
    T., 150
McKELVY,
    J., 131
McKENZIE,
    H., 124
    N., 135
    NANCY, 94, 105,
        114, 152
McKINZIE,
    NANCY, 134
    WM., 134, 152
McKNIGHT,
    D.F., 121
    ROBERT, 119
McLAND,
    AUGUST, 161
McNEAL,
    NEAL, 85
    NEIL, 95
McNEIL,
    JAMES, 134, 145
    NEIL, 114, 125,
        134, 152
McNIEL,
    NEAL, 105
McPOR,
    WILLIAM, 95
McQRAIG,
    DANE, 56
McRAE,
    A., 94, 105,
        114, 134
    ALEXANDER, 124,
        152
McRANGER,
    MARY, 85
McREA,
    A., 85
McREDDON,
    ALEXANDER, 57
McTUAGA,
    DAN, 61
MADDEN,
    J., 177
    S., 92, 102,
        131, 141, 159,
        164
    S.S., 24
    SAM, 68, 149
    SAM G., 161
    SAMUEL, 69, 111,
        172
    SAMUELS, 183
MADEN,
    S., 82
MADLIN,
    S., 122
MAHERRY,
    F., 131
MAILIN,
    WILLIAM, 88

MAKEN,
    WM., 162
MAKERS,
    WILSON, 134
MALICE,
    M.A., 146
MALIE,
    MARTHA, 127, 137
    WILLIAM, 127
MALIN,
    JAMES, 41(2)
    MARTHA, 98, 107,
        117
    W.M., 147
    WILLIAM, 41, 98,
        107, 137
    WILLIAM M., 41
    WM., 78, 87
    WM. M., 117, 146
MALLORY,
    E.L., 36
MAMMON,
    M., 135
    WM., 151
MANARD,
    JOHN, 153
MANDIN,
    SAMUEL, 60
MANNERS,
    WILLIAM, 85
MANNON,
    M., 96, 105
    MATHERN, 153
    MATHIS, 125
MANNOR,
    M., 86
MARABLE,
    HENRY H., 58
MARBURG,
    JOHN, 153
MARCHANDS,
    WILLIAM, 119
MARCHANKS,
    WM., 139
MARCHANTS,
    R. MARCH, 149
MARCHBANK,
    GILES, 80, 110
    GILLIS, 90
    J., 80
    JONES, 17
    RUBEN, 110
    S., 80
    STEPHEN, 89, 90,
        100
    W., 80
    WILLIAM, 89
MARCHBANKS,
    GILL, 101
    JAMES, 89, 100
    R., 120
    REUBEN, 55
    STEPHEN, 109

PRESSOR (continued)
  J.F., 130
  J.T., 140
  JAMES, 130, 132,
    161, 164
  JOHN, 122, 132,
    162
  JOHN T., 161
  JON T., 142
  MATHEW, 132
  SAMUEL, 132
  THEO, 142
  THEOPHELAS, 122
  THEOPHILUS, 150
  THOMAS, 132,
    142, 162
  WM., 162(2)
PRETTLE,
  SAMUEL, 161
PREVITE,
  W.F., 130
PREWETT,
  W.F., 121
PREWITT,
  W.C., 141
PRICE,
  ASA, 16
  JOHN, 134
  MARTH, 153
PRINCE,
  JOHN, 79, 89,
    99, 108, 118,
    128, 138(2), 147

PRINCE (FRINCE?),
  M., 96
PRITCHARD,
  PLEASANT, 29
PRITCHELL,
  JRAND ?, 137
PRIVETTE,
  W.C., 130
PROSK,
  ROBERT, 78
PRUITT,
  W.C., 149
PUCKETT,
  EDWARD I., 47
  JOSIAH, 1
PULL,
  WILLIAM, 17
PULLEY,
  MARY, 104, 113
  SALEY, 5
  THOS. W., 94
PULLY,
  MARY, 84
  T.W., 151
PUNKNIS,
  E., 24
PUPILS,
  JOSHUA, 50

-Q-

QUILLIN,
  JAS., 183
  JOHN, 161
QUILLING,
  DAVID, 161

-R-

RAGSDALE,
  JOHN, 95, 105,
    115
RAIDWELL,
  ROBT., 85
RAINEY,
  DAVID, 99, 119
RALLS,
  JOHN, 125
RAMBY,
  SHADRACK, 110
RAMLY,
  CARROLL, 151
RANDLE,
  JOHN, 113
RANEY,
  DAVID, 108
RAPER,
  J.S., 99
RARBURG,
  JESSE, 85
RASBERRY,
  JESS, 140
  JESSE, 162
  JESSY, 20
  JOHN, 141
RASBONG,
  JESSE, 122
RASBORG,
  JESSE, 154
RASBURG,
  A., 154
RASBURY,
  JOHN, 150
RASWELOL,
  LEWES, 119
RATLIFF,
  ELIZABETH, 108
RATTOFF,
  ELIZABETH, 117
RAWLS,
  JOHN, 85
RAY,
  ISAAC, 90
  WILLIAM, 90
RAYES,
  J.J., 142
RAYSDALLE,
  JOHN, 134
RAYSHALL,
  JOHN, 84
REA,
  ALEXANDER M.S.,

72
READERS,
  DANIEL, 137
READN ?,
  JAMES, 118
REASLY,
  R.S., 122
REAVES,
  T., 122
REAVS,
  JAMES, 1
REDDEN,
  B., 81, 121, 132
  _____, 76
REDDIC,
  KENNETH, 95
REDDICK,
  C.B., 104
  CALVIN, 19(2)
  CHAS. B., 20
  E., 85
  E.B., 114
  ELENEZER ?, 104
  K., 4
  KENIST, 1
  KENNETH, 57,
    105, 114, 144,
    153
  KINNITH, 5
  RUSH, 2
REDDICKS,
  JAMES, 143
REDDNER,
  KENNITH, 134
REDDRICK,
  C.B., 124
  CALVIN, 151
  E., 174(2)
  EBENEZER, 123
  KENNETH, 2
REDES,
  MARY, 125
REDEY,
  SAM, 86
REDICK,
  C.B., 85
  K., 85
REE,
  H., 110
  HALLAWAY, 35
REEDER,
  JAMES, 118
REEDOR,
  DANIEL, 128
REEVES,
  DEWEY, 17
  DREWRY, 166
  E.A., 119
  E.G., 139
  EDEY, 180
  F., 112
  F.R., 141, 150
  GEORGE, 109,

128, 138, 147,
  180
JAMES, 180
JAMES M., 3,
  179, 180
MR., 118
T., 111
TIMOTHY, 102,
  148
WM., 96
REEVS,
  E.A., 128
REGNOBLE,
  CONSTABLE, 14
REMPS,
  HY., 84
RENAL,
  JAMES, 134
REYLAN,
  ADAS, 163
REYNOLDS,
  JOHN, 152
  SARAH, 168
RHODES,
  MARY, 106
RICHARDSON,
  JAMES, 112
  T.H., 60
RICHISON,
  ELIZABETH, 138
RIDDICK,
  C.B., 95
  C.R., 134
  E., 113
RIDUS,
  JAMES M., 2
RIGHT,
  WM., 85
RILLICK,
  WILLIAM, 120
RILLY,
  JOHN, 79
ROADS,
  MARY, 115, 135
ROBBINS,
  CHARLES, 125
  CHARLIE, 85
  HARTY, 86
ROBERSON,
  DAVID O., 162
  H., 152
  HENRY, 134
ROBERTS,
  H., 25, 26(2)
ROBERTSON,
  A.T., 51
  E.A., 153
  HENRY, 85
  J., 112
  JAMES, 122
  JOHN, 79, 89,
    99, 108, 118,
    138, 147

P.T., 51
R., 135
SAMUEL B., 129
T., 153
THOMAS, 139
WILLIAM, 34
WILLIAM B., 51
_____, 102
ROBINS,
CHARLES, 145,
153
CHARLIE, 96,
106, 115
ROBINSON,
CHAS., 50
HENRY, 114
JOHN, 128
WILLIAM B., 50
ROBISON,
DAVIS O., 181
ROBORS,
HENRY, 94
ROBURN,
HENRY, 105
ROCHELL,
ROBT., 171
ROCHELLE,
ROBERT, 47
RODDEN,
B., 111, 142,
150
RODDS,
MARY, 96
RODGERS,
J.J., 122
S., 29
SIM, 29
ROE,
C.C., 23
ROGER,
SION, 165
ROGERS,
ELIJAH, 28
J.J., 112, 132
MARY, 137
S., 24, 25
ROLING,
A., 84
ROLINS,
CHRLES, 134
ROLLS,
G.B., 135
GREEN B., 116
JAMES, 135
JOHN, 96, 115,
134, 145, 153
ROMEY,
SHADROCK, 90
ROMLY,
S., 101
RONNLY,
C., 143
RONTO,

MARY, 121
RONTON,
J., 142
ROOVRALL,
_____, 135
ROP,
DAVID, 115
ROSEBERG,
JESSE, 15, 16
ROSEBERRY,
JOHN, 95
ROSEBURY,
JESSIE, 95
ROSENVILLE,
LEWIS, 83
ROSS,
D.E., 153
DAVID, 86, 96,
105
J.H., 153
JOHN, 106
S., 23
SAM, 34
ROSVALE,
LOUIS, 93
ROSWELL,
LEWIS, 110, 130,
139
ROWE,
WILLIAM, 83, 85,
106
ROYERS,
J.J., 132
RUDER,
D., 147
RUMLY,
S., 149
RUMONS,
T.L., 172
RUNENON,
JOHN, 162
RUNNBY,
LEWIS, 72
RUNNEON,
JOHN, 28, 38,
39, 47, 62, 70
JOHN, JR., 28
LEWIS, 28, 47,
70
MARTIN, 47, 70
RUNNEOUS,
JOHN, 182
RUSHING,
A.D., 132, 151
ABEL, 8, 11
ABLE, 31, 35,
41, 43
ANDY, JR., 37
ASA, 83, 103,
113
ASA D., 93, 142
BALARD, 91
BENTON, 11

BURRELL, 11
D., 11, 82, 111,
121, 131
DENIS, 67
DENNIS, 102, 140
E., 93, 103, 150
ELIZABETH, 83,
113, 132, 142
F., 103
F.M., 93, 113,
132, 142
G.W., 132, 150
GEO. W., 142
HARDY, 21, 23,
83, 93, 103,
112, 122, 162,
182
HARVEY, 23
J., 131(2)
J.D., 66, 103,
113, 132
J.H., 154
J.J., 10, 66,
83, 93, 112,
142, 150
JACK, 8
JACKSON, 31, 66,
67
JAMES, 150
JANE, 112
JNO. D., 142
JOE, 35
JOEL, 11, 12,
31, 60
JOHN D., 38, 83,
93, 132, 151,
175(2)
NANCY, 8, 10
P., 82
PHILLIP J., 113
R., 102, 112,
121, 122, 140,
144, 150
R., JR., 131
R.P., 103, 114,
121
R.T., 121, 135,
144, 154
RACHELE, 122
RICHARD, 44, 140
RICHARD P., 67
ROBERT, 8, 10,
11, 85, 95, 104,
114, 134, 152

ROBERT Y., 31
SARAH, 8, 9(2),
10, 11, 31, 35,
85, 95, 104,
114, 134
STEPHEN, 10, 11
T., 72
W., 111, 121,

131, 142
W.G., 9
W.H., 81, 92,
102, 112, 122,
150
WALLACE, 39
WILLIAM, 15, 37
WILLIAM G., 8
WILLIS, 67, 82,
91, 102, 140
WM. G., 11
WM. H., 132, 161
_____, 131
RUSSELL,
J., 131
JAMES, 102
JOSEPH E.S., 58
ROBT., 167
RUST,
JAMES T., 160
JAS., 182
RUTHERFORD,
JAMES, 1, 2, 3

-S-

SADDLEN,
JOHNSON H., 160
SAGLES,
SAMUEL S., 178
SAMUEL,
JOHN, 110
SANDERS,
A., 120, 148
ABRAHAM, 90,
110, 161, 182
ABRAM, 130
DENESY, 101
DENPE, 91
G., 108
GILFORD, 99,
118, 138, 147
GILLIFORD I., 79
HURHAI, 101
J., 120
J.S., 88
J.W., 140
JOHN, 88, 90,
99, 101, 118,
130, 138, 139
JON, 149
THOS., 5
SARDINS,
GUILFORD, 128
SARRATT,
C.M., 26
CHARLES M., 162
CHARLIE, 12
SARRETT,
JOSEPH, 141, 162
JR., 121
SAVAGE,
JOHN G., 4

SAWREY,
  ELIZABETH, 79
  RICHARD, 78
SAYES,
  E.W., 138
  S.S., 80
  WARREN, 148
SAYLE,
  JOHN, 14
SAYLES,
  D.T., 36
  E.W., 119
  ELI, 109
  J.S., 24, 25,
    179
  JAMES, 50, 89,
    100, 161(2)
  JAMES S., 12,
    13, 49, 69, 164,
    179, 183
  JOHN, 162, 182
  MARION, 89
  MARVIN, 12
  T.W., 57
  WARREN, 100, 128
SCHNIDER,
  PETER S., 123
SEALMAN,
  G., 4
SELF,
  PETE, 108
  PETER, 79, 88,
    99
SELPH,
  PETER, 138
SEMOINS,
  E., 178
SEMOMIUS,
  IASIOH, 134
SEOF,
  PETER, 118
SERAFORD,
  NEMBERN, 171
SERRATT,
  MAHALD, 182
  MARY, 160
  WM., 141
SETTLE,
  B., 67
  D., JR., 67
  D.C., 121
  D.L., 81, 102,
    131, 141(3)
  SAM, 67
SETTLES,
  D.L., 111
  DANIEL, 92
SETTLINS,
  Z., 121
SEVENDEL,
  WM., 148
SEVENDELL,
  TOM, 34

SEVENDLE,
  ASA, 160
  G.C., 148
  GARETT, 162
  NATHAN, 129, 138
  THOMAS, 119
  WM., 139
  WM. E., 129
SEVENDLER,
  ASA, 128
SEVILLE,
  THOS., 100
  WILLIAM, 100
SEVINDLE,
  ASA, 80, 119
  N., 80
  NATHAN, 148
  T., 80
  THOMAS, 148
  WILLIAM, 119
  WM., 80
SHARES,
  NELLY, 2
SHELLBERG,
  DELTON, 16
SHELLING,
  MATILDA, 95
SHELLY,
  W., 130
SHEMWOOD,
  _____, 146
SHEPARD,
  J., 111
SHERLEY,
  JAMES, 127
SHERLY,
  JAMES, 137, 138,
    146
SHIFF,
  JAMES, 59
SHILLEY,
  D.N., 134
  MATILDA, 85
SHILLING,
  JACOB, 6
  MATILDA, 105,
    115
SHILLINGS,
  D.N., 152
SHIRES,
  NEELY, 96
SHIRLEY,
  JAMES, 12, 78,
    87, 98, 107
SHORES,
  WILEY, 125
SHORT,
  H., 23(2)
  HYRAM, 149
  MALICHIE, 162
  N., 25, 101,
    120, 139, 149,
    182

NEEDHAM, 34,
  110, 183
NEEHAN, 90, 162
  SARAH, 161, 183
SHOVE,
  NELLY, 3
SHOWERS,
  NETTY, 85
SHUNT,
  N., 130
SIMMONAS,
  R.P., 145
SIMMONS,
  B.P., 125, 153
  B.T., 135
  EDWARD, 17, 172
SIMS,
  J.G., 141
  JOHN, 93
SINAUBLY,
  ABNER, 66
  W.M., 66
SITFOOT,
  HENRY, 113
SLANTER,
  SAMUEL, 145
SLAUGHTER,
  SAMUEL, 153
SLOAN,
  PEGGY, 78
SMALEY,
  A., 10
  JOHN, 95
SMALLEY,
  A., 10, 82, 103
  ABNER, 9(2), 10,
    32
  ABORIN, 9
  I.P., 84
  J.P., 115
  JOHN, 104, 114,
    115
SMALLY,
  A., 121, 131,
    149
  ABNER, 111
  J.P., 152
  JAMES T., 144
  JOHN, 134, 144,
    152
  T.G., 134
SMAWLEY,
  JOHN, 71
SMITH,
  ABSALOM, 15
  C., 99
  D., 85
  D.A., 104
  DAVID, 95, 161
  DEZA, 89
  DIZA, 79
  E., 22
  ELENDER, 129,

  138, 148
  ELIZABETH, 148
  ELNDER, 119
  EVINS, 166
  G., 140
  GILLION, 130
  HERMAN, 99
  HIRIAM, 89
  HYMAN, 108
  HYNANS, 119
  HYRAM, 138, 147
  ISAAC, 79, 108,
    119, 128, 147
  ISIAH, 88
  J.B., 138
  JACK, 108
  JAMES, 127, 137
  JOHN, 109, 128,
    138
  JONATHAN, 12
  LEVI, 80
  LEVY, 100, 109
  LILLIAN, 110
  LILLIE, 51
  LINE, 41
  MAHALA, 119
  MAHALY, 128
  MELTON, 105, 132
  N.H., 151
  NATHAN, 89
  PAUL, 53
  REBECCA, 86
  SELA, 89
  SHADNICK, 79
  THOMAS, 104
  THOS., 85, 94
  W., 102
  WILLIAM, 79, 89,
    94, 104, 108,
    115, 128, 138
  WILLSON, 119
  WM., 84, 89, 99
  _____, 162
SMOTHER,
  S., 120
SMOTHERS,
  GILLEN, 101
  GILLIN, 91
  GILLUM, 149
SNIDER,
  H.B., 143, 151
  T.G., 123
  THOS., 113
SOP,
  HUGH A.L., 133
SORRATT,
  ALETA, 182
  ATITECE, 162
  MAHALA, 162
SORRETT,
  J., 131
  WM., 131
SOTHERLAND,

TAYLOR (continued)
  JOSE, 165,
    166(2)
  NANCY, 94, 104,
    113
  STEPHEN, 29
  W.M., 84
  WIDOW, 30
  WILLIAM, 144
  WM., 105, 115,
    152
  WM. E., 100
  _____, 139
  _____, 100,
    148
TEDDEN,
  ELISHA, 119
  JOEL, 119
TEDDER,
  E., 148
  ELGA, 28
  ELIJAH, 28
  ELISHA, 129, 139
  JOE, 138, 148
  JOEL, 17, 18
  JOS., 129
TEDDERS,
  ELISHA, 17
TEDDOR,
  E., 109
  ELISHA, 100
  JOEL, 80, 90,
    100, 109
TEER,
  JACOB, 123
TEFFLE,
  ANTHONY, 98
TELLER,
  A., 34
TELLETT,
  SAND, 35
TEMPOLE,
  D., 79
TEPPETT,
  EZICHIE, 137
  L.R., 99
  WHITFIELD, 137
TEPPITT,
  LARKING, 118
TERRY,
  SCOTT, 77
TERY,
  JACOB, 143
TEVI,
  JACOB, 94
THOMAS,
  DAVID D., 5
  J.K., 103, 112
  J.R., 92, 121,
    131, 141
  JOHN, 86, 103
  M., 149
THOMASON,

GEO., 109, 148
GEORGE, 119,
  128, 139
GREGORY, 89
JAMES, 110
JONAS, 90
M., 110, 120,
  130, 139
MIDESON, 101
U., 90
THOMASSON,
  JAMES, 101
THOMPSON,
  C.H., 122
  CHARLES, 160
  E.H., 112
  JOHN, 62
  L., 81, 91, 130,
    149
  L.H., 112, 121
  LEM, 103
  LENA, 141
  LENNIEL, 161
  P., 81, 91, 112,
    121, 130, 149
  R., 102
  ROBERT, 179
  W.C., 102, 112,
    130
  W.M., 182
  WILLIAM, 13, 15
  WILLIS, 118, 162
  WM., 111
  WM. C., 141
  Z., 14
THOMSON,
  G., 80
  PERRY, 141
THORNO,
  J.R., 81
THORNTON,
  AARON, 47
  ARAN, 162
  ARON, 182
  ELIZABETH, 11,
    160
  GEORGE, 100
  J., 111, 131,
    141
  JNO., 182
  JOHN, 37, 93,
    121, 154, 162
  LOUISE, 112
  LUKE, 47
  PRESLY, 146
  W.P., 182
  WM., 162
THRASHER,
  G., 110
  JEMIMA, 83
  MIMA, 100
  NANCY, 110
TICE,

JACOB, 105
JOB, 114
JOHN, 83, 93,
  103, 113, 132,
  142, 151
TILLEY,
  JOHN W., 16
TIPPEN,
  JAMES, 133(2)
TIPPETT,
  ALFORD, 88
  EZEKIAL, 87
  L., 146
  LARKIN, 137
  W., 146, 147
  WHITFIELD, 78,
    87, 98
TIPPITT,
  ALFORD, 118
  LARKIN, 127
  WHITFIELD, 108,
    118
TITTLE,
  H.Z., 80
  SAM F., 70
TOMASON,
  ARNOLD, 101
TOMPKINS,
  THOS., 154
TOTTLE,
  SAM, 34(2), 35
TOUES,
  WIDOW, 147
TOWNON,
  MAY, 90
TOWNSEND,
  A., 120
  ALBERT, 110
  ALLEN, 130
  E., 176
  ELI, 175
  HAMILTON, 115
  HARRETT, 175
  HARRIETT, 85,
    96, 106
  HARRIT, 125, 176
  HARRITT, 135,
    145, 153
  JOESAILLA, 130
  MARY, 38, 101,
    110, 120, 130,
    140, 149, 163
  NATHANIEL, 38,
    163
  PENSELLA, 120
  STEAPHEN, 162
TOWNSOMS,
  MAY, 80
TOWNSON,
  MARY, 38
  NATHANIEL, 38
TRAVIS,
  M.L., 156

TUN,
  JOAB, 152
TURNER,
  B., 81, 92, 110
  BENSON, 103
  BENTON, 120
  JAMES, 113
  JOHN, 94
  N.B., 167
  R.B., 106, 117
  SARAH, 88
  THOMAS R., 89
  WM. T., 151
TUTTLE,
  HORATION, 89
  I.J., 139
TYNER,
  WM., 148
  WM. H., 139
  WM.H., 129

        -U-

UBSSEL,
  WM., 151
UTLEY,
  ABLE, 162
  BUMEL, 119
  BURNIE, 139
  H., 26
  J., 24
  J.W., 21, 23,
    24, 25(2)
  JAMES W., 22
  JOHN, 23
  JOHN W., 60, 160
  Q. ?, 72
  S., 36
  SETH, 119, 139,
    159, 160
UTLY,
  A., 81, 92, 102,
    112, 149
  B., 80
  BURREL, 148
  BURRELL, 89,
    100, 109
  J.W., 26, 27(2),
    95, 105, 114
  S., 36, 109
  SETH, 62, 80,
    89, 100
UTTEY,
  A., 130
  ALICE, 121
  J.W., 134
  JOHN W., 144
  SETH, 128
UTTY,
  ABEE, 141
  BURK, 128
  J.W., 121

www.ingramcontent.com/pod-product-compliance
Lightning Source LLC
Chambersburg PA
CBHW080420270326
41929CB00018B/3104